A Biohistory of 19th-Century Afro-Americans

A Biohistory of 19th-Century Afro-Americans

The Burial Remains of a Philadelphia Cemetery

Lesley M. Rankin-Hill

BERGIN & GARVEY
Westport, Connecticut • London

Library of Congress Cataloging-in-Publication Data

Rankin-Hill, Lesley M.
    A biohistory of 19th-century Afro-Americans : the burial remains
of a Philadelphia cemetery / Lesley M. Rankin-Hill.
        p.   cm.
    Includes bibliographical references and index.
    ISBN 0–89789–435–9 (alk. paper)
    1. Afro-Americans—Pennsylvania—Philadelphia—History—19th
century.   2. First African Baptist Church Cemetery (Philadelphia,
Pa.)   3. Afro-Americans—Pennsylvania—Philadelphia—Antiquities.
4. Human remains (Archaeology)—Pennsylvania—Philadelphia.
5. Philadelphia (Pa.)—History.   6. Philadelphia (Pa.)—Antiquities.
I. Title.
F158.9.N4R36   1997
974.8′1100496073—dc20   96–7172

British Library Cataloguing in Publication Data is available.

Library of Congress Catalog Card Number: 96–7172
ISBN: 0–89789–435–9

First published in 1997

Bergin & Garvey, 88 Post Road West, Westport, CT 06881
An imprint of Greenwood Publishing Group, Inc.

Printed in the United States of America

The paper used in this book complies with the
Permanent Paper Standard issued by the National
Information Standards Organization (Z39.48–1984).

10 9 8 7 6 5 4 3 2 1

Dedicated to my mother and father

Esperanza Victoria Valdés

Randolph Alonzo Rankin

and to

my family, friends, and mentors

who were instrumental and inspirational

and

have now "gone to a better land"

Juan Valdés

Onelia Roque Valdés

Randolph Alphonso Rankin

Randy James Rankin

Maryann Snow Bates

Sylvia Helen Forman

Wm. Montague Cobb

J. Lawrence Angel

Contents

Illustrations

FIGURES

PLATES

Acknowledgments

This endeavor could only have been accomplished with the effort and support of many people. My sincere gratitude and appreciation is extended to all those individuals and institutions that have made this dream a reality. My deepest gratitude goes to my mother, Esperanza V. Valdés, for her diligent and thorough editing, understanding, motivational efforts, support, and "suffering with me"; and to my husband, Seabern Hill, who has always supported and invested in me throughout the many years. He taught me to "just do it."

The research that this study was based upon was supported by the following institutions and programs: the University of the District of Columbia, College of Liberal and Fine Arts (especially Dean John Butler and Associate Dean Sue Reddick); the Smithsonian Institution, Museum of Natural History; Minority Faculty Fellowship; Department of Energy, Los Alamos National Laboratory, Historically Black Colleges and Universities Faculty Fellowship; the Southwestern Bell Humanities Faculty Fellowship at the University of Oklahoma; and the University of Oklahoma Junior Faculty Fellowship.

I would like to acknowledge the following people for their technical and/or professional services: Wanda Downs (who really runs the department); Amelia Marie Adams; Diane Ghalib, for her excellent commissioned illustrations; Paula Allen; Jaime Butler; William Scates; Diane Mayes; Don Mayes; Arion Mayes (especially the late night La Bag runs); Michael Brown; John Carter; Murray Dennis Bates; Dr. Michael Blakey; Terri Judd Warren; Sean Jenkins, Mary Kay Davies; Jennifer Kelley; Dr. Debra Sellers; the Pennsylvania Historical Society staff and especially, John Lee Davis, who took me out of the computer dark ages with patience, humor and caring. A special acknowledgment goes to Henry Williams, who invited a stranger into his home to review Robert Ulle's papers (Dr. Ulle's papers led me to the discovery of the female FABC beneficial society).

This book is based on my original dissertation research, and I would like to express my appreciation for the significant contributions of my professors–

mentors at the University of Massachusetts at Amherst: George J. Armelagos, who took the risk twenty-four years ago and has always been my staunchest supporter, there could be no better advisor; Sylvia Helen Forman, who made me "toughen up," nurtured and bullied me, and is deeply missed; R. Brooke Thomas, who has inspired and motivated me; Andy Anderson, who taught me to enjoy statistics and, through his example, made me a better teacher. In addition, I want to recognize the inspiration, training, opportunities, and magical moments given to me by three great scholars: J. Lawrence Angel, for giving me the opportunity to work on the First African Baptist Church cemetery population; C.L.R. James, who impelled me to return to doctoral studies and told me that I, too, could be a "Renaissance Person"; and the most influential, Wm. Montague Cobb, who became my mentor and taught me so much about science, anthropology, activism, Afro-Americans, himself, and, most importantly, "not to let the bastards get you down" (in Latin, of course).

I thank Maryann Snow Bates for her friendship and intellectual camaraderie. Throughout graduate school, fieldwork, and writing a book, she was my inspiration and role model. Her consistent caring and tenacious motivation kept me going even after her death.

I wish to thank my grandmother, aunts, uncles, and cousins who have been my cheering squad; my mother-in-law, Pauline Rice, for her support, and Clyde and Jerry Snow for taking me in and providing steady encouragement. A very special thank you to Chunga, Guarionex, and Bayoan for being "mi familia."

I would also like to thank my editors, Lynn Flint, Elizabeth Murphy, and Jodie McCune, at Greenwood publishing group for their support, confidence, and patient advice.

A Biohistory of
19th-Century
Afro-Americans

Chapter 1

Introduction

The First African Baptist Church (FABC) Cemetery remains were accidentally discovered and eventually excavated during the 1980s. Who were these people long forgotten and invisible under the soil and pavements of Philadelphia? These were not the aristocratic intelligentsia; their pictures are not found in the historical society. These were not the members of the Philadelphia Black elite. These were invisible people in life and death. The FABC congregation members interred in the forgotten cemetery represent the Philadelphia Afro-American community during the first half of the nineteenth century. In particular, they are representative of the poorest segment of that community: the people who did the laundry, cleaned houses, and carted the heavy loads from the docks into the city. Those people who, to a great extent, led faceless lives forged in hardship. When they died they were buried in graves sometimes four burials deep, so close together that many burials overlapped. Eventually, the cemetery was relegated to deep obscurity under a parking lot—not remembered until a backhoe blade hit a grave.

This book focuses on who those people buried in the First African Baptist Church Cemetery were and the conditions and experiences of their lives. The search for those invisible people was predicated on two assumptions: (1) that the material lives of the poor and the powerless can be reconstructed utilizing diverse sources and (2) that "dead people do tell tales." In other words, their stories are written on the bones and teeth that are left behind. Therefore, through searching documents, historical accounts, maps, and drawings, the material lives of nineteenth-century Philadelphia Afro-Americans was revealed. Through combining archival research and the assessment of the FABC skeletal remains, the health status of this Afro-American community was brought to light.

The mid-nineteenth century was a time of changing social, political, and economic conditions in Philadelphia for all segments of the population, especially for Afro-Americans. Notwithstanding stressful environmental and socio-economic conditions, Afro-Americans in Philadelphia had institutions such as beneficial societies and churches that provided both economic and social support as well as spiritual sustenance. The First African Baptist Church cemetery population represents a sample of that Afro-American community. The FABC skeletal population provided unique opportunity to explore and reconstruct the experiences of Afro-Americans during the antebellum period in environments other than southern plantation slavery. This book focuses on bringing the scope and method of physical anthropology into an area of study that has not been previously examined from a multidisciplinary biocultural perspective. The health, lifestyles, conditions, and constraints of urban-free Afro-American populations are explored from an integrative biocultural framework that interrelates socio-historical, demographic, and biological factors. Skeletal biological methods include paleodemographic and paleopathologic assessment of health and disease status.

FIRST AFRICAN BAPTIST CHURCH CONGREGATION

The First African Baptist Church was founded in 1809 by thirteen persons, including the Reverend Henry Simmons (Plate 1.1). The first thirty member meeting house was established at 11th and Vine Streets with the aid of the Euro-American First Baptist Church and an "attitude of benevolent paternalism" (Parrington and Roberts 1984:29). The Baptist Association of Philadelphia seated delegates from the African Baptist Church from its inception, unlike the Methodist, Presbyterian, and Episcopalian entities that first opposed the establishment of Afro-American churches.

Brooks (1922), in his official history of the First African Baptist Church, states that in 1816 "a rift occurred in the congregation" surrounding the membership and aid to incoming ex-slaves, creating a schism in the congregation. A more detailed explanation is not available from either historical accounts or documents. Records of the National Baptist Conference only refer to the schisms and go on to recognize two congregations, with both congregations retaining the First African Baptist Church name.

The splinter group, consisting of many of the original congregation's founding members, including Reverend Simmons, established a new meeting house two blocks away at 13th and Vine Streets. The dissident church ran into financial difficulties in 1822, and its property was sold at a sheriff's sale. The congregation relocated the church and established a burial ground on Reverend Simmons's land located at 8th and Vine Streets (Milner 1981). This location of the FABC site, where the meeting house and cemetery were situated in the Spring Garden district, are illustrated in Figure 1.1.

The cemetery, accidentally discovered in 1980, is the burial ground of this dissident FABC congregation. The cemetery was used from circa 1822 until 1843. The Philadelphia Board of Health condemned the cemetery in 1841 due to overcrowding. Apparently, the congregation continued to use the cemetery since interments are recorded for 1842 and a second Board of health condemnation was decreed in 1843. Historical documents do not offer any information on the FABC congregation from 1841 until the death of Reverend Simmons in 1851, when all his properties were sold. Therefore, the fate of this dissident FABC congregation appears to be lost. The original mother church, after years of declining membership (Brooks 1922), exists today at another location.

Plate 1.1
Reverend Henry Simmons, Pastor, First African Baptist Church, Philadelphia

Source: Albert Newsam Litho Collection, The Historical Society of Pennsylvania.
First African Baptist Church, Philadelphia.

Figure 1.1
Map of Philadelphia Indicating Location of the FABC Site

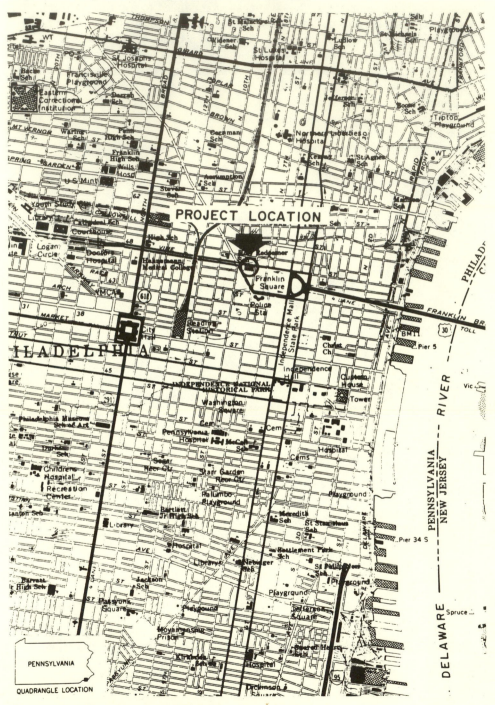

Source: John Milner Associates, Philadelphia, Pennsylvania.

Reverend Simmons's properties were razed in the 1850s and replaced by a safe factory and a row of houses constructed along Chester Street. The cemetery became the backyards, walls, and privies of these homes, which stood on the site until the 1960s when they were demolished and replaced by a parking lot. Therefore, the FABC cemetery burials were preserved until their discovery and excavation in the 1980s (Parrington and Roberts 1984).

Archaeology

Excavation of the Philadelphia Commuter Rail tunnel led to the discovery of the First African Baptist Church cemetery located in today's "Center City" area. Following the discovery in November 1980, the cemetery was resealed for its protection. A document search was conducted to identify, date, and locate the cemetery in historical context. A four-year legal process ensued to determine legal responsibility and the proper course of action. Public hearings were held, and the present-day FABC congregation was consulted. The culmination was the placement of the site on the National Register of Historic Places.

Michael Parrington, of Milner Associates, excavated the cemetery in 1984 and 1985, uncovering approximately 140 burials that represent members of the First African Baptist Church congregation interred circa 1822–1843. Burials were sent to Dr. J. Lawrence Angel of the Smithsonian Institution in Washington, DC, for skeletal analysis. The author, through a Smithsonian fellowship, was able to undertake the study presented in this book.

The archaeological investigation mapped the cemetery as consisting of two main rows running north and south (Figure 1.2). Many graves were closely aligned, with as little as six inches between them; multiple interments of as many as six burials in each of several plots were common. This pattern of interments is probably an indicator of the congregation's relative poverty and the general overcrowding in this part of Philadelphia during the nineteenth century (Parrington and Roberts 1984). Several pieces of pottery, single shoes on top of six coffins, and single coins placed near the head in eight burials—all considered customs of African origin—were the only artifacts found with the burials (Parrington 1985; Parrington and Roberts 1984; Parrington and Wideman 1986). Other artifacts or grave markings were lost to surface destruction when the housing, factory, and parking lot were constructed, thus obscuring information concerning individual identity or other cultural mortuary practices of the congregation.

AFRO-AMERICAN RESEARCH AND BIOHISTORY

The experience of Afro-Americans in the Americas has been of interest to historians, anthropologists, sociologists, and, more recently, to scholars of

Figure 1.2
FABC Cemetery Map

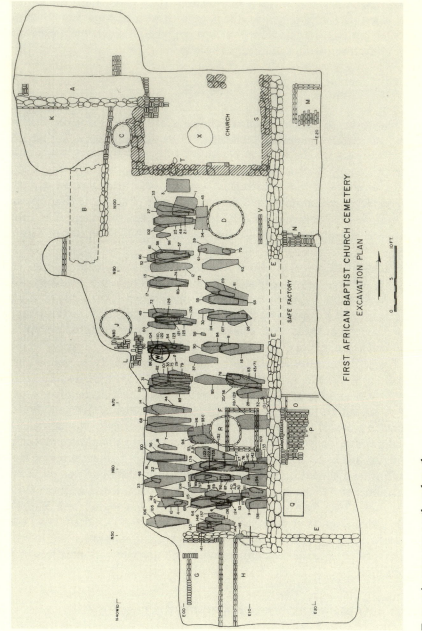

FIRST AFRICAN BAPTIST CHURCH CEMETERY
EXCAVATION PLAN

Two main rows run north and south.
Source: John Milner Associates, Philadelphia, Pennsylvania.

Black/Afro-American studies. Despite the diversity of disciplines involved, research on the experience of Afro-Americans in the New World can be characterized as yielding an overproliferation of works but an underdevelopment of approaches and scope. This criticism is not directed to the work of any specific discipline, but to all of the fields that at one time or another have considered Afro-Americans, their history, their social conditions, and/or the reconstruction of the "Black experience" of some research interest and social or scientific significance. There is a plethora of studies on a fairly narrow range of topics and themes concerning Afro-Americans. These have included, for example: the reasons for and origins of New World slavery; comparative slave system studies debating the existence of substantive differences between colonial powers' treatment of slaves; the economic efficiency or inefficiency of plantation slavery systems; the harsh treatment by American colonists that "stripped" Afro-Americans of their African heritage and culture; the emancipation of the slaves and Reconstruction (1860–1880) as the catalysts to the deterioration of Afro-American socioeconomic conditions, which therefore created a breeding ground for modern Afro-American conditions and problems.

The scope of anthropological research concerning Afro-Americans has been primarily represented by cultural anthropological studies of race relations (Harris 1964; Pitt-Rivers 1967), family social organization (Gonzalez 1970; Stack 1970), language (Dillard 1970; Reisman 1970), music (Lomax 1970; Szwed 1970; Whitten 1970), cultural patterns (e.g., religious systems) (Aguirre-Beltran 1946; 1958; Bourguignon 1970; Mintz 1951, 1961; Price 1970) and adaptive strategies of New World Afro-Americans (Despres 1970; Klumpp 1970; Valentine and Valentine 1980). Physical anthropological work has focused on comparative anthropometrics, growth, and development studies; differences between racial groups; racial typologizing; discussions concerning race and intelligence; and, more recently, skeletal biological assessments. Afro-American archaeological research has been extremely limited. Archaeological studies have primarily focused on reconstructing the lifestyles of Afro-American communities in the northeast United States (Baker 1982; Bridges and Salwen 1982; Paynter 1990; Schuyler 1982) and southern plantations (Otto 1975; 1982, Singleton 1985).

Boas (1906, 1909) was the first anthropologist to seriously advocate a research focus on Afro-Americans during the early twentieth century. He proposed the creation of an "Africa Institute" of anthropological research focusing on the accomplishments of Africans, anatomical studies, and statistical analyses. This was to fulfill a twofold purpose: to eradicate racism by showing whites the positive attributes of Afro-Americans' African ancestors and disproving the biological, psychological, and moral inferiority myths concerning them; and to improve the Afro-Americans' self-images and conditions by making them less "despondent," more hopeful, more proud of their heritage and ambitious to change their conditions. In addition, he suggested that anthropological research should focus on the American "Negro" as an excellent example of a population undergoing culture change and environmental adaptation. Although Boas's innovative views have produced the modern configuration of American anthropology, his ideas concerning Afro-Americans were heeded by few.

Anthropologists focused on "plantation America," on race relations in the Americas, on the Caribbean as a plural society, and on the family and household composition of migratory wage laborers vis-à-vis the larger society. In the United States, a few anthropologists worked in the Deep South, but most avoided working with Negroes in the urban North, leaving the field to sociologists, political scientists, and "Urbanologists" who continued to specialize in urban problems and race relations. While anthropologists thought that their findings were being ignored or distorted, it seemed to sociologists and others that anthropology—the discipline based on a tradition of field work and comparison—consistently ignored the great subculture at our door, that of the urban black American. (Whitten and Szwed 1970:30)

A call for a new emphasis on Afro-American anthropology was presented at the 1967 American Anthropological Association symposium "Negroes in the New World," which culminated in the volume edited by Whitten and Szwed (1970) called *Afro-American Anthropology*.

Pervasive in many historical studies of Afro-Americans is the concept that somehow slavery in the New World stands as an isolated historical deviation of which the western world should be ashamed, apologize for, rationalize and/or study as a separate phenomenon. Others have studied New World slavery from a more universal context, as Williams contends:

Slavery was an economic institution of the first importance. It had been the basis of Greek economy and had built the Roman Empire. In modern times it provided the sugar for the tea and the coffee cups of the Western World....It produced the cotton to serve as a base for modern capitalism....Seen in historical perspective, it forms a part of that general picture of the harsh treatment of the underprivileged classes, the unsympathetic poor laws and severe feudal laws, and the indifference...[of] the rising capitalist class. (1971:4)

Thus, enslaved Africans were placed into a system that was already formulated. In the English colonies, Afro-Americans were legally and in practice treated as indentured servants until the legislation of the 1660s. Williams maintains in his controversial work *Capitalism and Slavery* that

the origin of Negro slavery...was economic not racial; it had to do not with the color of the laborer, but the cheapness of labor....The features of the man, his hair, color, and dentition, his "subhuman" characteristics so widely pleaded, were only the later rationalizations to justify a simple economic fact: that the colonies needed labor and resorted to Negro labor because it was cheapest and best. (1971:14)

Southern plantation slavery is the central focus of the majority of historical studies. The themes discussed earlier were essentially explored within the context of New World slavery as separate and distinct sociohistorical phenomena based on racism and hatred. Much of the debates concerning slavery can be described as two polarized approaches to antebellum American history: that of social historians versus that of economic historians.

Despite the voluminous anthropological, historical, and sociological literature, several areas of research have been ignored. These include such topics as: (1) the heterogeneous nature of Afro-American populations because of diverse African provenience and admixture with diverse Europeans and/or Native Americans; (2) the experience of urban Afro-American slaves and freedmen during the Antebellum period; (3) the living conditions, health status, and life styles of nonslave Afro-Americans; (4) changing American sociocultural conditions (e.g., industrialization) and their impact on Afro-American conditions; (5) and the health status and biological adaptability of Afro-Americans. In addition, multidisciplinary, integrative research approaches to New World Afro-American populations have rarely been undertaken.

Cliometricians (economic historians) have been interested in quantitatively analyzing the "traditional" accounts of the period, but little emphasis has been placed on the socioeconomic and health statuses of free Afro-Americans in the premodern period. Within the economic analysis of the nonslave labor market, Fogel and Engerman do discuss the conditions of free Afro-Americans briefly:

Data in the 1850 census suggest that the economic condition of the average free northern Negro may have been worse than that of the average free Negro in the south. A comparison between New York and New Orleans reveals that New York Negroes lived in more crowded housing, had a lower proportion of craftsmen and less wealth per capita than free Negroes in New Orleans. For Blacks during the antebellum era, then, freedom and slavery were not separated by a sharp dividing line. (1974:244)

Due primarily to the annexation of Louisiana between 1790 and 1810, there was a 150 percent increase in the nation's Afro-American population (Genovese 1972). After these dramatic increases rate at the turn of the century, there was a radical and consistent decline in the increase of freedmen due to the increasing restrictions on manumission, the expulsion of freedmen, and a general deterioration of the free Afro-American's conditions of life in the slave states, particularly during the period of 1830–1860 (Curry 1981; Genovese 1972). In 1860 there were close to half a million free Afro-Americans in the United States, roughly half of them in the slave states.

According to Curry (1981), societal restraints in the urban north were more effective and onerous than the legal prohibitions of the south. Even without legal barriers, Afro-Americans were prevented from undertaking occupations that were potentially lucrative although menial, unskilled, and nonseasonal (e.g., cartage, for it was extremely difficult to obtain necessary licenses). They encountered strong opposition when trying to enter the artisan trades in the northern cities, finding it almost impossible to be accepted as apprentices or journeymen.

While this prejudice has been attributed primarily to the Irish immigrants of the early 1800s, there is evidence indicating that this type of occupational prejudice existed prior to the influx of the immigrants of the nineteenth century (Curry 1981; Du Bois 1899).

Sociohistoric and demographic studies on the urban experience of Afro-Americans have been limited. There exists a body of nineteenth and early twentieth-century literature about "coloureds" and free Negro elites in New Orleans and Philadelphia, written by "Negro intellectuals" of the period (e.g., Du Bois 1899; Willson 1841). This literature is useful in understanding the experience of an extremely small and unique group of Afro-Americans, but it also illustrates the stringent constraints of early American society, as well as the conditions that permitted this small amount of social mobility.

One of the more important reasons for understanding the experiences of free Afro-Americans is what it can illustrate about the society at large:

Probably the best indication of a society's attitude toward the enslaved peoples within its ranks is the role that the freedmen plays within the predominantly slave regime.... For the community of freedmen under slavery is a microcosm of what the post-emancipation freedmen society will be....In short, the position of the freedmen under slavery is a prime indicator of the pattern of assimilation and the attitude of the white classes to the African Negro within their midst. (Klein 1967:193)

In many New World societies, freedmen were accepted as another social class with rights, privileges, and resources distinct from slaves (e.g., Cuba, Brazil, Peru, and New Orleans, Louisiana). In others, it was difficult to obtain manumission, and freedmen were considered divisive, feared, and treated not much better than slaves, with no "place" in the society (as in the United States, with the probable exception of Louisiana). Despite the obviously significant impact of this tenuous social status on the individual and the Afro-American community, research is virtually nonexistent. How did Afro-American ex-slaves and freeborns survive in an urban environment that was hostile, where they were relegated to marginality and had to live in a wage economy in a nonagricultural setting where food supplementation (hunting, gathering, and small-scale farming) was not possible? What were the conditions that manumitted slaves found upon receiving or buying their freedom; was it different from that of freeborn Afro-Americans? The comparison of the urban and rural settings for both slave and free Afro-Americans should also be a major concern of Antebellum research, since:

Nothing—not the fact that one was an American, or a Philadelphian, or a property holder, or a father, or a barber, or a Methodist, or a voter, or a Mason—was one-third so significant as the fact that one was black in a society that legally, socially and politically viewed Negroes as innately inferior and undesirable as occupiers of urban space. Surely few things in the life of the urban black were more self evident than the existence of this community of exclusion, suppression, and, withal, resentment. (Curry 1981:242)

The urban environment of colonial America was not a very healthy one. In particular, the residentially segregated poor and Afro-Americans both endured unsanitary conditions, exposure to infectious diseases, and dark, dank, congested neighborhoods. These environmental conditions coupled with the socioeconomic status of Afro-Americans (slave and free) must have posed severe psychosocial and biological stress on individuals and the Afro-American community at large.

AFRO-AMERICAN BIOHISTORY

During the last twenty years, Afro-American biohistory has evolved into the study of both the biological and sociocultural factors that have affected and/or influenced the health, fertility, morbidity and mortality of Afro-Americans in the New World within an historical context. Afro-American biohistory is a meeting ground for the many disciplines that focus on the health and disease of African slaves and their descendants in the Americas. This expansive and complex area of research is not easily delineated because of its broad geographic, temporal, and topical range. The geographic range of Afro-American biohistorical studies includes the entire New World. The majority of these studies focus on plantation societies of the southern United States (Cardell and Hopkins 1978; Gibbs, et al. 1980; Kiple and Kiple 1977a), British West Indies (Craton 1976; Higman 1979; Kiple 1984; Sheridan 1975), Cuba (Eblen 1974; Fraginals 1977), and Brazil (Cooper 1986; Goodyear 1978), the major slaveholding territory in South America. Temporally, Afro-American biohistorical studies span the fifteenth through nineteenth centuries, beginning with the first Africans arriving with the conquistadors and ending at the close of the nineteenth century when slavery was completely abolished from the hemisphere (1886 in Cuba).The topical scope of the field, as discussed above (for detailed discussion on Afro-American health studies see Rankin-Hill 1990, Chapter 2), encompasses issues of interest to economists, demographers, historians, physicians, political scientists, and anthropologists.

Afro-American biohistory is not only the study of those Africans and ancestors who were slaves, but of those "Afro-American societies" that were forged throughout the African Diaspora in the New World. Biohistorical studies must consequently take into account the diversity of these populations created by time, history, culture, geography, and ecology. Therefore, Afro-American biohistory should be considered as a field that studies the adaptations of humans of African origins to biological, environmental, and sociocultural stresses of involuntary migration and resettlement in the New World.

The cross-disciplinary nature of Afro-American biohistory has served both as a catalyst and a hindrance to the growth and direction of the field. Major works, such as Curtin's (1969) *Atlantic Slave Trade* and Fogel and Engerman's (1974) *Time on the Cross*, were milestones for their informational, methodological, and theoretical approaches to Afro-American biohistory. Curtin's challenge for broader multidisciplinary research paradigms and methodological innovations has elicited numerous studies, which have basically emulated or replicated his work or that of Fogel and Engerman. A few of these works did take on Curtin's challenges, significantly contributing to the body of knowledge in the field. Yet little has been accomplished in expanding the conceptual limits of the field. In fact, much of the emphasis has been on the intricacies of quantification and data manipulation, and not on different approaches of interpreting and/or examining the data generated.

Pervasive in many multidisciplinary studies is the extraction of relevant facts from other disciplines without regard to context or paradigm, resulting in a tendency toward generalization and reductionism of medical and clinical data. Genetic immunities, such as sickle cell trait to malaria, and deficiencies, such as lactase enzyme, are commonly assumed to be part of the biological make up of all Afro-American populations. These assumptions are usually employed without considering the ecological context, biological history of the population, and/or clinical substantiation of these genetic traits in the population. Therefore, Afro-American biohistorical studies have been predominantly reconstructive and descriptive in paradigm, using indirect and inferential methods of health assessments. Limitations of these paradigms have occurred due to the failure to consider a broader approach that would include: (1) a biocultural approach, which would focus on the interactions of culture and biology; (2) the investigation of adaptive strategies; (3) the consideration of an ecological context of health and disease; (4) a focus on localized Afro-American groups or populations, which would provide a means of assessing biological, cultural, and environmental conditions cross-culturally; (5) the consideration of intrapopulational variation.

These approaches are fundamental to modern physical anthropological research and could contribute new information, perspectives, and reevaluations to Afro-American biohistorical research.

AFRO-AMERICAN BIOHISTORY AND PHYSICAL ANTHROPOLOGY

Physical anthropology has contributed significantly in the past to our understanding of Afro-American anthropometry and growth and development during the late nineteenth and early twentieth centuries, as discussed earlier. The discipline has evolved, in the last decades, from a focus on race and racial differences to a focus on human biological and ecological adaptation. Modern physical anthropology, on the other hand, offers a unique contribution to Afro-American biohistory in both scope and method. The most significant contributions of physical anthropology can be (1) models in studying human populations from a biocultural perspective; and, (2) skeletal biological analyses. Thus, it provides less indirect methods of health assessment—information that was not previously available—and infuses a broader theoretical scope to Afro-American biohistorical studies.

THE BIOCULTURAL FRAMEWORK

Human populations, in order to survive and reproduce, develop means of coping with the limitations, resources, and conditions of the environments they inhabit. These means of coping are cultural and biological adaptations to both the general and/or specific conditions of the environment. This ecological view is fundamental to studying the processes of human biocultural adaptation. Environments include three components: the inorganic (climate, water, soil); organic (from pathogens to predators); and the sociocultural such as human-created pollution or agricultural alteration of the natural environment (Armelagos, Goodman, and Jacobs 1978; Dubos 1965; Hunt 1978; Thomas, Winterhalder, and McRae 1979). These environmental properties, whether made by nature or humans, are not static. Fluctuations are common and extreme changes possible; therefore, human responses to environmental conditions are always dynamic and involve continuous adjustments in equilibrium.

Cultural adaptive responses to environmental conditions can include material culture (e.g., clothing, tools), social systems, behaviors and ideology (e.g., symbolic communication, information).   A population's behaviors, beliefs, structures, and products can mediate, exacerbate, or create environmental conditions that in turn require a response, thus creating a dynamic process of biocultural adaptation.

Biological adaptive responses can be studied from a hierarchy of increasing organizational complexity at the physiochemical, cellular, organ system, organism (individual), population, and ecosystemic levels (Mazees 1975). Each succeeding level of this hierarchy forms the dominant environmental focus of the preceding level. For example, the environment of the cell is the organ, that of the individual is the population, and that of the population is the ecosystem. As outlined by Mazees (1975:11) adaptive domains, or areas of response, for the individual organism include:

- reproduction
- health (morbidity, mortality, disease resistance)
- nutrition
- nervous system
- growth and development
- generalized stress resistance
- physical performance
- affective functions (happiness, tolerance)
- learning and expressive ability

These same adaptive domains are assessed in relation to size, density, distribution, composition, and organization at the populational level.

Health and disease depend on an organism's ability to maintain homeostasis (a constant or balanced internal environment) at each hierarchical level, notwithstanding the innumerable variations of the external environment. Internal environmental constancy is achieved through the orderly performance of the body's physiological and biochemical processes. When deviations or "stressors" threaten or have an actual effect on one or more of these adaptive domains, then disease is experienced. Disease can also be the manifestation of inadequate, inappropriate, or maladaptive responses (Cannon 1939; Dubos 1965).

Through the application of a biocultural framework, biological and cultural interactions within a specific environmental context can be identified and their effects on populational patterns of health and disease determined. In addition, multicausal and synergistic relationships that affect the type, onset, duration, and magnitude of disease can then be investigated.

BIOCULTURAL MODEL

The basic biocultural framework can be modeled to address a particular area of research or problem. The paleoepidemiological research model (Figure 1.3) proposed by Goodman, et al. (1984) to investigate the skeletal biology of archaeological populations, is an example of a biocultural model. In skeletal biological studies, the bones and teeth of prehistoric and historic populations are examined for pathology and growth disturbances. (A detailed discussion of skeletal biological methods is presented in Chapter 2.) These are indicators of physiological disruption (stress) and provide a means of assessing the general health status of a population. Data generated from skeletal biological analyses must be placed within the context of a population's lifeways and history to explain the conditions that produced these disruptions. The paleoepidemiological model provides a means of asking processual questions about the causes and results of physiological disruptions and/or stresses experienced by populations. The authors describe the conceptual framework of the model as follows:

Stress is a product of three sets of factors: environmental constraints, cultural systems, and host resistance. These may vary over time and space. If uncorrected, these constraints will result in increased physiological disruption. Cultural systems may act to buffer the impact of the environmental constraints. However, cultural systems may also magnify existing stresses or produce novel ones. If stress is not adequately buffered by extra-individual means, its effects may be buffered only by individual host resistance. Host resistance varies by age and sex. Genetic factors also play an important role in resistance to certain diseases. When host resistance and environmental constraints are held constant, variation in stress levels may be related to cultural differences. (Goodman, et al. 1984:15)

Figure 1.3
Generalized Model for the Biocultural Analysis of Skeletal Remains

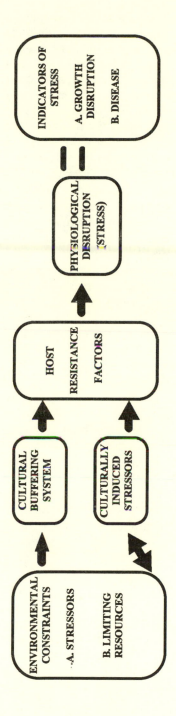

Source: Goodman, et al. 1984.

The first component of the biocultural model is the environmental context of a population; this is the source of all necessary resources. Yet, environmental conditions may produce situations to which the individual and population must adapt and respond, thus producing constraints that may affect survival or impose limitations on the biological development of individuals and the population. These constraints can include a broad range of factors, from fluctuations in the availability of necessary resources (such as food or energy) to climatic conditions to sanitation. Environmental constraints are also intimately linked to a population's cultural system, such as levels of technology, social organization, and information processing by the group.

Therefore, in this model, the environmental constraints include both stressors such as severe climate and rough topography, and limiting resources, such as availability of potable water, land, and seasonality of food. The cultural system is examined for both its buffering mechanisms and functions in response to the environmental constraints, and the stressors produced by the culture itself. Cultural practices, organization, and beliefs can buffer environmental constraints in numerous ways: for example, extended kin groups that come together and share food in times of trade scarcity, the division of labor by sex and age, or concepts of nature that promote conservation rather than degradation of the environment. Culturally induced stressors can include practices such as early weaning of children or technology-associated pollution of the water supply.

Host resistance factors account for the variation in the impact of stressors at the individual and populational levels. Host resistance, therefore, encompasses the biochemical, genetic, immunological, and physiological constitutions of individuals. Resistance or susceptibility to stressors are thus contingent upon the biological life-cycle stage and general health status. Therefore, individuals and segments of a population, based on age and/or sex, can be differentially at risk to disease, nutritional, and environmental stressors.

Utilizing this paleoepidemiological model with the appropriate archaeological, ecological, cultural, and biological information specific to a skeletal population, can provide a powerful means of investigating the processes affecting human health and disease that occurred in the past. In addition, the application of a biocultural research approach and model to studies of human health allows for hypothesis testing and new perspectives on modern health problems

The second area of significant physical anthropological contribution to Afro-American biohistorical studies is the methodology of skeletal biology in assessing the health and disease status of archeological populations. As discussed above, the relevance of these methods is in their placement within a biocultural framework. Afro-American skeletal populations, although not abundant, have and will become available for study under several conditions: (1) the intentional cemetery excavation due to land redevelopment or threat of environmental damage; (2) the accidental discovery of an abandoned cemetery; (3) historical and archaeological excavation projects.

A BIOCULTURAL APPROACH TO AFRO-AMERICAN BIOHISTORY

The utilization of a biocultural framework in Afro-American biohistorical research expands the scope and changes the focus in several ways. The major shift is in focusing on localized populations or groups, rather than on hemispheric population studies or aggregated groups such as slaves from disparate states or regions; this focus is a shift in emphasis to the interactions of biology, environment, and culture in studying the disease process in a population rather than searching for specific disorders with single specific etiologies. It also introduces the consideration of adaptation and multicausality into the analysis and reconstruction of the life styles, health, and disease of Afro-American populations. Therefore, biohistorical studies focus on the temporal, ecological, cultural, and biological conditions specific to an Afro-American population. This biocultural approach should produce more in-depth and detailed information about a population that could later contribute significantly to comparative studies of Afro-American populations in the Diaspora. Furthermore, a biocultural framework provides a means both of testing hypotheses generated from earlier biohistorical research and of formulating new hypotheses.

Heterogeneity, both biological and cultural, of Afro-Americans in the Diaspora is an important factor to consider. The localized populational focus can deal with this in two ways: by accounting for the biocultural heterogeneity of the population and through studying intragroup variation. The ethnic and admixture history of an Afro-American population (especially outside of the United States) can be determined from hemispheric population studies (Curtin 1969; Du Bois 1899; Eblen 1973). These studies identify the patterns of African provenience and destinations of slave populations. They are supplemented by ethnographical, ethnohistorical and historical information concerning cultural exchange/syncretisms and interpopulational relationships between colonists (British, Dutch, French, Portuguese, and/or Spanish), Amerindians, and Afro-Americans.

On a cautionary note, the intent is not to advocate research on "race" and/or determining the degree of admixture, since "race" in biological terms is not a particularly useful means of classifying human beings. Rather, ethnic information becomes only another factor of intragroup variation such as cultural practices, beliefs, and social stratification when examining differential patterns of disease incidence and prevalence within a population. In addition, this biocultural localized population approach offers an opportunity to study Afro-American biohistory within an ecological context as called for by Gibbs, et al. (1980). Therefore, health and illness can be examined within the environmental conditions and constraints experienced by the Afro-American population. These environmental factors include: geography and climate (for example, the jungles of Brazil, the tropical conditions of Cuba, the southeastern U.S. coastal plains); the type of subsistence (plantation farming, urban laborers, small-scale farming); types of foods available and their seasonality; exposure to pathogens; and sociotechnological alterations of the environment.

Previously in Afro-American biohistorical studies, disease resistance or susceptibility was always explained from a genetic perspective. Rarely were intrapopulational differences or adaptational explanations considered. In actuality, the adaptive abilities of Afro-Americans is a critical factor in the entire process of enslavement, involuntary migration, and resettlement in the Americas (Cobb 1939), including disease resistance and susceptibility. Thus, the application of a biocultural framework to Afro-American biohistorical research would bring together an expanded research paradigm, a new set of foci and perspectives in exploring the experiences and health of Afro-Americans in the Diaspora.

The remainder of this book focuses on the biocultural study of free, urban, nineteenth century Afro-Americans in Philadelphia, as represented by the First African Baptist Church (FABC) Congregation cemetery population interred ca.1822–1843. It utilizes the Goodman, et al. (1984) model (as set forth in Figure 1.3) for paleoepidemiological research to examine the biohistory of this long-forgotten Afro-American community. Chapter 2 summarizes the research design and methodology. Chapters 3 and 4 present the environmental and sociohistorical contexts of the Afro-American community—a synthesis of health and illness in nineteenth-century Philadelphia, in general, and for Afro-Americans, in particular. A synthesis of the FABC skeletal evidence and comparisons with other Afro-American skeletal series are presented in Chapter 5. Chapter 6, the concluding integrative chapter, pulls together the FABC data (Chapters 3–5) into a biocultural analysis.

Chapter 2

In Search of the Invisible People: Methods and Materials

I am invisible, understand, simply because people refuse to see me.

—Ralph Ellison 1952:3
Invisible Man

Setting out to discover the fabric of the material lives of free Afro-Americans in nineteenth century Philadelphia presented a serious problem, that of their invisibility in the historical record. This is a common problem whenever one studies nonelite people in the historical past, especially members of the underclasses. These are the people who facilitated the lives of the wealthy and the powerful of society; they built cities, provided goods and services, and, to a great extent, were the essential elements of a growing society. However, they remain obscure in the history books, literature, and publications of the period. Elites leave significant documentation of their lives in a variety of forms such as tax, probate, and land records; church records; social registers; newspaper accounts; minutes of social/charitable organizations; city directories; and personal diaries. These materials have a high probability of being archived, stored, inherited, collected, and eventually reposited (e.g., local historical societies, libraries). The few sources of documentation (e.g., church records, almshouse records, beneficial societies) for the poor and underclasses of a society are likely to be lost. Yet Philadelphia, because of its particular social, religious and economic characteristics, provides a relatively good source of information concerning Afro-Americans. As a center for Abolitionists and Quakers, Philadelphia became a hub of activity which generated invaluable records and information (albeit limited) concerning Philadelphia Afro-Americans and their material lives. In addition, because of the city's national historical role there are diverse sources of national and city history that can potentially offer up documentation. The research design included utilizing multiple methods: (1) a document and literature search; (2) demographic analyses consisting of paleodemographic and historical demographic methods; and (3) skeletal biological analyses based on paleopathological and histological methods. Data from these assessments were analyzed statistically and later considered within the biocultural framework presented in Chapter 1.

DOCUMENT AND LITERATURE REVIEW

The objectives of this review were to identify historical materials and relevant literature pertaining to nineteenth-century Philadelphia that would provide a means of: 1) reconstructing the environmental and sociohistoric contexts of its inhabitants and with primary emphasis on Afro-Americans; (2) describing the Afro-American population as to demographic, socioeconomic, religious, and sociocultural factors; (3) clarifying what segment(s) of the Afro-American population the FABC congregation members represented; and (4) describing morbidity and mortality patterns that would facilitate the interpretation of skeletal biological assessments.

Areas of particular focus for this document and literature review included: the social and legal status of free Afro-Americans in Antebellum Philadelphia; the history of slavery and emancipation in the state and city; the environmental and living conditions, such as sanitation, housing, water, and food supply; and the history and role of Afro-American churches in Philadelphia and the First African Baptist Church, in particular. To this end, several institutions and library collections were visited/consulted. These included the Historical Society of Pennsylvania, Philadelphia Baptist Association, Balch Institute, Afro-American Museum, Philadelphia Social History Project Archives at the University of Pennsylvania, Temple University Urban Archives and Collection, City of Philadelphia Archives, State of Pennsylvania Archives, Library of Congress, and the National Archives.

Data Sources

National and local data sources were identified for descriptive populational and sociodemographic information concerning Afro-Americans in nineteenth-century Philadelphia.

United States Census

The United States Censuses for the City of Philadelphia and adjoining districts (1810–1850) were reviewed for population enumeration by age, sex, and legal status of Afro-Americans. Comparability of the censuses was a significant problem due to the inconsistent use of geographical and age classifications. Therefore, the censuses for 1830–1840 were selected for demographic analysis because of their high degree of comparability.

Pennsylvania Abolition Society 1838 Census

The Pennsylvania Abolition Society (1838, 1856) and the Society of Friends (1847) conducted detailed surveys of Philadelphia Afro-American households, which are archived in manuscript form at the Historical Society of Pennsylvania. The Philadelphia Social History Project (PSHP) xeroxed and entered data directly into machine-readable form These censuses are available through the University of Pennsylvania Population Research Center in magnetic tape or diskette format with a code book. The computerized censuses also include unique codes, developed by the PSHP (Hershberg 1973), for occupational categories listed in the census and for geographically locating households.

The 1838 census was selected as the primary data source for two reasons: first, the denomination and color of church attended by the head of household was identified only in that census; and, second, due to temporal factors, the 1838 census had the highest probability of including FABC congregation members interred in the cemetery and/or their respective households. Plate 2.1 shows a sample page, on which Reverend Henry Simmons, FABC pastor, is listed.

The 1838 census was utilized to examine religious affiliations, socioeconomic indicators, and birth status (freeborn or ex-slave) of Afro-American heads of household

Interment Records

A partial interment list for the FABC cemetery (1825–1842) was originally abstracted by Stephanie Pinter from the City of Philadelphia, Board of Health cemetery returns for Milner Associates (archaeologists). The list includes names, ages, and causes of death for most individuals, and the place of death in a few instances. This list represents approximately 48 percent of the burials recovered from the cemetery (Appendix B). These cemetery returns were reviewed for further information and verification.

The database was also studied for more specific information regarding "African Baptists" and FABC congregation members, and the original manuscripts were scrutinized for accuracy, clarification, and details that may not have been entered into the computerized data base. In addition, the Abolition Society minutes that established "The Committee to Visit the Coloureds" and the subsequent committee minutes and published reports were reviewed for details and contextual explanation of the census, the census takers, and the data generated.

Vital Rates

Medical historical sources describing and/or quantifying Philadelphia health conditions and vital rates were sought for the first half of the nineteenth century. Vital rates for the period of 1807–1827 and 1830–1840 were found in the American Journal of the Medical Sciences as reported by Gouverneur Emerson (1827, 1837, 1848), a Philadelphia physician. These vital statistics, based on the Philadelphia Board of Health bills of mortality, give data on population size, death rates, seasonal patterns of mortality, and causes of death.

Other Sources

Throughout the search, several documents were found that contributed to the study. These included: a deed and title transfer of Reverend Simmons's property by his wife; a Penny Collection Book for the First African Baptist church that was used to cross-check with the 1838 census; a charter for an unmarried female beneficial society for FABC, with names that were also cross checked with the census; and an 1838 Almshouse record book for "coloured" women and unpublished manuscripts by members of the Philadelphia Social History Project. Also found was a lithographic portrait of Reverend Henry Simmons by A. Newsam, one of the foremost Philadelphia portrait artists of the period. This portrait was one of only four Afro-Americans found in the Newsam Collection at the Historical Society of Pennsylvania.

DEMOGRAPHIC ANALYSIS

Paleodemography and Historical Demography

Paleodemography and historical demography provide invaluable populational information when used concomitantly within skeletal biological studies. "Paleodemography is the study of vital rates, population distribution, and density in extinct [and extant] human groups, especially those for which there are no written records" (Buikstra and Konigsberg 1985:316). Fundamental to paleodemography is the aging and sexing of each individual skeleton in a population (Angel 1969). Despite recent criticisms of paleodemography (Bocquet-Appel and Masset 1982) and reassessments (Armelagos and Van Gerven 1983; Buikstra and Konigsberg 1985; Greene, et al. 1984; Johansson and Horowitz 1986), paleodemography continues to provide an essential means of understanding the vital rates, population structure, and change of archaeological populations. Historical demography studies vital rates, population structure, and change based on available documents. Birth, death, marriage, and/or tax records are examined to determine morbidity, mortality, and fertility in a population. In both prehistoric and historic populations, scrutinizing the age-sex structure and population density can provide relevant information concerning health status. The emphasis of these studies is on life expectancy, probability of dying, and patterns of mortality. Combined with archaeological data and skeletal evidence of physiological stress, the impact of nutritional inadequacy and disease on differential mortality can be assessed. The use of life

Plate 2.1
Pennsylvania Abolition Society 1838 Census Manuscript Page

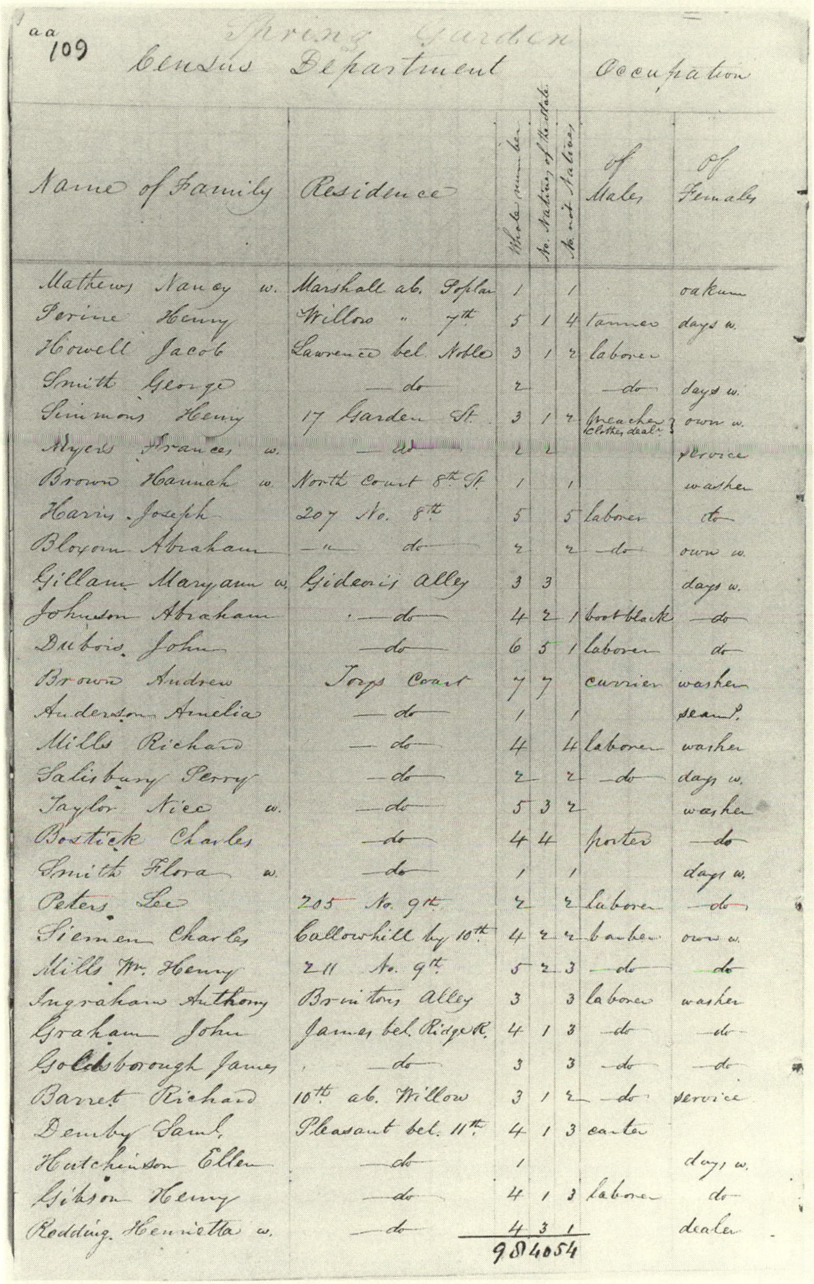

Spring Garden

aa 109 Census Department	Residence	Whole number...	In station of the state, do not station	Occupation of Males	of Females
Name of Family					
Mathews Nancy w.	Marshall ab. Poplar	1	1		oakum
Torine Henry	Willow " 7th	5	1 4	tanner	days w.
Howell Jacob	Lawrence bel. Noble	3	1 2	laborer	
Smith George	do	2		do	days w.
Simmons Henry	17 Garden St.	3	1 2	preacher clothes deal.	own w.
Myers Frances w.	do	2	2		service
Brown Hannah w.	North Court 8th St.	1	1		washer
Harris Joseph	207 No. 8th	5	5	laborer	do
Bloxom Abraham	do	2	2	do	own w.
Gillam Mary ann w.	Gideon's Alley	3	3		days w.
Johnson Abraham	do	4	2 1	boot black	do
Dubois John	do	6	5 1	laborer	do
Brown Andrew	Toys Court	7	7	currier	washer
Anderson Amelia	do	1	1		seam.
Mills Richard	do	4	4	laborer	washer
Salisbury Perry	do	2	2	do	days w.
Taylor Niec w.	do	5	3 2		washer
Bostick Charles	do	4	4	porter	do
Smith Flora w.	do	1	1		days w.
Peters Lee	205 No. 9th	2	2	laborer	do
Siemen Charles	Callowhill by 10th	4	2 2	barber	own w.
Mills Wr. Henry	211 No. 9th	5	2 3	do	do
Ingraham Anthony	Brintons Alley	3	3	laborer	washer
Graham John	James bel. Ridge R.	4	1 3	do	do
Goldsborough James	do	3	3	do	do
Barret Richard	10th ab. Willow	3	1 2	do	service
Demby Saml.	Pleasant bel. 11th	4	1 3	carter	
Hutchinson Ellen	do	1			days w.
Gibson Henry	do	4	1 3	laborer	do
Redding Henrietta w.	do	4	3 1		dealer
		98	40 54		

Note: Reverend Henry Simmons is the fourth entry at 17 Garden Street.
Source: The Historical Society of Pennsylvania, Pennsylvania Abolition Society Facts Book IV.

tables can be an effective assessment technique to ascertain mortality differences between, or within, segments of the population's (age-specific or sex-specific) mortality patterns (Moore, et al. 1975). Model life tables, such as those developed by Weiss (1973); and Coale and Demeny (1966) for isolating abnormal characteristics in mortality profiles, and Farley (1965) for nineteenth century Afro-American mortality, have been important developments in historical demography and paleodemography. Through these demographic analyses, population parameters can be generated and long-term trends in adaptation, health, and disease examined.

In this study, the demographic analysis combined paleodemographic and historical demographic methods and information. Data was compared on life expectancy, survivorship, mortality, and morbidity from information derived from skeletal remains and those identified in the sources described above, when appropriate.

Paleodemographic analysis based on the skeletal aging and sexing of FABC burials (Angel, et al. 1987) provided an essential means of understanding the vital rates and population structure of this archeological population. Studying the age-sex structure and populational patterns of mortality revealed relevant information concerning the health status of FABC congregation members. Utilizing skeletal age at death, a life table was constructed using Lotus 123 software. Paleodemographic assessments focused on life expectancy, survivorship, and patterns of mortality (age and sex). This data was then compared to other Afro-American paleodemographic studies (Kelley and Angel 1983; Rathbun 1987; Rose 1985,) and to model life tables (Weiss 1973).

Historical demographic data from the U.S. census, vital rate reports (Emerson 1827, 1837, 1848), and the FABC partial interment records were used to compare with paleodemographic patterns. These comparisons focused on age-sex ratios, mortality patterns, and seasonality of deaths. In addition, historical demographic studies (Condran 1980; Condran and Cheney 1980) for Philadelphia during the latter half of the nineteenth century were used to place the paleodemographic and historical demographic assessments into context.

THE FIRST AFRICAN BAPTIST CHURCH CEMETERY SKELETAL REMAINS

The First African Baptist Church Cemetery consisted of 144 burials (Parrington and Roberts 1984); of these, 135 skeletons were recovered. There were 75 adult and 60 subadult skeletons. The adults consisted of 36 males and 39 females. The majority (55%) of subadults were infants under twelve months, 23.3 percent aged 1–5 years old, and 21 percent aged 6–16. The FABC adult age and sex distribution is summarized in Table 2.1; Table 2.2 summarizes subadult age distribution.

Table 2.1
FABC Adult Skeletons

Age Group	Males	Females
16–20	1	2
21–30	3	15
31–40	8	8
41–50	14	10
51–60	8	1
61–over	2	3
Totals	36	39
N=75		

Table 2.2
FABC Subadults

Ages	Number
0–12months	34
1–5years	14
6–16years	12
Total	60

Condition and Availability for Study

Taphonomic processes and/or construction related factors affected the recovery and preservation of the FABC skeletal remains. Therefore, the preservation of the skeletal material varied greatly. Of the 75 adult burials, 10 (13.3%) crania and 3 (4%) skeletons were missing. The remaining crania (86.7%) and postcranial skeletons (96%) ranged from very fragmentary to excellent condition. Skeletal remains were classified as to condition of preservation, with crania and post-crania assessed independently, for each individual. The criteria for scoring the condition of skeletons (very fragmentary, poor, fair, good, or excellent) depended on the proportion of the skeleton that was recovered (how complete) and the condition of the bone surfaces and joints for assessment purposes.

SKELETAL BIOLOGICAL ANALYSES: METHODS OF HEALTH ASSESSMENTS

Human bone provides an excellent source of health status information because it is metabolically initiated, nutritionally tempered, physiologically controlled, and biomechanically shaped (Vaughn 1975). Bone provides a measure of biological and cultural factors that have affected the health of an individual/population. Biological factors include nutrient intake, metabolism, genetics, aging, hormonal interactions, and biomechanical stress; and, together with behavioral factors—such as, diet, type and levels of activity, life style and reproductive history—all affect the health and disease status of the human skeleton.

The skeleton is a dynamic system that undergoes growth and development throughout the individual's life span. The average human between conception and age twenty has an active period of bone growth, with a peak period of bone mass development between ages twelve and forty. From age thirty to death, a process of bone resorption predominates, whereby bone mass decreases (Martin, et al. 1985). The biological and behavioral (cultural) factors indicated above can interfere in these normal processes, causing disease episodes and/or periods of delayed growth. These experiences can be indelibly recorded on the skeleton and dentition, leaving behind a means of assessing the individual's general health and disease history, although the duration and severity of nutritional inadequacy determines the extent of evidence recorded on the skeleton. Through observing these "historical remnants" of bones and teeth, both macroscopically and microscopically, the physical anthropologist has a means of measuring a population's health. Several types of skeletal analyses can be undertaken to be later placed within a biocultural and sociohistoric context. Analyses at the macroscopic level can include: anthropometric measurements, assessment of growth and development, and paleopathological analysis of the skeleton and dentition. Microscopic analyses can include bone histology and chemical analyses. In addition, the reconstruction of the population's demographic patterns provides another data source to assess the general health status in terms of morbidity and mortality.

Anthropometry, Growth, and Development

Measurements of the skeleton allow for a comparison of the population under study with other populations and previously established standards. Anthropometric measurements and the respective indices serve as a way to determine stature, growth patterns, and degree of sexual dimorphism in a population. In addition, anthropometrics can be useful in the determination of race, if used cautiously. Anthropometric measurements and growth assessment provide data that can then be correlated with paleopathological analyses to clarify and elaborate the health status of a population.

Paleopathology

The focus of paleopathological analysis is on populational health status, as identified by specific and nonspecific stress indicators. Stressors are considered to be extrinsic variables that affect the organism's ability to function. Biological responses to stressors are not always identified in skeletal remains:

Reaction is mediated by the physiological state of the individual and can be completely buffered, leaving no osseous record. However, disease states lasting as few as four days can interrupt growth, producing markers such as lines of growth arrest in long bones. Chronic stresses can permanently affect growth and development and alter adult skeletal dimensions. (Buikstra and Cook 1985:444)

Even with extensive environmental reconstruction and substantial archaeological data, it is difficult to ascertain the exact source of stressors in studying archaeological populations. In addition, the skeletal system, which has numerous biological functions and interfaces with several other systems, tends to react in limited generalized ways to stressors as an adaptive mechanism. And, it is usually the last system to react to malnutrition and disease stress.

Many disturbances, by acting on the same process may produce similar results, and the identification of a single causative agent may not be possible. This is particularly true in the case of nutritional deficiencies, in which the synergistic effect of multiple deficiencies, or of interactions with infectious disease, is frequently a complicating factor. (Huss-Ashmore, et al. 1982:399)

FABC PALEOPATHOLOGICAL ANALYSIS

A paleopathology form that allowed for both quantitative and qualitative assessment of each burial was devised. In conjunction with the form, a coding format for pathologies, demographic, and burial information was constructed as a guide for scoring. This standard format for coding pathologies by each bone (location, condition, severity, and status) facilitated the data entry and subsequent statistical analysis process. Quantitative (coded) data was entered onto eighty column sheets, verified, and then entered into a computerized data base program. Demographic and burial information recorded for each individual included: sex, age, age group and burial group, and condition of crania and postcrania. Each adult skeleton was examined for evidence of pathology, trauma, and/or joint degeneration.

Pathologies were coded by bone location, severity, and status at time of death (remodeled or unremodeled); this included pathological lesions of specific etiology (e.g., tuberculosis), nonspecific infections (e.g., periostitis), indicators of undernutrition (e.g., porotic hyperostosis), and fractures. Criteria for scoring lesions diagnosed as porotic hyperostosis and periostitis were based on those developed by Mensforth, et al. (1978). Congenital, biomechanical, and nonspecific anomalies were also recorded by bone and location. Nonquantitative evidence related to biomechanical use, such as hypertrophy of muscle attachment areas, was also observed, described, and recorded.

Data from other paleopathological studies of FABC undertaken by other investigators were also included in this analysis. These included: (1) linear enamel hypoplasias and hypocalcifications analyzed from raw data forms provided by Blakey (1986); these data were entered into a data-base management program by type of defect, age of onset, and duration for four permanent and deciduous teeth (upper and lower central incisor, upper and lower canine) for each adult and subadult (when available); (2) age, sex, and stature information for each burial was abstracted from the "measurement and morphological observation" forms of Angel (Smithsonian Anthropological Archives); (3) subadult pathologies as assessed by Angel (Smithsonian Anthropological Archives) and Ortner (reported by Kelley 1988) were also abstracted and recorded.

Paleopathological assessments entailed the examination of skeletal remains for evidence of infection, malformation, trauma, and degeneration. These pathologies were then assessed as to degree of severity and status (healed or unhealed). The major types of pathologies for which the FABC skeletal remains were examined and the criteria for diagnosis are presented in the following sections.

Porotic Hyperostosis

Porotic hyperostosis, a nonspecific pathology of the skull vault (frontal, parietals, and occipital bones), orbits, and immature long bones, is usually diagnosed by its distinctive characteristics of thickened bone, sievelike appearance, and the "hair-on-end" pattern observed radiographically (Goodman, et al. 1984; Huss-Ashmore, et al. 1982; Steinbock 1976). The pathological lesions of porotic hyperostosis develop due to anemias of nutritional (e.g., iron deficiency anemia) or congenital hemolytic etiologies (e.g., sickle cell and thalassemia). Anemic conditions lead to increased red blood cell production as compensation for the high turnover rate of abnormal red blood cells. This process results in the expansion of skeletal marrow cavities (diploe) between the cranial tables (Steinbock 1976)—thus the thickened and sievelike appearance of the exposed hypertrophied trabecular bone (lesion) of the diploe, which can be observed due to the significant thinning of the outer bone layer.

Etiological diagnoses are possible when other bones of the skeleton have responded to an anemic condition. Radiographic assessment is usually necessary for the differential diagnoses of genetic hemolytic disorders (Steinbock 1976), although some pathologic changes may be observed macroscopically. Distinctions include: (1) the greater involvement of the prenasal sinuses, mastoids, and maxilla in thalassemia; and (2) long bone thrombosis, cortical thickening, narrowing of the medullary cavity, and aseptic necrosis of epiphyses in sickle cell anemia, as well as vertebral compressions confined to the central portion of the centrum (Steinbock 1976).

The pathological lesions known today as porotic hyperostosis have been well documented in the archeological literature (Angel 1966; El-Najjar, et al. 1978; Lallo, et al. 1977; Mensforth, et al. 1978; Moseley 1965; 1967; Palkovich 1987; Steinbock 1976). Although identified in the late nineteenth century (Goodman, et al. 1984) as a pathology, porotic hyperostosis has been the subject of a long history of debates concerning etiology and terminology (Hill and Armelagos 1990; Steinbock 1976). The comprehensive term porotic hyperostosis (Angel 1966, 1967, Steinbock 1976) includes the porous and pitted appearance of the ectocranial surfaces of the skull, thus subsuming terms used for specifying cranial location (e.g. cribra orbitalia, cribra frontalis). Armelagos and Hill (1990) have suggested that the small pinpoint porosities on the cranial vault, at times attributed to osteoporosis, should also be diagnosed as porotic hyperostosis.

Primarily a pathology of infancy and childhood, porotic hyperostosis has also been observed in adult skeletons, with higher incidence rates for females of child-bearing ages (Carlson, et al. 1974). The frequency and distribution of lesions tend to cluster within specific age groups, associated with peak periods of growth and development requiring increased iron metabolism (Lallo, et al. 1977, Mensforth, et al. 1978). The incidence of healed lesions are indicative of mortality and morbidity patterns of a population, since the remodeling process (healing) points to the individual's exposure to early stressors and survival despite an initial episode of iron deficiency (Mensforth, et al. 1978). In addition, subadults with active lesions tended to die at a slightly higher rate in early childhood (Huss-Ashmore, et al. 1982).

In New World populations (Amerindian), porotic hyperostosis has been primarily associated with nutritionally induced iron deficiency anemia rather than congenital anemias. Since the New World was apparently free of endemic malaria prior to colonization, congenital hemolytic disorders were not found in the Americas. Therefore, maize-dependent diets have been considered the underlying cause of iron deficiency anemia in New World archaeological populations (Goodman, et al. 1984; El-Najjar, et al. 1978; Steinbock 1976). These high carbohydrate, low protein, ascorbic acid-deficient maize and beans diets, although appreciably high in iron content, were low in iron absorption. The bioavailability of iron is affected by dietary constituents such as chelating agents (ascorbic acid, sugars, sulfur-containing amino acids) that promote iron absorption. By contrast, agents such as phosphates and phytic acid inhibit the absorption of iron by binding it into insoluble molecules (Beal 1980; Mensforth, et al. 1978). Food processing, such as boiling for long periods of time at high temperatures, may have further reduced the bioavailibity of iron and other essential nutrients (such as folic acid and vitamin B^{12}) necessary for normal development of red blood cells.

Several investigators (Goodman, et al. 1984; Huss-Ashmore, et al. 1982; Lallo, et al. 1977; Mensforth, et al. 1978; Palkovich 1987) have concluded that the interaction of cultural, ecological, and biological factors must be considered in order to account for the etiology and incidence of porotic hyperostosis in a population. Many of these studies have demonstrated the importance of the synergistic relationship between infection and iron deficiency anemia. Carlson and coworkers (1974) found that subadults (0–10 years) in prehistoric Sudanese Nubian populations exhibited higher incidence of porotic hyperostosis due to low iron grain-dependent diets, weaning stress, and parasitic infections. Similarly, Lallo and coworkers (1977) found an increase in porotic hyperostosis as maize dependency increased in Dickson Mound Amerindians. Lallo and coworkers maintain that infectious and parasitic diseases and weaning practices, interacting with iron deficient diets, led to nutritional deficiencies and infectious conditions, which resulted in the inhibition of iron absorption and porotic hyperostosis at Dickson Mounds. Palkovich (1987) found that endemic maternal malnutrition, which predisposed infants to early infections, was the underlying factor in the high incidence of porotic lesions in southwestern Arroyo Hondo subadults. Walker (1986), in his study cf the Channel Island, California, Amerindians, further emphasized the problem by considering only a dietary etiology for porotic hyperostosis. Although Channel Islanders consumed a marine based diet rich in iron (13–19 clams provide 7mg and 13–19 oysters provide 5.6mg of iron—compared to 6.6mg for 3oz. of beef liver), its bioavailability was compromised due to diarrheal diseases. Thus, the underlying causes were the combination of water contamination, parasitic infections, and seasonal malnutrition.

Mensforth and coworkers (1978) used refined age categories in their assessment of Libben site subadults, combined with diagnostic distinctions (healed and unhealed) for both porotic hyperostosis and periostitis. They demonstrated that infectious disease was the initial condition that made individuals more susceptible to iron deficiency anemia (porotic hyperostosis). When both infectious disease and porotic hyperostosis occurred in an individual, the infectious lesions were usually more severe (Lallo, et al. 1977; Mensforth, et al. 1978).

Therefore, paleopathological identification and assessment of porotic hyperostosis as to severity, lesion status (remodeled and unremodeled), age and sex-specific categories provide a broader understanding of the: (1) relationship between maternal and infant health status; (2) differential patterns of morbidity and mortality; and, (3) the interaction of nutrition and infectious disease, in archeological populations.

When examining Afro-Americans skeletons, the assumption that porotic hyperostosis is due solely to nutritionally induced anemias could lead to the loss of significant information. The utilization of an ecological approach that includes differential diagnosis would remedy this potential problem. Clearly, some African slaves brought the hereditary material for sickle cell anemia with them to the New World, allowing the possibility of sickle cell disease in Afro-Americans. In addition, heterozygous (sickle cell trait) Africans and their descendants, who labored in the malarial conditions of the coastal plains of the southern United States and Central and South Americas during the eighteenth and nineteenth centuries, may have had a selective advantage (Gibbs, et al. 1980) and maintained the sickle cell gene. The possibility of hereditary anemias, therefore, should not be excluded in the paleopathological assessment of Afro-American skeletal remains.

Cranial bones for each FABC individual were scored for porotic hyperostosis by severity of porosity (slight, moderate, and severe), location, and status (unremodeled and remodeled). Lesions were scored as "unremodeled" when they exhibited sharply defined margins in the cribiform mesh with macroscopically visible porosity. Lesions with smooth lamellar texture, displaying bone filling of the peripheral pores and an absence of porosity, were scored as "remodeled" (Mensforth, et al. 1978). Diagnosis of porotic hyperostosis was based on the assessment of porosity/pitting on the parietals, frontal and occipital bones, and expanded diploe. Long bones were also examined for macroscopic evidence of pathological changes related to sickle cell anemia. Subadults were examined by Ortner and reported by Kelley (1988).

Periostitis

The incidence of infectious disease, as determined by periosteal bone lesions (periostitis), can also be an important indicator of physiological stress in a population. Periostitis, when analyzed within a cultural and ecological context that integrates paleopathological data from several stress indicators, provides a measure of acute and chronic infectious disease in a population (Goodman, et al. 1984; Magennis 1986). Important to understanding populational health is the differential diagnosis between infections of known etiology, such as tuberculosis and treponemas (e.g., syphilis), and those of nonspecific etiology (Ortner and Putschar 1981; Steinbock 1976). The majority of infectious disease lesions are caused by a wide range of microorganisms, and may be subsumed under the general term periostitis and osteomyelitis (Steinbock 1976). Lesions confined to the outer periosteal surface of the bone are commonly referred to as periostitis. When infection involves the entire bone tissue, including the marrow cavity, the term osteomyelitis is used more frequently. Osteomyelitic lesions may be caused by bone trauma, infection of the surrounding tissue, or a wide range of blood borne microorganisms (Ortner and Putschar 1981).

Periostitis, commonly observed on long bones, may also occur on the cranial tables (endo- and ecto-cranial). The tibia and femur are the most frequently affected bones. Since the tibia tends to exhibit the highest frequency of periostotic lesions compared to other bones, it usually provides the maximum number of affected individuals. Periosteal reactions result from an elevation of the fibrous outer layer of the periosteum due to the compressing and stretching of blood vessels. Subperiosteal hemorrhage then occurs which, in turn, reduces the blood supply to the bone. If the physiological disruption is severe and long term, the periosteal bone tissue will die (necrosis). Otherwise, the periosteum will resume normal growth when the disruption ceases (Goodman, et al. 1984;

Steinbock 1976), thus producing a healing or remodeling process that can be assessed as remodeled or unremodeled (active). Host resistance, nutritional status, and virulence of the microorganism can affect the severity and distribution of periosteal lesions. They may be acute and localized, or chronic and systemic, affecting several bones at a time. Goodman, et al. (1984) maintain that the effective analysis of periostitis should include bone location, severity, status (unremodeled or remodeled), and narrow biologically relevant age categories.

Often, one pathophysiological state predisposes an individual to one or several other diseases.   Therefore, consideration of synergistic processes is critical. Lallo and coworkers (1977) demonstrated at the Dickson Mounds site that increasing agriculturalism, population density, sedentism, and decreased nutritional adequacy elevated the incidence of infectious disease morbidity and mortality.

Cranial and post-cranial adult skeletons from FABC were macroscopically examined for periostitis. Lesions were scored for severity, bone location and status (unremodeled and remodeled). The criteria for scoring lesions was based on Mensforth, et al. (1978):

- *Remodeled lesions*—generally display considerable resorption and redistribution of the new subperiosteal bone as it becomes incorporated into the normal cortex or table of the affected bone. The remodeled bone is very smooth, dense, and more mature in appearance.... Occasionally, the more involved cases exhibit trace hypervascularity and loss of normal bone contour.
- *Unremodeled lesions*—characteristically display a fibrous, vascular, porous, and somewhat irregular new layer of bone which gives the appearance of a "scab" over the normal cortex or table of the bone. (Mensforth, et al. 1978:24–25)

The frequency and distribution of periosteal lesions were then assessed by sex, age group, and association with iron deficiency anemia (porotic hyperostosis).

Trauma

Trauma involving the skeleton is generally caused by cultural factors such as warfare or technology (e.g., occupation), and physiological conditions (e.g., osteopenias) that affect bone directly (Ortner and Putschar 1981). Skeletal evidence of trauma can include fracture, dislocation, deformity due to disruption in nerve and/or blood supply, or distortion of shape/contour of bone. Broadly defined, fractures are "any traumatic event that results in the partial or complete discontinuity of a bone" (Ortner and Putschar 1981:55). Trauma also includes wounds due to weapons (swords, axes, arrows, spears), surgical procedures (trephinations), or breaks induced by pathophysiological conditions.

Mensforth and Lovejoy (1985), in assessing the accuracy of skeletal aging of Ohio Amerindians from the Libben Site, used several biological aging phenomena including the frequency and distribution of fractures (based on Lovejoy and Heiple's 1981 Libben fracture study). Fractures attributed to old age are primarily those of the proximal femur and distal radius (colle's fracture), which characteristically occur when the individual extends the arm to break an accidental fall either "precipitated or exacerbated by the degenerative effects of aging" (Mensforth, and Lovejoy 1985:97). Osteoporosis or bone loss is a significant underlying factor in the occurrence of these age-related fractures. Through the aging process, the rates between bone formation and removal, once balanced, become disproportionate, with bone loss exceeding bone formation. Thus, cortices become thinner and more brittle, leading to a higher risk of fracture in the weight-bearing joints such as the proximal femur or the inability to withstand accidental falls. Investigators (Buhr and Cook 1959; Mensforth, and Lovejoy 1985) maintain that similar age and sex patterns of old age fractures are displayed in different populations, although overall fracture rates vary due to cultural and technological factors. Age-associated fractures were few, despite the high overall rate of fracture per individual at Libben (Lovejoy and Heiple 1981). Distal radius fractures, both in modern populations (Buhr and Cook 1959) and Libben, remained low for both sexes until age forty, followed by a marked increase in frequency for females after age forty-five (Mensforth, and Lovejoy 1985). The differential distribution of this old age fracture at Libben had a female to male sex ratio of 4:1. Proximal femur fracture incidence did not accelerate until age sixty in modern populations (Buhr and Cooke 1959). The occurrence of only one transcervical femoral fracture in Libben and none in FABC suggests that a significant portion of either population did not survive beyond age sixty (Mensforth, and Lovejoy 1985).

Mensforth, and Lovejoy (1985) found that the majority of fractures observed in the Libben population were due to accidental causes, and that those due to interpersonal aggression were virtually absent. Variance in the frequency of occurrence of Libben fractures was accounted for by the "years at risk" of individual members. Therefore, the longer people lived, the more likely they were to have a fracture. In Lovejoy and Heiple's (1981) study of Libben long bone fractures, they observed two life-cycle periods of elevated fracture rates based on the "years at risk" analysis. These two periods included the older segment of the population aged over 45; and the adolescent/young adulthood group aged 15–25.

Degenerative Joint Disorders

The human skeleton has two basic types of joints: (1) diarthroses, where the articular surfaces are covered with cartilage, united by a fibrous capsule that is lubricated by synovial fluid—this type of joint allows for a wide range of movement (e.g., hip, elbow); and (2) synarthroses, or joints with no joint cavity, where two bones are joined by connective tissue, thus limiting the range of movement (e.g., intervertebral disks, the pubic symphysis joining the innominates). The degeneration of these joints, in skeletal remains, can be studied as indicators of biomechanical stress, trauma, biological aging. Life style and activities play an important role in either buffering an individual from joint degeneration (arthritis) or enhancing the likelihood that the condition will appear. Therefore, the pattern, distribution, severity, and onset by age and sex in adults can be used to interpret the role of cultural activity in the etiology of degenerative joint disorders (Goodman, et al. 1984).

Paleopathological diagnosis of degenerative disorders (arthritis) in dry bone entails a less complicated process compared to that of clinical diagnosis, primarily due to the absence of soft tissue. Hence, diagnoses of degenerative disorders in skeletal remains are limited to: osteoarthritis (degenerative joint disease), traumatic arthritis, rheumatoid arthritis, infectious arthritis, vertebral osteophytosis, ankylosing spondylitis, and gout (Steinbock 1976). Osteoarthritis and vertebral osteophytosis are the most common degenerative disorders observed in skeletal remains and yield the greatest amount of information concerning activity patterns. Based on morphological differences, rather than pathology, the degeneration of the vertebral bodies has been classified separately as "osteophytosis" despite the similar, if not identical, process of osteoarthritic degeneration of the diathrodial joints (Merbs 1983).

Osteoarthritis is a common, progressive, chronic, noninflammatory disease of the diathrodial joints causing increased disability throughout the aging process. It primarily affects individuals thirty years and older, with slightly higher frequencies in males (Steinbock 1976). The weight-bearing joints such as the hips and knees, and those joints exposed to chronic trauma (shoulder, elbow, temporo-mandibular) are most frequently affected. The occurrence of osteoarthritis is rarely confined to one joint in an individual (Merbs 1983).

Functional stress and biomechanical "wear and tear" are considered the primary causes of osteoarthritis, although nutrition, genetics, and viral infections can also exacerbate the degenerative process. Biomechanical stress is most apparent at the articular surfaces of long bones and flat bones (e.g., innominate, scapula). Joint degeneration does not develop as an inflammatory disease/condition in the early stages. It is a progressive, age-related process that includes: cartilage breakdown, reduced bone vascularization, decreased ability for bone self-repair, and decreased secretion of lubricating fluid. This process leads to the exposure of subchrondral bone, and the articular surfaces become pitted, eroded, and "lipped" around the margins. The areas subjected to the greatest biomechanical stress and strain undergo more intense degeneration, usually producing pitting and erosion on the central portions of articular surfaces first, due to the centrifugal motion of the joint (Merbs 1983). New bone growth (exophytic), which occurs along the margins of the articular cartilage and in fossae located within joint capsules, is commonly referred to as "lipping." The direction of these marginal osteophytes is usually governed by lines of mechanical force exerted on the area of growth and by the contour of the joint surface from which it protrudes (Merbs 1983).

The articular surfaces are eventually denuded of cartilage due to the continuous unlubricated rubbing of bone on bone. This process produces a shiny "ivory-like" or "polished" appearance, which is referred to as eburnation (Martin, et al. 1979; Merbs 1983; Ortner and Putschar 1981; Steinbock 1976). This is followed by a roughening of the articular surfaces, and excoriated grooves form lines of mechanical stress eventually leading to gross deformity (Merbs 1983).

Age-related patterns of osteoarthritis have been observed in numerous studies of old world (Angel 1971, 1979) and new world populations. These studies have included populations that utilized different subsistence strategies including hunter-gatherers (Kelley 1979; Merbs 1983), hunter-gatherer/agriculturalists (Pickering 1979), and horticulturalists and agriculturalists (Martin, et al. 1979). In general, osteoarthritis began between ages 30 and 35 and increased with age, regardless of the severity of joint degeneration. Studies of middle-aged adults generally show a higher incidence in males (30–40 years old), but, when older adults (50 years old and above) are included, females have higher frequencies (Merbs 1983). Males tended to have higher overall incidences of osteoarthritis than females, although differential patterns of joint involvement by sex were reported in most studies. Martin and coworkers (1979) studied degenerative joint diseases in Dickson Mound Amerindians and found an association between osteoarthritis and periosteal reactions. Individuals with multiple joint involvement showed a statistically higher percentage of periosteal reactions. Both infectious lesions and degenerative joint disease appeared to be a function of age, and the more severe arthritic involvements consistently showed more severe infectious reactions.

According to Merbs, certain occupations and sports activities, in particular those that tend to concentrate stress on specific articular joints, "may produce pathology, or premature aging in the parts of the articular system under greatest stress" (1983:19). Two examples are osteoarthritis of the elbow for tennis players or baseball pitchers and degeneration of the fingers in seamstresses. In his review of the activity-related osteoarthritis and osteophytosis literature, Merbs (1983) found that: (1) jobs which included heavy lifting, particularly if the lifting entailed more than a minimal duration of time, were associated with higher incidence of osteoarthritis; (2) lifting was also associated with osteoarthritis of the knee; (3) heavy work (e.g., pneumatic drill operating), including lifting, was associated with the occurrence of osteoarthritis of the elbow; (4) incidence was higher for men who were craftsmen or construction workers than for the general population; and (5) cotton workers exhibited osteoarthritis of the cervical spine and the joints of the hands, although vertebral disk degeneration was significantly less than for miners. Merbs's research of a Canadian Inuit skeletal population (Sadlermuit of North Point) identified degenerative joint disease patterns associated with specific activities of these hunter-gatherer-fisher people (e.g., shoulder osteoarthritis with harpoon throwing).

Several investigators have developed systems for assessing arthritic involvement, coding the severity of condition from slight to severe (Jurmain 1977; Martin, et al. 1979; Ortner and Putschar 1981; Steinbock 1976). These methods have been considered a problematic assessment (Steinbock 1976) because of the qualitative nature of the assessment and the possibility of high interobserver variation. However, if the researcher presents details of analysis and photographs of the stages, the analysis can be useful.

In the FABC population, degeneration of joint surfaces were scored from "absent" to "severe" for each joint surface per bone, after Steinbock (1976). In addition, to facilitate comparability, the scores for the articular surfaces comprising a joint were aggregated in order to report the presence or absence of degenerative changes by major joint complexes (e.g., knee included distal femur, patella, proximal tibia, and fibula).

Osteophytosis

Osteophytosis, the counterpart of osteoarthritis of the vertebrae, is characterized by the thinning, decrease in lubrication, and eventual destruction of the intervertebral disks. The intervertebral disks consist of the nucleus pulposus, the annulus fibrosus, and two hyaline cartilage plates. The nucleus pulposus is the interior of the disk, which in younger individuals is a semigelatinous tissue and in the adult becomes more collagenous and reduced in fluid. The annulus fibrosus is the peripheral portion of the disk consisting of fibrous tissue. The vertebral bodies are united firmly along the margins by fibers from the annulus, which are intertwined with the longitudinal anterior and posterior ligaments of the spinal column. The intervertebral disks have several functions, including shock absorption and movement. "The nucleus pulposus equalizes pressures, is important in fluid exchange, and serves as the axis of movement between adjacent vertebrae. The annulus provides stability by binding the vertebral bodies together and acting as a check ligament" (Merbs 1983:18). Degeneration causes tearing of some of the annulus fibers from the marginal ridge; the nucleus pulposus becomes compressed and protrudes anteriorally against the longitudinal ligaments. The resultant pressure leads to the formation of new subperiosteal bone at the point of anterior ligamental attachment. These marginal osteophytes ("lipping") on the vertebral bodies can become large enough to impinge on the adjacent vertebra. Eventually, the intervertebral disk will be completely destroyed and the two osteophytes will often fuse (ankylosis). Osteophytes usually occur on multiple vertebrae. Osteophytosis usually occurs in thirty to sixty year olds, and ranges in severity from slight lipping to partial or complete fusion of the vertebrae. McKern and Stewart (1957) attempted to utilize the age-related pattern of osteophytosis as a skeletal age indicator. Both Yesner (1981) in a study of Aleut skeletons and Gunness-Hey (1980) in an Eskimo series found an earlier onset of osteophytes, beginning as early as age twenty and, thereafter, increasing in a "directly age-related pattern." Clark and Delmond (1979) also found a distinct age-related pattern for both males and females in Dickson Mound populations.

Dental Enamel Defects: Hypoplasias and Hypocalcifications

The dentition is an excellent source of individual and populational health status information since dental health is directly related to dietary habits (Wells 1964).

No structures of the human body are more likely to disintegrate during life than teeth, yet after death none have greater tenacity against decay.... [P]athology of these organs is similar to that of other tissues and they may be affected by congenital anomalies, injury, infections, new growths, degenerations or deficiency states. (Wells 1964:121)

Paleopathological analysis also included the examination of FABC dentitions for enamel defects, which are indicators of nutritionally and/or disease-induced metabolic disruptions.

Formation of the human dentition is initiated during the gestational period, within the maxilla and mandible, from the fifth prenatal month and continuing on to approximately six years of age. Both deciduous (primary or "milk") and permanent dentitions are formed through the process of enamel matrix formation, amelogenesis. The enamel matrix is secreted by ameloblasts, forming enamel sequentially with age. The incisal aspect (cusp) is formed first, followed by successive bands of mineralizing enamel until the cervical border reaches the root completing the crown (Blakey 1981;Blakey and Armelagos 1985; Goodman and Armelagos 1985).

Episodes of metabolic stress, such as disease and/or malnutrition that interfere with calcium availability (Blakey and Armelagos 1985) or absorption, can result in developmental enamel defects. Hypoplasias and hypocalcifications are enamel defects produced during different phases of tooth formation. Enamel hypoplasias are deficiencies in enamel thickness due to a cessation of the enamel-forming (ameloblast) activity. This arrested calcium deposition during the initial phase of enamel development involves only the transverse bands of enamel laid down during that period. Therefore, hypoplasias occur as transverse linear lesions, appearing as grooves or serial pitting.

The secondary phase of dental development entails the mineralization and/or calcification of enamel. Insults during this phase result in a reduced calcified salt content in teeth. These areas of "hypocalcification" are transverse bands of normal thickness with an opaque coloration (chalky white or yellow brown), usually involving deeper enamel than hypoplasias, and a hard outer enamel "skin" without indentation (Huss-Ashmore, et al. 1982; Blakey and Armelagos 1985).

Several authors have reported a differential pattern among teeth in the incidence of enamel defects (El-Najjar, et al. 1978; Goodman and Armelagos 1985; Swarstedt 1966). All have concluded that the greatest frequency of defects occurs on the maxillary central incisor and mandibular canine. Goodman and Armelagos (1985) propose that the inter-tooth differences reflect variations in susceptibility to hypoplastic defects of tooth type. The most frequently affected teeth are those that are more developmentally stable and under greater genetic control. In addition, the earlier developing teeth have earlier peak frequencies of defects than later developing teeth. Swarstedt (1966) advocated the analysis of all teeth for defects as opposed to the traditional single tooth analysis, because of intertooth variability. Thus, his approach allows for (1) verifying that the underlying stress producing the defect was systemic and not local in origin; and, (2) establishing a more comprehensive chronology of episodes by utilizing teeth that develop at different ages. Alternately, Goodman, et al. (1980) proposed using the "best tooth approach" as was illustrated in the Dickson Mounds Amerindian study in which 95 percent of systemic episodes were recorded on one or both of the maxillary central incisor and the mandibular canine.

Studies of adult permanent dentition of archeological and preindustrial populations have found generally low frequencies of defects established prior to the second year and after the fourth year of life (Goodman, et al. 1984; Corruccini, et al. 1985; Huss-Ashmore, et al. 1982; Rose 1985; Schultz and McHenry 1975). Goodman (1988), in a study of enamel hypoplasia chronology, compared two urban industrial samples: Sarnat and Schour's (1941, 1942) Chicago series and a sample from the Hammon-Todd osteological collection, comprised of lower socioeconomic Cleveland area adults born between 1855 and 1913. The Chicago series reported high frequencies of hypoplasias during the first year of life (66.6 %) and a large portion of the remainder occurring before age three. The Hammon-Todd, which produced data with a high frequency (63.0%) of defects between 2.0 and 4.0 years, generally duplicated the chronological pattern observed for nonindustrialized populations, and significantly varies from the Chicago sample. As Goodman (1988) has indicated, the Sarnat and Schour (1941,1942) should not be considered the "universal" pattern, especially for industrialized populations. This has been further corroborated by the FABC hypoplasia data. Goodman, also suggested that these chronological similarities between industrial (Hammon-Todd) and non-industrial populations might be associated with at least two factors:

First, it is suggestive that teeth are most susceptible to defects near the middle third and that this common period of increased susceptibility may promote similar chronological patterns of defects. Second, it may be that the common peak frequency of hypoplasias between 1.5 and 4.0 years reflects a time of increased environmental stress and/or increased vulnerability for children in most populations. Weaning may be at least one of a series of potentially important nutritional, immunological, and socioeconomic factors. (Goodman 1989:789)

Analysis of deciduous dentition enamel defects provides a means of link-ing the health experiences of childhood with survival, and indirectly with the health status of reproducing females in the population (Buikstra, and Cook 1985; Blakey 1981; Blakey and Armelagos 1985; Sciulli 1977). A differential pattern between defect types has been observed in the deciduous dentition: hy-poplasias are generally low, while hypocalcifications are high in a stressed population (Sciulli 1977), and Blakey (1981) suggests that this might reflect intrauterine protection of the fetus. It has also been proposed that individuals with greater numbers of defects and with prenatal onset experienced earlier mortality than those whose primary onset occurred primarily during the pro-longed lactation and weaning period (Blakey and Armelagos 1985). These authors have reported a pattern of mortality between ages one and three for those with prenatal onset defects, and at least four years of age for those with postnatal formation of defects. Therefore, a most significant finding based on information from the deciduous and permanent dentitions is that the individu-als most stressed during infancy did not survive long enough to erupt a secon-dary dentition.

Enamel defects for FABC deciduous and permanent dentition data were analyzed separately for both hypoplasias and hypocalcifications. The chronol-ogy of deciduous enamel development was based on Shaw and Sweeney (1973) and Goodman, et al. (1980) for the permanent dentition. Blakey and coworkers used a chronometric method (Blakey 1981; Blakey and Armelagos 1985), which measured the distance between the cemento-enamel junction and both the incisal and coronal borders of a defect. The measurements were then con-verted into the developmental ages at which the defect began to develop (onset) and the age at which normal development resumed. Episodes were represented by the number of discontinuous periods of defective development without tem-poral overlap. This measurement and method of defining episodes provided a means of estimating the age of onset, the period over which stress occurred (duration or chronicity), and the ages at which stresses ceased and resumed for each individual (Blakey, et al. 1989). Enamel defects recorded provided a record for the prenatal period (from the fifth month in utero) through childhood (6.5 years), therefore including the deciduous and permanent dentitions.

Bone Morphometry and Histology

There are three basic types of bone that make up the human skeleton: compact cortical bone, trabecular (spongiosa, cancellous) bone, and woven bone (Vaughan 1975). Cortical bone is found in long bone shafts, which surround the marrow cavities and tend to be hard. Trabecular bone is made up of a net-work of interlacing partitions that enclose the cavities containing red or fatty marrow. Trabecular bone is found in vertebral bodies, the ends of long bones, and the majority of the flat (e.g., ilium, sternum, rib) bones (Vaughan 1975).

Woven bone (fiber or fetal), the most immature form of bone tissue, is formed by healthy neonatal and early postnatal skeleton. It is also prevalent in individuals with specific disorders (such as osteogenesis imperfecta or Paget's disease) or bone fractures (Stout and Simmons 1979).

Histological analysis of bone provides a means of studying the overall state of an organism. Bone structure can be studied at the macroscopic and microscopic levels. Cortical bone has been the most extensively studied in archaeological populations, primarily due to its better preservation, compared to trabecular and woven bone (Stout and Simmons 1979; Stout and Teitlebaum 1976). Macroscopic studies primarily entail the assessment of bone quantity; these morphometric studies include measurements of any cortical bone (cortical thickness and cortical area) present; noninvasive methods such as photon absorbtiometry have been used to determine bone density. Microscopic studies entail the assessment and measurement of bone at the cellular level, and constitute a means of assessing the quality of bone as it relates to the dynamic relation between bone formation and resorption.

Bone mass in the human skeleton increases during childhood, when bone formation exceeds resorption, and remains relatively stable from young adulthood until middle age. Bone mass then decreases throughout middle age (beginning at age 30), when resorption or bone loss exceeds formation. This bone loss makes cortices progressively thinner and more porous (Martin, et al. 1985), frequently leading to osteopenia or osteoporosis. These terms are often used interchangeably, the latter more frequently to indicate an age-related disorder. Thus, osteoporosis is defined as an age-related bone pathology, usually associated with loss of calcium and characterized by reduction in bone density, increasing porosity, and brittleness. Osteopenia is diagnosed when these conditions are observed in younger individuals, an indicator of nutritional deficiencies (Vaughn 1975) and/or impaired growth and development.

In skeletal biological studies, primarily for reasons of preservation, the denser, more compact cortical bone of long bone shafts is utilized to diagnose osteopenia/osteoporosis and assess the quality/quantity of bone. The femur, the most commonly used bone for archaeological populations, is tubular when viewed in cross-section (Figure 2.1), with an endosteal (inner) and periosteal (outer) surface covered with a membrane (Martin, et al. 1985). The dense region between both surfaces is the cortex (cortical or compact bone), which surrounds the marrow cavity composed of trabecular bone. It is the cortex that is studied macroscopically and microscopically in order to assess bone quantity and quality. Macroscopic assessment of cortical bone primarily provides information on the quantity of bone present at a gross level, while microscopic assessments supply data for both bone quantity and quality, at the tissue level. Therefore, morphometrics at the macroscopic or organ level provides a means of indirectly assessing the growth and development of individuals.

FABC Bone Histology: Cortical Thickness and Cortical Area

Every adult and subadult skeleton available was sampled for histological study. Based on common practice in the field, the left femur was selected for sampling. Whenever a left femur was missing or extremely fragmentary, the right femur was selected. Pathology or trauma of the left femur (such as a bone cyst or fracture) also required the selection of the right femur, since bone turn over activity is increased in both pathological and fracture conditions (Frost 1985; Ortner 1976; Stout and Simmons 1979).

Each femur was measured for total length, and the midpoint was marked. Two centimeters proximal and distal to the midpoint were marked, and a transverse cross-section totaling 4 centimeters was taken. Femoral sections were cut with a diamond blade saw or a hand coping saw, depending on the preservation and density of the bone. The proximal and distal ends of the samples and the burial number were then marked on the sample for consistency and accuracy in thin section preparation. Each sample was cut in thirds, with the first and third sections reserved for future study and the central section utilized for this research. The sample was cleaned ultrasonically in acetone for approximately ten minutes, air dried, and then embedded in dimethylene triamine epoxy. This embedding medium reduced the time of embedding significantly compared to methyl methacrylate. Complete curing takes one to fourteen hours, depending on the method of curing and the size of the specimen. If curing is undertaken by heating on a hot plate or in an oven at less than 90 degrees Fahrenheit, the curing time is less, whereas curing at room temperature requires eight to fourteen hours.

Thin sections were prepared by cutting slices approximately 200 microns thick on a Buehler Isomet and then mounting them on a clean, warmed microscope slide with the same epoxy at a 5:1 ratio. After allowing to dry and ascertaining that no air pockets had formed between the slide and the specimen, the slide was ground down to 80–100 micron thickness and was then polished. The determination of the final thin section thickness was based on the quality of bone microstructure visualization under the microscope. Thickness was ascertained by using a Helios dial caliper. The methods and materials selected were chosen based on pretesting of FABC rib and femoral sections, representing the best and worst preserved skeletal material based on gross inspection. Pretesting was undertaken while training with Debra Martin (Hampshire College), David Mann (Los Alamos National Laboratory, Thin Sectioning Lab—Earth and Space Science Division), and Mitchell Shaffler (University of Utah, Bone Biology Laboratory).

When thin sections were prepared for analysis, approximately 50 percent of the individual sections presented problems in visualization due to organic compounds lodged within the haversian systems and lamellar bone, despite the acetone cleaning prior to embedding,. Several sample sections were ground to lower thicknesses of 35–85 microns as opposed to the standard 80–100 microns, which also did not improve visualization. Samples were also stained with basic fuchsin, as well as washed in xylene as a clearing agent, in order to enhance visualization. This method proved only to stain the debris darker than the microstructure. It was decided to forego the microstructural analysis until a better methodology and funding were obtained to resolve the visualization problems.

Femoral cross-sections of fifty-four adults (twenty-eight males and twenty-six females) and seven subadult skeletons were studied macroscopically. Morphometrics of FABC femoral cross-sections were taken utilizing two different measurement techniques; these included mean cortical thickness and total cortical area. Cortical thickness was taken at eight preselected equidistant points with a Helios needle point dial caliper to the nearest tenth of a millimeter. The eight thickness measurements were summed and averaged for each individual. This method duplicated the technique of Martin, et al. (1987) for the Cedar Grove post-Reconstruction Afro-American sample from Arkansas. Cortical area was calculated by measuring the periosteal and endosteal perimeters of femoral cross-sections and then subtracting the endosteal perimeter (marrow cavity) from the periosteal area in order to obtain a total cortical area measurement. Cortical area measurements were taken using a digitizer and the Bioquant image analysis system morphometrics software package. The formula used to calculate cortical area was similar to the one developed by Sedlin, et al. (1963) for calculating percent cortical area (PCA), although intracortical was not accounted for, therefore the measurement was called "cortical area" only.

Formula: $\dfrac{\text{periosteal area - medullary cavity area}}{\text{periosteal area} \times 100}$ = cortical area

Cortical thickness for each individual was compared between and within age and sex groups, in order to determine the existence of differential health and disease patterns. Children and adults were considered separately. A populational analysis was followed by a comparison to other Afro-American and African populations that have been studied histologically, such as Cedar Grove Cemetery (Martin, et al. 1987) and Nubians (Martin and Armelagos 1979, 1985; Van Gerven, et al. 1985).

FABC skeletal biological and histological assessments were compared to assessments of other Afro-American skeletal series. The studies that were utilized for comparison represent the larger populations that have been reported in the literature.

Figure 2.1
Femoral Cross-Section with Equidistant Lines for Cortical Thickness
Measurements

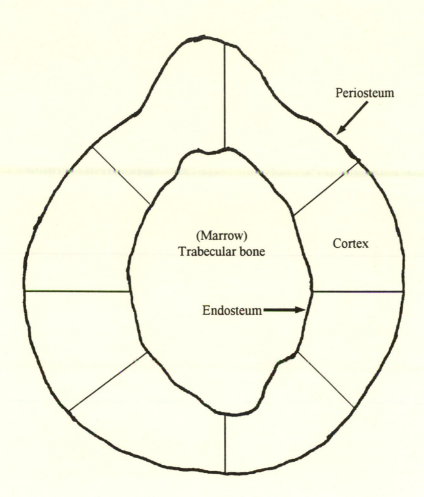

Illustration by Diane Ghalib, 1995.

AFRO-AMERICAN SKELETAL BIOLOGICAL STUDIES

The limited Afro-American skeletal series which have been studied represent a broad spectrum of Afro-American life styles and biohistory throughout the eighteenth, nineteenth, and early twentieth centuries. These skeletal biological series include: South Carolinian plantation slaves (Rathbun 1987); Maryland industrial slaves (Kelley and Angel 1983); ex-slaves and their descendants from rural Arkansas (Rose 1985); urban slaves from New Orleans (Owsley, et al. 1987); poor and destitute urban dwellers (Blakley and Beck 1982) from reconstruction period Atlanta; slaves from several small (1–9 burials) southern farms or plantations (Angel, et al. 1987); and the only Caribbean series, Babardian sugar plantation slaves (Handler and Corrucini 1986). Availability of the majority of these Afro-American skeletal populations for analysis has been limited (two weeks to several years) due to their historical status and/or exhumation conditions. Only one skeletal series has been curated, that of Catoctin Furnace (Kelley and Angel 1983); the remainder have been reburied or scheduled for reinterment.

There are three general patterns observed in skeletal series of Afro-Americans, which concur with biohistorical life style and health analyses (see for examples Kiple and Kiple 1980b; Rankin-Hill 1990): (1) high infant and child mortality; (2) periods of malnutrition and disease indicated by linear enamel hypoplasias and non-specific infectious lesions; and, (3) high incidence of degenerative joint diseases and muscle attachment area hypertrophy, evidencing the physically strenuous lives of Afro-Americans. Differential patterns are observed among and between these skeletal series in longevity by sex, general health status, type, and incidence of trauma. These studies demonstrate the need for regionally, temporally, historically, and culturally focused studies of Afro-American populations. Comparisons and conclusions regarding Afro-American skeletal biological studies have varied based on several factors: the preservation of the skeletal remains, which affects the types of analyses possible; the methodologies undertaken by different investigators; and the presentation of data. The following section reviews research on the major Afro-American skeletal series, briefly describing provenience and general skeletal biological assessments of health status and diseases. Results of FABC skeletal biological analyses and more detailed comparisons, where data were available, follow.

Newton Plantation, Barbados, West Indies

Corruccini coworkers (1982) have undertaken the only large study of an Afro-American slave population from the Caribbean. This series represents a population involved in an intensified sugar plantation economy. This slave cemetery, associated with the Newton plantation in Barbados, consisted of 103 individuals interred between 1660 and 1820. The skeletal remains were poorly preserved, and the majority of the osteological analysis was based on craniodental characteristics. These analyses indicated a mean age at death of 29.3 years, with only 50 percent of the skeletons "confidently" sexed; analyses were combined and not differentiated by sex. Historical data available on Newton plantation's slaves aided the evaluation of the demographic patterns determined from the scarce skeletal remains. These data "show vastly greater infant and child mortality, stability with relatively low mortality ages 10–35, then consistently greater mortality by age 40 than is indicated by skeletal aging" (Handler and Lange 1978:286).

Hypoplasias followed a nonrandom pattern: one age of banding per affected individual always extended across all the teeth that calcified at the same period, indicating an age of 3 or 4 years for the event (Corruccini, et al. 1985:450). The high frequency of severe hypoplasias suggests that these Caribbean plantation slaves experienced periodic episodes of near-starvation, considerable weaning trauma, and metabolic stress.

St. Peter Street Cemetery, Louisiana

The St. Peter Street Cemetery in New Orleans, Louisiana, dating between circa 1720 and 1810, was studied by Owsley, et al. (1987). St. Peter's served as New Orlean's principal cemetery during the city's first seventy years under both Spanish and French rule. Until the discovery of the African Burial Ground (circa 1694–1794) in New York City, the burials in this cemetery represented the earliest urban Afro-American skeletal population that had become available for study.

The sample consisted of twenty-nine individuals, twenty-three adults aged twenty and over, and six subadults (one infant, two aged 5–9, and three aged 15–19); of these, thirteen (45%) were identified as Afro-Americans and were most probably slaves, although their life styles would differ significantly from their counterparts on plantations. Primary occupations for New Orleans urban slaves would have included "domestics employed as cooks, nurses, house maids, butlers and coachmen" (Owsley, et al. 1987:22). Others were engaged in skilled trades such as carpentry, bricklaying, painting, cabinet making, and butchering.

Preservation was "relatively poor, and a comprehensive survey of total skeletons was seldom possible" (Owsley, et al. 1987:10). Each skeleton was studied for anthropometric and paleopathological indicators of health status. Females appear to have had a shorter life span than males, with a peak mortality at 20–24 years of age and slightly higher rates of death, while male peak mortality was at 40–49 years. But Owsley and coworkers caution that an "inherent sample bias may misrepresent the actual mortality curve of the colonial population"(1987:10) due to small sample size and the under-representation of infants and children.

Hypertrophy of muscle attachment areas was frequent in males, indicating strenuous labor, while less frequent and pronounced in females. Arthritic changes in the postcranial skeleton, primarily osteophytes, usually of slight to moderate severity, were also exhibited by males. Owsley, et al. concluded that "the evidence presented suggests that the slaves buried in this cemetery may have lived slightly better lives than those on rural plantations" (1987:24).

Catoctin Furnace, Maryland

The Catoctin Furnace Cemetery in Frederick County, Maryland, dates from the late 1790s to 1820. The skeletal population studied represented only one-third of the cemetery population, because the rest of the cemetery had been covered over by a state highway. This skeletal material became available during the widening of the highway and constitute a small sample of thirty-one individuals (fifteen adults, fourteen children under age twelve, and two teenagers). These individuals were members of an iron working slave community, and primarily represented familially related individuals (Kelley and Angel 1983). This is a poorly preserved population, extremely friable and fragmentary due to soil conditions.

Females were at greater risk of dying earlier in this industrial slave community, as indicated by a mean age at death of 35.2 years for females and 41.7 for males, a pattern of earlier female mortality comparable to Cedar Grove. In general, Catoctin slaves were healthy with "no extreme cases of deficiency...found in this sample, which substantiates the idea that the ironworkers were relatively well-fed" (Kelley and Angel 1983:31). However, these slaves may have experienced episodes of infection and/or nutritional deficiency, as suggested by the incidence of dental hypoplasias (71% males and 43% of females) and tibial bowing, indicating possible rickets. The frequency of males with hypertrophy of muscle attachment areas, and the location and degree of severity of joint degeneration, especially in the vertebrae, points to the strenuous life style of this population.

38CH778, South Carolina

Inadvertently discovered during construction-related ground leveling, site 38CH778 was the slave cemetery associated with a plantation outside of Charleston, South Carolina (Rathbun 1987). Thirty-six individuals, interred between 1840 and 1870, were recovered and subsequently reinterred. Skeletal remains consisted of twenty-eight adults (thirteen male, fifteen female) and eight subadults. Skeletal biological analyses included: demographic, anthropometric, paleopathologic, biochemical (trace element analysis), and histomorphometric (cortical thickness).

Rathbun (1987) reported high rates of dental pathology, growth interruption, and elevated levels of bone strontium, which suggested a diet high in carbohydrates and vegetable materials for the 38CH778 slave sample. Males appear to have been at greater risk of earlier mortality, with a mean age at death of thirty-five years, versus forty years for females. This pattern of male susceptibility was also observed in indicators of childhood metabolic stress, such as linear enamel hypoplasias (92% males versus 70% for females) and Harris lines (45% males and 18% females). Anemias were also prevalent, characterized by both adult (36%) and subadult (80%) incidence of cribra orbitalia and significant diplotic expansion of the cranial vault. Rathbun hypothesizes that these

Table 2.3
Afro-American Skeletal Series

Site/Location	Time Periods	Total No. Burials	Life Style	Preservation	Analysis/Status[1]
Newton, Barbados	1660–1820	103	plantation slaves	fragmentary	months/reinterred
Colonial sites	1690–1820	29	plantation slaves	poor–good	indefinite/available[1]
St. Peter's Cemetery, New Orleans	1720–1810	13	urban slaves	poor	3 years/reinterred
Catoctin Furnace, Maryland	1790–1820	31	industrial slaves	poor/fragments	indefinite/available[1]
FABC 8th Street, Philadelphia	1821–1843	144	ex-slaves/freeborn	poor-good	3 years/reinterred
FABC 11th, Street - Philadelphia	1810–1822	89	ex-slaves/freeborn	poor–good	5 years/reinterred
38CH778, South Carolina	1840–1870	36	plantation slaves	poor–good	1 year/reinterred
Oakland Cemetery - Atlanta, Ga.	1866–1884	17	poor and indigent	fragments-excellent	? /reinterred
Cedar Grove Cemetery Arkansas	1890–1927	78	rural farmers	poor-excellent	2 weeks/reinterred

Note: 1 = Remains available Smithsonian Institution, Museum of Natural History.

lesions represented both acquired iron deficiency and hereditary hemolytic disorders, such as sickle cell anemia. Nevertheless, other evidence of hereditary anemia is not reported. Nonspecific systemic and localized infections were also frequent in the 38CH778 population, with the highest frequency in subadults (80%). The majority of adult (64%) skeletons exhibited evidence of infection, although sex differences were not statistically significant (69% males, 60% females). Strenuous labor was also a significant factor in the lives of these slaves, as shown by the high frequency of degenerative joint disease with markedly higher frequencies of schmorl's nodes and muscular hypertrophy in males (Rathbun 1987).

Cedar Grove, Arkansas

The Cedar Grove Baptist Church cemetery (Rose 1985) was the burial site of a post-Reconstruction (1890–1927) rural Afro-American population that consisted of descendants of the local plantation freedmen. The revetment of the Red River by the Army Corps of engineers led to the salvage excavation of burials scheduled for destruction. The seventy-eight burials excavated comprised 73.6 percent of the total cemetery population and represented 40 percent of the cemetery's usage time since its founding in 1834. The skeletal remains were assessed using demographic, anthropometric, paleopathologic, and histologic methods.

Demographic patterns suggested that the Cedar Grove sample represented a highly stressed population. Females and infants constituted a high percentage of the cemetery population, an indication of high infant mortality (27.5%) and of a life expectancy of fourteen years at birth. Adult (above age 20) mean age at death was 41.2 years for males and 37.7 years for females. Thus, females had an earlier and higher mortality rate than males, a pattern opposite to that of the slaves of 38CH778, South Carolina, but similar to that of other Afro-American populations (e.g., Catoctin Furnace). Health status determined by paleopathological studies indicated

high frequencies of anemia, rickets, scurvy, and protein malnutrition, all resulting from inadequate diets. Protein malnutrition is further indicated by the presence of the weanling diarrhea syndrome characterized by high systemic periostitis rate (41.2%), active cribra orbitalia (58.5%) and a modal childhood age at death of 18 months. These data suggest an almost exclusive reliance upon the traditional Black dietary staples of fatback and corn. (Rose 1985:308–309)

High frequencies of degenerative bone disorders signified strenuous physical labor. Comparison of the national Afro-American census statistics for the period with the skeletal biological data "clearly demonstrates that national trends in the deterioration of Black diet and health are reflected in the experience of the Cedar Grove community" (Rose 1985:309). Table 2.3 summarizes the major Afro-American skeletal series that have been studied and assessments published.

Chapter 3

The Philadelphia Afro-American Community

HISTORICAL BACKGROUND

Obtaining a legal declaration as "a free person of color" was not an easy process for Afro-Americans in the slaveholding states during the Antebellum period. Afro-Americans, when manumitted or emancipated, moved to the urban centers of both the southern slaveholding states and the north. Urban centers, especially in the south, provided employment, some degree of anonymity, and greater freedom to ex-slaves than did remaining in rural areas (Curry 1981).

While the largest free Afro-American population in the slaveholding south and the country was in Baltimore, Maryland, from 1820–1860 (Hershberg 1975; Parrington and Roberts 1984; U.S. Census 1820, 1830, 1840, 1850, 1860). Philadelphia at the turn of the century (1790–1810) was the largest; by 1820, it constituted the second largest free Afro-American population nationally and the largest outside of the slaveholding states. Both historical and geographical factors contributed significantly to this unique situation in early nineteenth century Philadelphia. Quakers, following their religious tenets, opposed the institution of slavery. Committed to the abolition of slavery in Pennsylvania and in the colonies, the Quakers were at in the forefront of the abolition movement early in the eighteenth century. They were highly successful in the state due to their large numbers, antislavery activism, and representation in the Pennsylvania legislature. These factors eventually led to the adoption of abolitionist legislation and the enfranchisement of slaves during the late eighteenth century. As a result of liberal laws and the gradual abolition of slavery, Pennsylvania became a focal point for Afro-Americans seeking freedom and opportunity.

Pennsylvania's geographic location as a boundary state to the slave states of Maryland, Delaware, Virginia, and the District of Columbia made Pennsylvania, and Philadelphia in particular, a "natural gateway between the North

and the South" (Du Bois 1899:25). As an urban commercial center and port
city, Philadelphia provided ex-slaves and freeborn Afro-Americans opportunities for nonagricultural, although limited, employment as laborers, blacksmiths,
craftsmen, and domestics. Thus, Philadelphia became a haven for fugitive and
manumitted slaves and, after the Civil War, for emancipated Afro-Americans.

Afro-Americans have lived in the Philadelphia area since the mid 1600s.
They were originally imported as slaves during the active colonial slave trade
for domestic services and skilled labor. Concomitant to the brisk slave trade,
there was a rising movement among the citizenry to stem the slave importation
due to fears of job competition and slave insurrections (Du Bois 1899; Parrington and Roberts 1984). White laborers released from indentured service con-
tended that slaves, who were hired out by masters as laborers and mechanics,
were competing with them for the available jobs. Therefore, they protested the
practice and advocated the curtailment of slave importation into the state. Although there were attempts to control the size of the Afro-American population
in the 1700s by imposing duties on slaves brought into the colony, there were
more than 6,000 slaves in Philadelphia County in 1780 (Scharf and Wescott
1884).

The Quaker abolitionist movement brought freedom to many Afro-
Americans during the eighteenth and nineteenth centuries, further increasing
the Afro-American population. William Penn, owner/founder of Pennsylvania,
manumitted his slaves in 1701 and encouraged manumission of slaves in the
colony. In 1780, the Pennsylvania legislature passed the "Act for the Gradual
Abolition of Slavery," providing for large-scale manumissions beginning in
1808. Furthermore, in urban centers, slaves who received payments for crafts
and skilled labor were able to manumit themselves and family members. Consequently, in the city of Philadelphia by 1790, most Afro-Americans were free,
whereas slaves only numbered 390 (Scharf and Wescott 1884).

The period between 1780 and 1820, in Philadelphia, can be characterized
as one of progress, growth, and, to some extent, opportunity for Afro-Americans.
Between 1790 and 1800 alone the Afro-American population of the city increased by 176 percent, compared to a 43 percent increase in the Euro-
American population (Du Bois 1899).

Nineteenth-century Philadelphia was growing as an industrial center,
drawing large numbers of immigrants, primarily Irish and Germans. The Afro-
American population was also growing as the emancipations mandated by the
Abolition Act of 1780 were implemented and the number of fugitive slaves increased (Du Bois 1899; Scharf and Wescott 1884). Philadelphia's populational
increases, by decade between 1820 and 1840, are summarized in Table 3.1.
Although, the Afro-American population consistently increased throughout the
period, Euro-American growth was significantly greater. The combination
of new industries and growing immigrant populations led to

Table 3.1
Population of Philadelphia City 1820–1840

Decade	Free Whites	Free Coloreds
1820	55,017	7,228
1830	70,653	9,495
1840	83,158	10,509

Sources: United States Census 1820, 1830, 1840

a fierce economic struggle, a renewal of the fight of the eighteenth century against Negro workmen...and soon to natural race antipathies was added a determined effort to displace Negro labor....[T]he tide had set against the Negro strongly, and the whole period from 1820 to 1840 became a time of retrogression for the mass of the race, and of discountenance and repression from the whites. (Du Bois 1899:26)

Hence, the first half of the nineteenth century was a volatile period for Afro-Americans living in Philadelphia, characterized by discrimination, violence, and declining socioeconomic conditions and legal status (Hershberg 1976b; Nash 1988; Parrington and Roberts 1984). Euro-American mobs periodically rioted, beginning in 1829 and continuing through 1842, clubbing and stoning Afro-Americans in the streets, in planned raids, attacking their homes and destroying several churches (Du Bois 1899; Nash 1988; Parrington and Roberts 1984; Scharf and Wescott 1884). Catholic Euro-Americans were also attacked during this period, although not as frequently or violently (Nash 1988; Scharf and Wescott 1884). Free Afro-Americans, mostly adolescents of both sexes, were also kidnapped and sold into slavery between 1827 and 1828 (Federal Writer's Project 1941). Mob attacks after 1842 continued to occur sporadically until the end of the Civil War. Politically and legally, Afro-Americans suffered major losses despite the fact that they protested and petitioned against legislation that would curtail their limited rights under the Pennsylvania constitution. Eventually, Afro-Americans were disenfranchised in 1838, losing the right to vote in Pennsylvania, a right they had exercised since 1790. Institutionalized and informal mechanisms for Afro-American repression were thereby established.

SOCIOECONOMIC CONDITIONS

Philadelphia had become a major center (by 1800) for Afro-American institutions such as churches, beneficial societies (precursors to Afro-American insurance companies), and schools. It was also home to a small number of financially successful Afro-American businessmen (Walker 1983) and intellectuals (Curry 1981; Du Bois 1899; Nash 1988; Winch 1988). The majority of

Philadelphia Afro-Americans remained in the poorest socioeconomic class. Few owned property, and all had limited rights and privileges. Most of these Philadelphians, whether freeborn or ex-slaves, were employed as unskilled laborers. Women and children also had to work outside the home to contribute to family survival. Yet, continued Euro-American efforts to limit the access of Afro-Americans to the growing number of factory jobs and the skilled trades were quite successful. *The Register of Trades of the Colored People* published by the Pennsylvania Abolition Society for 1837 noted that 23 percent of skilled artisans did not practice their occupations because of "prejudice against them." This number increased to 38 percent in 1856, with all skilled artisans employed in unskilled labor. Therefore, job discrimination was effective and ongoing, with Afro-Americans "excluded from new areas of the economy, uprooted from many of their traditional unskilled jobs, denied apprenticeships for their sons and prevented from practicing the skills they already possessed" (Hershberg 1981:376).

After 1838, the ramifications of the changing employment conditions and subsequent effects on family structure are evidenced by the increasing numbers of Afro-American men and women living within white households as domestics, outside the traditional family unit. The disparate female-male sex ratio (.67/.61) prior to 1860 illustrates the impact of better employment opportunities for women (domestic service) and out-migration of males due to deteriorating employment (Emerson 1848; Hershberg 1981). Furthermore, for Afro-Americans there was a 10 percent decrease in the per capita value of personal property and a 2 percent decrease in total wealth between 1838 and 1847. Real property owners declined by 3 percent, although the number of households increased by 30 percent between censuses (Hershberg 1981).

Afro-American residential patterns, which are measured by both the distribution and the density (number) of Afro-American households within a grid (a grid unit is an area roughly one by one and one-quarter blocks) (Hershberg 1973, 1981), show that residential segregation of Afro-Americans, which had increased since the 1820s, rose steadily until the Civil War. Between 1838 and 1847 the average density increased 13 percent in all grid units inhabited by Afro-Americans, but more significant was the 10 percent increase in Afro-American households within the densest grid units, those consisting of one hundred or more Afro-American households (Hershberg 1981).

The majority of these Afro-American households were located on small alleys off of main streets such as Race-Vine, which had as many as eight of these alleys or courts. Many alleys consisted of "a group of buildings, from two to a dozen or more, either in a single row or arranged around a court, reached from the street by a narrow walk, between two buildings facing the main street [Figure 3.1]. Privies were erected at the end of a court, or in the middle" (Hastings 1967:165). Usually these houses were of two or three and a half stories and only one room to a floor. Therefore, these were crowded and dark dwellings inhabited by Afro-Americans and lower class (unskilled laborers)

Euro-Americans. Residential density patterns for Afro-American households between 1820 and 1837 are given in Figure 3.2.

CHURCHES AND BENEFICIAL SOCIETIES

In the post–Independence War period (1780–1800) in Philadelphia, the increasing number of ex-slaves had to forge new lives and survive in a hostile new environment. In responding to the needs of recently freed ex-slaves for socioeconomic stability, moral support and leadership, Richard Allen and Absalom Jones, both ex-slaves, established the Free African Society in 1787. This first mutual aid, quasi-religious society was patterned after the Euro-American craft societies, ethnic benevolent societies, and the Society of Friends, whereby the moral as well as socioeconomic well-being of members was monitored (Du Bois 1899; Nash 1988). In time, the Free African Society would lead to the establishment of the independent Afro-American church movement.

Historically, 1794 was a landmark year for Philadelphia Afro-Americans; Absalom Jones founded St. Thomas's African Episcopal Church and Richard Allen established the Bethel African Methodist Church (Walker 1983; Nash 1988). Until then, Afro-Americans had attended Euro-American churches where the Afro-Americans worshipped in pews set apart from the congregation and were required to stand when seats were only available in the "white pews" (Du Bois 1899; Hershberg 1975; Nash 1988; Scharf and Wescott 1884). The impact of these Afro-American churches was dramatic. By 1838, only 5 percent of the churchgoing Afro-American community attended 23 predominantly Euro-American churches . The other 95 percent of the churchgoing population were distributed among the Afro-American denominations. The denominational distribution of Afro-Americans based on the 1838 census is detailed in Table 3.2. The majority attended the African Methodist churches (59.9%), followed by Baptist 6.2 percent, Presbyterian 5.9 percent, Episcopalian 5.4 percent, Catholic 1.5 percent, and other denominations 9 percent. Socioeconomic differentiation between these denominations did exist, although not as distinct "social classes." Hershberg (1975) and Nash (1988) consider Presbyterians and Episcopalians (11.3%) the "elites" of the Afro-American community, relatively speaking, based on occupation, land ownership, and other socioeconomic variables; while Methodists and Baptists were at the lower end of the socioeconomic "scale."

St. Thomas and Bethel established the independent Afro-American church movement as an

important instrument for furthering the social and psychological liberation of recently freed slaves…[based on] a growing feeling of strength and a conviction that black identity, self-sufficiency, self-determination, and the search for freedom and equality in a recalcitrant white world could best be nourished in the early years of the republic through independent black action. (Nash 1988:133)

Figure 3.1
Nineteenth-Century Alleyway Housing

Illustration by Diane Ghalib, 1995.

Figure 3.2
Residential Pattern Afro-American Households, 1820-1838

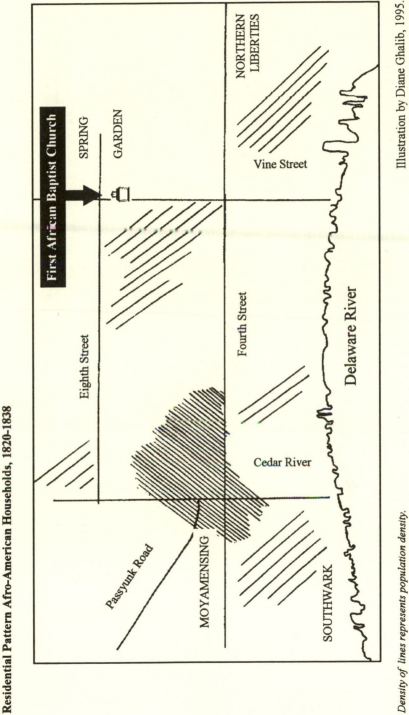

Density of lines represents population density.

Illustration by Diane Ghalib, 1995.

Table 3.2
Distribution of Afro-American Households by Denomination and Color of Church

Denomination	Afro-American	Percent	Euro-American	Percent	Totals	Percent
African Methodist	1,973	59.9	31	0.9	2,004	60.8
Baptist	204	6.2	48	1.5	252	7.6
Episcopalian	178	5.4	1	0.0	179	5.4
Presbyterian	194	5.9	0	0.0	194	5.9
Catholic	48	1.5	44	1.3	92	2.8
Lutheran	7	0.2	0	0.0	7	0.2
Dutch	0	0.0	1	0.0	1	0.0
Quaker	0	0.0	5	0.2	5	0.2
Unspecified	22	0.7	20	0.6	42	1.3
Non-church	—	—	—	—	519	15.8
Totals	2,626	79.8	150	4.5	N=3,295	100.0

Source: Pennsylvania Abolition Society 1838 Census.

Fulfilling this legacy, Afro-American churches had become the most important institutions in the nineteenth century Philadelphia Afro-American community. These churches and their affiliated beneficial societies were fundamental to Afro-American survival. In fact, Quaker and Abolition Society census data indicate that nonchurchgoing households fared worse socioeconomically (Hershberg 1975), having, for example, fewer children in school, lower household income, and fewer two-parent households.

HISTORICAL DEMOGRAPHY

Nationally, between 1820 and 1840, slaves comprised the majority (86%) of the Afro-American population. Slave males exceeded slave females, although not significantly (1–2%), in all age groups except the 14–35 age group in 1830. Free females exceeded free males (1–4%) during the same period in all age groups except for the under=14 (1820) and under-10 (1830 and 1840). A comparison of the age-sex distribution of slave and free Afro-Americans in the United States and Afro-Americans in Philadelphia for 1830 are presented in Figure 3.3.

The Afro-American population in Philadelphia between 1820 and 1840 was predominantly free, with less than 1 percent remaining as slaves (N=17 in the county). This high frequency of nonslaves attests to three significant factors: (1) the success of Quaker sociopolitical influence; (2) the impact of abolitionist legislation during the late eighteenth and early nineteenth centuries; and, (3) the city's role as a haven for ex-slaves, runaways, and freeborn Afro-Americans. Throughout the period, females exceeded males, averaging 60 percent of the Afro-American population, both in Philadelphia city and county. Little or no change occurred in the Philadelphia male population between 1830 and 1840, remaining constant throughout all age groups until decreasing at ages 36–55 and 55+. Female population size increased slightly between 1830 and 1840 in all age groups, except the age 55+ group. In 1830, there were more females aged 55+ than in 1840. The age-sex distribution of free Afro-Americans in Philadelphia City for 1830 and 1840, based on the U.S. census, are illustrated in Figure 3.4.

Censuses from the Antebellum period have consistently underenumerated populations. Condran and Cheney maintain "that the national estimates of undernumeration are not adequate for urban black populations...[t]he enumeration of black males in childhood and early adulthood is probably substantially worse than indicated in the Coale and Rives estimates of undernumeration" (1982:67). Therefore, both populational estimates and age-sex ratios for antebellum urban Afro-Americans must be approached with caution.

Despite the shortcomings of national-level demographic data, more detailed and accurate information is available for Philadelphia, thanks to the Pennsylvania Abolition Society and the Society of Friends (Quakers). The

Figure 3.3
Slave and Free Afro-Americans in the United States and Philadelphia (1830)

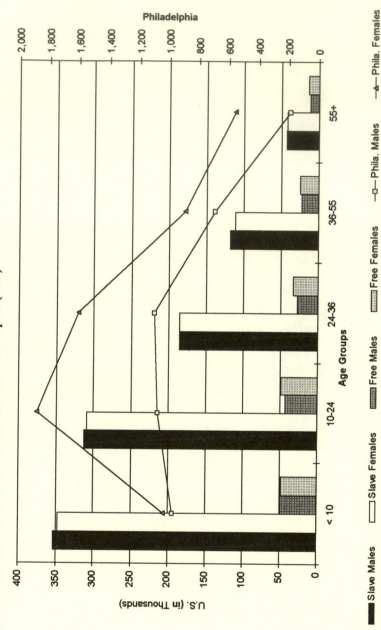

Source: United States Census 1830.

Figure 3.4
Free Afro-Americans: City of Philadelphia, 1830–1840

Age Groups

■ Males 1830   □ Females 1830   ⊞ Males 1840   ■ Females 1840

Sources: United States Census 1830 and 1840.

Pennsylvania Abolition Society (1838, 1856) and the Society of Friends (1847) undertook detailed surveys of Philadelphia Afro-American households. The 1838 census of Philadelphia's free Afro-American population was actually conducted in 1837 for a dual purpose of: defeating the pending legislation to completely disenfranchise Pennsylvania Afro-Americans in the new state constitution; and, disproving the common misconceptions that the free colored people were social nuisances and only filled the alms houses and jails (Hershberg 1981, Pennsylvania Society for Promoting the Abolition of Slavery 1838). Therefore, the 1838 census was both a means of documenting living conditions and establishing evidence that these were moral, hard working, contributing members of Philadelphia society. Cooperating with each other, the two organizations exchanged books and records and hired several of the same individuals to collect and organize the statistics for all three censuses. Hershberg states that "Taken together, the data gathered constitutes the richest information describing the total of any population group, white or black, urban or rural, in mid-nineteenth-century America" (1973:73). Therefore, the 1838 census was chosen as a major source of sociohistoric, demographic, and economic information for both the Afro-American community at large and "African Baptists" in particular.

The census surveyed household units, describing and reporting all information in aggregate form, collecting more than fifty items for each household. In contrast, the United States census between 1838–1856 collected no more than 12 items of information per household. Unique among categories evaluated by the 1838 census were the head of household's denomination, church attended, freeborn or slave status, how freedom was obtained, and the number of household members belonging to beneficial societies. Therefore, the 1838 census provides a significant source of general and specific information not available from other sources.

The 1838 census surveyed 3,295 Afro-American households for the city of Philadelphia and adjoining districts, which were eventually incorporated into the city of Philadelphia. These households were predominantly affiliated with Afro-American churches (79.7%), while only 4.6 percent attended Euro-American churches, and 15.8 percent were not affiliated with any church. Most households (n=1,973) were affiliated with the African Methodist Episcopalian church, the denomination that served as a significant catalyst in the development of the "Black Church" movement in America. The second largest denominational affiliation, with 204 households, was the African Baptist church (see Table 3.2).

Residential Distribution

Spatially, Afro-Americans resided primarily in the city during the first half of the nineteenth century. Since the districts adjoining the city were without geographically distinct boundaries, populational movement as to residence, occupation, and worship were unrestricted. Three of these districts (Northern

Liberties, Moyamensing, and Spring Garden) were home to a growing number of Afro-Americans throughout the nineteenth century. The majority of African Baptists (70%) resided in the city, while 13.2 percent and 11.2 percent resided in Moyamensing and Spring Garden, respectively. The remainder were distributed in small numbers in the other two predominantly Euro-American districts (Kensington and Southwark). Many members of the FABC congregation who did not live in the city proper lived in Spring Garden near the FABC church at Eighth and Vine streets. The distribution of Afro-American households by residential district is illustrated in Figure 3.5.

Households

Heads of households were predominantly male for both the overall population (71.6%) and the African Baptist (72.1%) households, as Table 3.3 illustrates. Widowed heads of household comprised 65 percent (n=606) of the female headed households for the population and 77 percent (n=44) of African Baptists. The 3,295 households contained a total of 12,084 Afro-Americans, with an average family size of 3.67. The African Baptist component comprised 6.2 percent of Afro-American households (n=204) consisting of 753 individuals, with an average family size of 3.69.

Occupations

The majority of Philadelphia Afro-Americans were employed as unskilled laborers (57.3% of the males and 72.8% of females). Only 11.5 percent of males and 8.9 percent of the females were involved in skilled jobs, such as blacksmiths or seamstresses. A small proportion of the population was involved in professional/high white collar (1%) or proprietary/low white collar (2.8% males, 3.3% females) occupations. Original census occupational responses numbered close to a thousand. The PSHP (1976) occupational coding

Table 3.3
Afro-American and African Baptist Heads of Households

Sex	Afro-Americans		African Baptists	
	No.	Percent	No.	Percent
Male	2,361	71.6	147	72.1
Female	934	28.4	57	27.9
Totals	3,295	100.0	204	100.0
Widows/all households	606	18.4	44	21.6
Widows/female households	606	65	44	77.2

Source: Pennsylvania Abolition Society 1838 Census.

Figure 3.5
Afro–American Households by Residential District (1838)

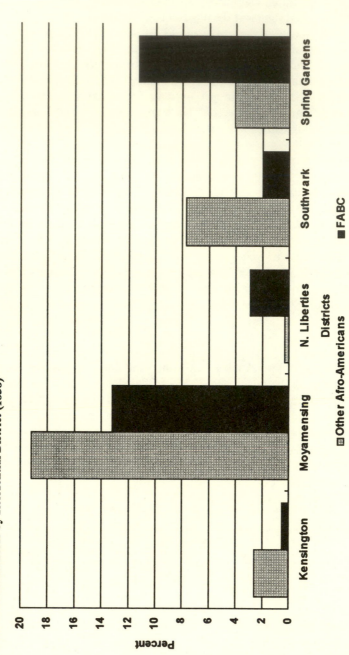

Source: Pennsylvania Abolition Society 1838 Census.

system, added to the database, includes variables that consolidate the manuscript occupations into more general categories.

Although these consolidation codes were used, 138 occupations were still listed for Afro-American males. The largest occupational category was laborer 27 percent, followed by waiters, porters, seamen, coachmen, carters and shoemakers, which accounted for the occupations of 55 percent of male-headed households; another 27 percent of households were either unreported (occupation) or headed by a woman. The remaining 18 percent of male occupations were dispersed among 131 consolidated categories including: tanners, whitewashers, grocers, blacksmiths, sailmakers, millers, etc.

Laborers (31%) and waiters (22%) were the two largest occupations reported for African Baptist males in the 147 male headed households; 28.3 percent were reported as porters, seamen, coachmen, carters, and shoemakers. The remaining 18.7 percent were dispersed among a variety of occupations, many skilled or semiskilled. These included: carpenter, blacksmith, cooper, cook, cabinetmaker, barber, miller, sexton, printer, dealer, grocer, preacher, and stevedore. A detailed comparison of the predominant occupational categories for African Baptist and all Afro-American male heads of household is presented in Table 3.4.

Consolidation codes for females listed forty-six occupational categories. The largest category (34%) was that of being a washerwoman (laundress), followed by that of domestic servant or dayworker (29%) outside of the home. Usually, daywork included washing, ironing, cooking, and cleaning for Euro-Americans (Nash 1988). Other occupations undertaken by Afro-American women included: mill worker, cook, dressmaker, and seamstress. A small proportion of the women (5%) were employed among forty disparate occupations, such as grocer, musician, teacher, shopkeeper, midwife, or sewer in a factory.

Significantly, all African Baptist women (except 1% who listed "own work") were employed. Laundressing (43%) and domestic/daywork (36%) were also the major sources of employment for African Baptist women, but proportionately higher than for the overall population. The remainder were employed as a dressmaker/seamstress, grocer, teacher, midwife, or shop keeper. For a comparison of the major female occupational categories for the overall Afro-American population and for African Baptists, see the summary in Table 3.5.

Status: Freeborn or Slave

The 1838 census identifies whether the head of household was a slave and how freedom was obtained; those that did not indicate a response have been determined to be freeborn (Hershberg 1976a). The reliability of this variable may be questionable for two reason: (1) the number of ex-slaves appears to be smaller than would be expected within the historical context of the time period;

and, (2) Henry Simmons, who is identified in the Philadelphia Baptist Association records as an ex-slave from Virginia, appears as freeborn in the census. Therefore, the high frequency of freeborn heads of household may be exaggerated because of underreporting on the part of Afro-Americans who were attempting to avoid re-enslavement or stigma. The status of both heads of household and household members for Afro-American and African Baptists

Table 3.4
Occupations of Male Heads of Households

Occupation	Percent Afro-American	Percent African Baptist
Laborers	27	31
Waiters	8	22
Porters	8	9
Seamen	4	7
Coachman	3	3
Carters	2	5
Shoemakers	2	4
Miscellaneous	19	14
NR/female head	27	5
	100	100
	N= 3,295	N=204

Source: Pennsylvania Abolition Society 1838 Census.

Table 3.5
Occupations of Female Heads of Households

Occupations	Percent Afro-American	Percent African Baptist
Washerwoman	34	43
Domestic	29	36
Cotton mill workers	6	—
Cooks	3	—
Dealers	3	—
Dressmakers	4	8
Whitewashers	2	—
No response/female	14	6
Miscellaneous	5	7
	100	100
	N= 3,295	N=204

Source: Pennsylvania Abolition Society 1838 Census.

are presented in Table 3.6.

Ex-slave household heads were freed under a variety of conditions. Generally, the manumitted classification represented those whose freedom was bought without specifying by whom or how. The categories of "self," "father," "husband," and "wife" indicated who bought the head of household's freedom. The categories "master" and "will" delineated freedom that was granted by a slave owner while alive, or after death as part of the estate. "Progressive freedom" indicated freedom that was granted through time, with increasing rights and privileges under the conditions of the Gradual Abolition Act of 1780. The "escaped" classification represented the few individuals that admitted being runaway slaves.

Only a small number of all Afro-American (9.5%) and African Baptist (12.3%) household heads reported being ex-slaves. Proportionately, more African Baptist households were headed by ex-slaves, although the majority of households were categorized as "born free." African Baptist households were more likely to have ex-slave members than the general population. The type of manumission with the highest frequency was "self," where the head of household had bought him/herself out of slavery. This may be associated with the high number of skilled Afro-Americans in Philadelphia and their increased opportunity to earn money for the master and themselves. African Baptist (36%) household heads tended to have a slightly higher proportion of self manumission than other Afro-American household heads (30.5%). The distribution for Afro-American and African Baptist households, specifying how the ex-slave head of household was freed, are shown in Table 3.7.

Hershberg (1971, 1976, 1981) maintains that, relatively speaking, ex-slave-headed households fared better socioeconomically than freeborn-headed households. He cites ex-slave households as having more two-parent households and greater total wealth, in particular when the head of household bought himself out of bondage. In general, the total wealth argument is not accurate when ex-slaves were African Baptists.

Table 3.6
Status of Household Heads and Members

	Afro-American		African Baptists	
Status	No.	Percent	No.	Percent
Freeborn Head	2,981	90.5	179	87.7
Ex-slave Head	314	9.5	25	12.3
Freeborn Members	2,489	75.5	139	68.1
Ex-slave Members	806	24.5	65	31.9
Households	N=3,295		N=204	

Source: Pennsylvania Abolition Society 1838 Census.

Table 3.7
How Heads of Households Freed

How Freed	Afro-Americans			African Baptists		
	No.	Percent Ex-slave	Percent All[1]	No.	Percent Ex-slave	Percent All[2]
Manumitted	146	46.4	4.4	12	48.0	5.9
Self	96	30.5	2.9	9	36.0	4.4
Escaped	2	0.9	0.1	0	0.0	0.0
Father	9	2.8	0.3	0	0.0	0.0
Husband	5	1.5	0.2	1	4.0	0.5
Master	38	12.0	1.1	2	8.0	1.0
Progressive	2	0.9	0.1	0	0.0	0.0
Wife	7	2.2	0.2	1	4.0	0.5
Will	9	2.8	0.3	0	0.0	0.0
Total	314	—	9.6	25	—	12.3

Source: Pennsylvania Abolition Society 1838 Census.
Note: 1 - All Afro-American households N=3295.
      2 - All African Baptist households N=204.

Beneficial Society Membership

Membership in beneficial societies could be a significant factor in a household's socioeconomic survival during times of crisis. Over half of all Afro-American and African Baptist households had members in a beneficial society, and 26 percent of African Baptist households had two or more members in a beneficial society. This multiple household membership may be associated with the predominant pattern of multiple adult households common in the nineteenth century Philadelphia Afro-American community. The number of household members belonging to beneficial societies for Afro-American and African Baptist households are summarized in Table 3.8.

African Baptist Churches

The code list for churches attended was sought in order to determine which households belonged to the First African Baptist Church congregation. Originally, the list could not be found either at the University of Pennsylvania Population Research Center, where the PSHP database is maintained, or at the University's Van Pelt library where PSHP documents are housed. A church-master list was compiled by reviewing the "church attended" listings for each census household from the original 1838 manuscripts, archived at the Historical Society of Pennsylvania. Eventually, the PSHP code list was found in the

Table 3.8
Household Beneficial Society Membership

	Afro-American		African Baptists	
Household Members	**Number**	**Percent**	**Number**	**Percent**
1	761	23	54	26
2	656	20	38	19
3	205	6	7	4
4 or more	122	4	6	3
Total households	**1,744**	**53**	**104**	**52**
No memberships	**1,551**	**47**	**99**	**48**
	3295	100	204	100

Source: Pennsylvania Abolition Society 1838 Census.

personal papers of Robert Ullo (deceased), a former member of the project. The PSHP list corroborated the master list.

The 1838 census database was searched for the pastors of both First African Baptist churches. These included: Reverend Henry Simmons (1822–1851) of the dissident church; and two pastors of the original "mother" church, Reverends John King (1813–1832) and James Burrows (1832–1844). In addition, a cross-link search between the census and the partial interment records of the Board of Health for the FABC cemetery was undertaken. First, names of adults interred after 1837 and then surnames for those interred prior to 1837 were searched for with addresses, when available. The latter was completely unsuccessful. The post 1837 search for the pastors found only Henry Simmons; the cross-link search matched three other individuals. The four cross-matches identified only the "first church attended," with no response for a "second church attended" (including Simmons).

African Baptist households were then grouped according to first church attended. Based on the church master list, four churches were identified. These included: the First African Baptist Church 8th Street (FABC); First African Baptist Church 11th Street (PSHP identified as Second African Baptist Church—SABC); Oak Street Baptist; and the Union African Baptist Church. The largest number of these households (N=117) belonged to FABC.

The two largest church memberships—FABC and Union Baptist Church—were compared for differences related to occupation, sex and free/exslave status of head of household, value of real property, beneficial society membership, family size, and total wealth; there were no significant differences. Since only 294 Afro-American households owned property, it did not appear to be a promising variable for finding differences between African Baptists, based on church affiliation. Nevertheless, the analysis proved to be edifying; of the fifteen African Baptists who owned property, seven were affiliated with FABC, and eight with Union African Baptist. Reverend Simmons owned

Table 3.9
Total and Average Wealth of African Baptist Household by Church

Church	Households	Total Wealth	Average Wealth
First African Baptist, 8th St.	117	$ 1,7615	$151
Union Baptist	10	95	90
Oak Street African Baptist	1	30	—
First African Baptist, 11th St.	76	15,970	210
All African Baptists	204	34,520	169
All Households	3,295	$ 843,451	256

Source: Pennsylvania Abolition Society 1838 Census.

the highest amount (value) of real property of all African Baptists, reported as $1,200. This certainly included the property occupied by the church and the cemetery. Nevertheless, African Baptists represented only 5 percent of the small number of Afro-American land owners.

Only total wealth, which is a combined figure of personal and real property, brought out differences between households. Comparison of the two largest church affiliations found that FABC held 46 percent of all African Baptist wealth, while Union African Baptist accounted for 51 percent, and First African Baptist Churches on 11th street and Oak Street African for 3 percent (N=11). The combined wealth of all African Baptists households, however made only 4 percent of the total Afro-American wealth. This fact would corroborate Hershberg's (1971, 1976) and Nash's (1988) contention that African Baptist represented the lower end of the Afro-American socioeconomic scale in Antebellum Philadelphia. The total and average wealth of African Baptists households by church affiliation, for all African Baptist and all Afro-American households, are presented in Table 3.9.

CONCLUSION

Philadelphia, during the first half of the nineteenth century, was a growing industrial center with increasing urbanization, geographical expansion, ethnic diversity, and population growth. For Afro-Americans, it was a volatile period characterized by discrimination, declining socioeconomic conditions, deteriorating legal status, and violence. Afro-Americans, in general, and African Baptists, in particular, represented the lower end of the socioeconomic scale, with a loss of land ownership, declining total wealth, and reduced access to skilled jobs throughout the period. Therefore, African Baptists primarily lived in the crowded residentially segregated neighborhoods, in large multi-adult households. These factors would have created environmentally, biologically, and psychologically stressful conditions for Afro-Americans to survive.

Figure 3.6
FABC Biocultural Model Based on Sociohistoric Information

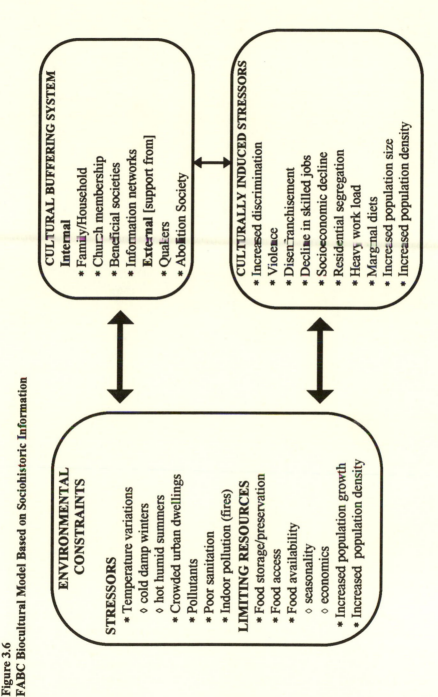

CULTURAL BUFFERING SYSTEM
Internal
* Family/Household
* Church membership
* Beneficial societies
* Information networks
External [support from]
* Quakers
* Abolition Society

CULTURALLY INDUCED STRESSORS
* Increased discrimination
* Violence
* Disenfranchisement
* Decline in skilled jobs
* Socioeconomic decline
* Residential segregation
* Heavy work load
* Marginal diets
* Increased population size
* Increased population density

ENVIRONMENTAL
CONSTRAINTS

STRESSORS
* Temperature variations
◊ cold damp winters
◊ hot humid summers
* Crowded urban dwellings
* Pollutants
* Poor sanitation
* Indoor pollution (fires)
LIMITING RESOURCES
* Food storage/preservation
* Food access
* Food availability
◊ seasonality
◊ economics
* Increased population growth
* Increased population density

A synthesis of the sociohistoric information within the context of the First African Baptist Church biocultural model is presented in Figure 3.6.

Chapter 4

Mortality and Health in Early Nineteenth-Century Philadelphia

The majority of Antebellum Afro-American health research has focused on the mortality and disease patterns of plantation slaves. Therefore, in attempting to ascertain the general health, disease experience, and mortality patterns of Antebellum Philadelphia Afro-Americans, one must turn to the medical historical and municipal sources of the period. The major sources of vital statistics for Philadelphia are the city bills of mortality, birth, and interment records maintained by the Philadelphia Board of Health. These manuscripts have been abstracted and reported by Emerson (1827, 1837, and 1848) in the *Journal of the American Medical Sciences*. These data were the primary sources for the ensuing analysis of mortality and health during the first half of the nineteenth century, into which the partial interment records for the FABC cemetery and the historical demographic literature for Philadelphia were incorporated.

The historical demographic literature available for Philadelphia primarily focuses on the last quarter of the century due to the improved quality and accuracy of the city's recordation and reporting of deaths. These studies validate observations and conclusions regarding patterns of mortality proposed in the earlier work of the period. Historical demographic studies also provide invaluable insights into the earlier half of the century because of the constancy of mortality patterns throughout the nineteenth century.

The early work of Emerson is based on the bills of mortality, of which the author maintains:

The authenticity of the Philadelphia bills of mortality may be regarded as resting upon very solid grounds. From authority vested in the Board of Health, this municipal power makes it obligatory upon physicians to give certificates designating the name, age, and sex of all who die under their care, and sextons are bound by still behavior penalties, not to permit the interment of any body, until each certificate is obtained, which he returns to the health office on the last day of every week, for publication. (1827:117)

Despite these assertions, the incomplete nature of these records presents several problems when studying mortality and health for the period. Reported causes of death were often vague or ill-defined, particularly in the case of infant and child deaths (Cheney 1984; Condran and Cheney 1982; Emerson 1848). In addition, during this period, classifications of illnesses changed several times, making comparisons between decades or years difficult. One improvement in the data did occur in 1821, with the inclusion of "color" in the death certificate, thus providing a means of assessing Afro-American mortality (1821–1826 and 1831–1840). Therefore, when cause of death is examined, generalization and, to some extent interpretation, are requisite due to the inconsistency and lack of specificity of mortality records.

The concomitant issuance of death registration and death certificates instituted after 1860 resulted in a significant improvement in the completeness and reliability of Philadelphia's recordation of deaths. Registered deaths were aggregated and published in annual reports of the Philadelphia Bureau of Health and included in a mayor's report for each year (Condran and Cheney 1982). However, the quality of cause of death data continued to vary due to changes in medical diagnosis, until the standardization of classifications in 1904. Birth and fertility data remained exceptionally poor until the early twentieth century, due to underenumeration of infants and incomplete registrations.

In general, the nineteenth-century mortality regime in Philadelphia was characterized by high crude death rates that fluctuated from year to year. The inadequacy of the extrapolated population figures, or the quality of death register, may account for some of the fluctuation, but genuine shifts in the levels of infectious disease from one year to the next are also responsible (Cheney 1984; Condran and Cheney 1982). The first half of the nineteenth century was a period of multiple epidemics and infectious disease experiences, a trend replicated in many urbanized areas nationally.

Any discussion of Afro-American mortality and health must be considered within the general framework of mortality and disease in Philadelphia during the period, due to the nature of the vital statistics available. The major causes of death for Philadelphia will be examined first; patterns of infant/child mortality and seasonality will follow; an overview of Afro-American mortality will conclude the discussion.

CAUSE OF DEATH AND PATTERNS OF MORTALITY

The age pattern of mortality in 1807–1826 had a bimodal distribution; the highest mortality in children under one year, accounted for 21 percent of all deaths, then declined to 8.7 percent in the second year of life, and continued to decline throughout childhood. Patterns of mortality by age for 1807–1826 are illustrated in Figure 4.1. Mortality began to rise in adulthood with increased but stable mortality between ages twenty and fifty, followed by a decline. Age pattern of mortality is not available for the 1831–1840 period with the exception of childhood mortality, which mimicked the earlier period and is discussed below.

Seasonal patterns of mortality in 1807–1826 are differentiated for adults and children (see Figure 4.2). Adult mortality appears to have been unaffected by seasonality, whereas childhood mortality increased through the spring months and peaked in June and July, primarily due to cholera infantum and diarrheal diseases, as discussed below. A similar pattern is observed in 1831–1840, but adult and child patterns could not be compared due to incompatible age classifications. Throughout the first half of the century, Philadelphia experienced numerous epidemics including: typhus (1819); cholera (1823, 1832 and 1834); scarlet fever (1832); and smallpox (1833–1834, 1835) (Emerson 1827, 1848). The impact of these epidemics is discernible in the mortality records of the period, although inaccurate diagnoses and the poor quality of recordation in the beginning years prevent a clear assessment.

Comparisons between the periods are limited, to some extent, by the changing diagnosis/classifications for cause of death. Therefore, comparisons were made only where the data allowed. The major causes of death for both periods (1821–1827 and 1831–1840) and the proportion of deaths for each cause (compared to all deaths for each period) are summarized in Table 4.1.

"Consumption," or tuberculosis, was the leading cause of death in Philadelphia throughout the century, primarily affecting adults. Only 14 percent of consumption deaths occurred in children, and usually those were over ten years old. According to Torchia (1977), a high proportion of consumption deaths should be attributed to Afro-Americans, who were differentially affected by an

Table 4.1
Frequent Causes of Death

Causes of Death	1807–1826 Percent	1831–1840 Percent
Cholera	7.19	8.33
Consumption (Tuberculosis)	15.04	14.23
Convulsions	7.04	6.00
Debility and Decay	6.17	3.84
Dropsy	6.55	6.83
Dysentery & Diarrhea	4.67	4.52
Fevers (scarlet, typhus, etc.)	12.93	7.53
Inflammations	8.97	*
Total No. of Deaths	N= 53,004	N= 49,678

*No longer a classification.
Sources: Emerson 1827, Table VI and III; Emerson 1848, Table E.

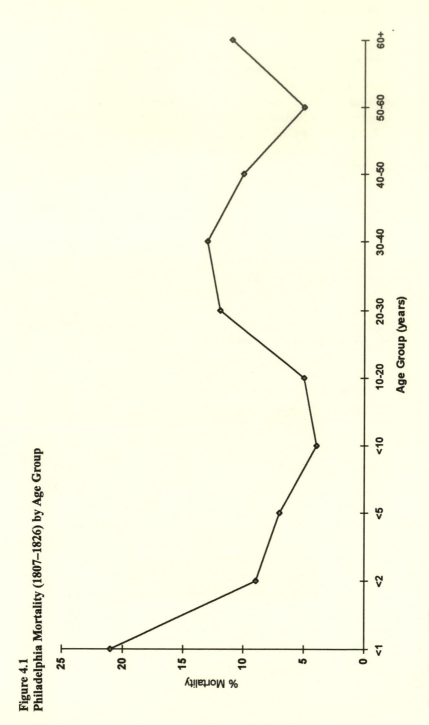

Figure 4.1
Philadelphia Mortality (1807–1826) by Age Group

Source: Emerson 1827.

74

Figure 4.2
Philadelphia Seasonal Deaths for Adults and Children 1807–1826

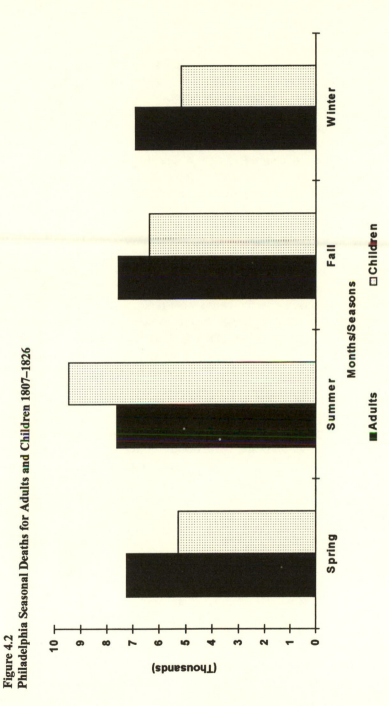

Source: Emerson 1827.

acute fatal form of tuberculosis. Actual rates by race are not available for the period.

Cholera was the second leading cause of death for almost three decades due to three epidemic outbreaks. The majority of cholera deaths (95.5%) were due to cholera infantum, thus affecting the infant mortality rate significantly. Convulsions were also, primarily, a cause of childhood death, since children accounted for 90 percent of all convulsion deaths.

The general category of "fevers" represented 12.9 percent of all deaths in 1807–1826, including a very low incidence of scarlet fever (1.9%). In 1830–1840, fever death declined despite a marked increase in deaths due to an epidemic of scarlet fever, which accounted for 4% percent of all deaths.

Deaths due to dropsy (inflammation) of the stomach and bowel, marasmus (calorie and protein malnutrition), debility, and decay (weight loss, loss of appetite and other nutritional disorders of unspecified etiology) may have been associated with cholera/diarrheal diseases. In addition, the high incidence of bowel and stomach inflammation, diarrhea, and dysentery, especially in adults, may be attributed to bacteria due to poor sanitation, contamination of water, and/or poor storage of foods.

The general classification of inflammations, including the lungs and chest, bowel and stomach, and the brain, were no longer in use by 1830. Instead, more precise classifications came into use. Diseases of the lungs were classified separately as consumption, pneumonia and bronchitis. Enteritis and hydrocephaly replaced the nonspecific diagnoses of inflammation or dropsy of the stomach, bowel, and brain, respectively, as separate causes of death. Hydrocephaly is an abnormal increase in the amount of cerebrospinal fluid that circulates through the brain and then drains into the venous system (Zimmerman 1980). Obstruction of the cerebrospinal fluid outflow or a failure to reabsorb into the cerebral sinuses results in an increased amount of the fluid. This increased fluid pressure on the brain, when occurring in children prior to the fusion of cranial sutures, produces an enlarged cranium and may lead to severe brain damage at any age (Ortner and Putschar 1981; Zimmerman 1980). Hydrocephaly is commonly associated with other congenital anomalies (such as spina bifida) or other infectious agents that produce acute cerebrospinal inflammation (e.g., virus, bacteria, protozoa, fungi).

Infant and Child Mortality

Throughout the nineteenth century, there were minor changes in infant and child mortality rates until after 1850; only modest improvements in life expectancy were seen before the 1880s (Condran and Crimmins 1980; Meeker 1972). Principal causes of infant and childhood deaths were acute infectious diseases. Improvements in the standard of living and the health reform movement of the late nineteenth century were the major factors in reducing the effects of infectious disease (Meeker 1972; Peterson 1979; Swedlund 1993). Rural rates of infant and child mortality were consistently lower than in the urbanized eastern United States.

The exception to these low rural rates were the high infant mortality rates for Afro-American slaves, which were 17 percent higher than that of the entire Antebellum population. Total losses of slave infants before the end of the first year, including reported stillbirths, accounted for 50 percent of all slave deaths (Steckel 1986b). "Thus, Model West life tables, which have low rates of infant and child mortality compared with older ages, are poorly suited to the slave experience" (Steckel 1986b:452). Condran and Cheney (1982) also reiterate this point regarding the similar age pattern of mortality for free Afro-Americans in Philadelphia, where the Model West life tables do not adequately represent the mortality experience of the population. "In fact, the deviations from Coale and Demeny West Model Life Tables for the black population were large enough to lead to the conclusion that these models should not be used with Philadelphia's black population" (1982:67). This is an important point of consideration, since many researchers assume that the sample under study is not adequate when it does not conform to model life tables.

Most of childhood mortality occurred during the first year of life and accounted for 47 percent of all childhood deaths; child mortality constituted 21 percent in 1807–1826 and 22 percent in 1831–1840 of all deaths. These rates may under represent the actual infant mortality rates because of underreporting and the lack of differentiation between fetal losses (due to spontaneous abortion) and stillbirths in the city's mortality bills. In fact, the majority of mortality figures reported by Emerson (1827, 1848) exclude from computations the number of stillbirths. The distribution of childhood mortality for both time periods, by age group, are presented in Table 4.2, illustrating the high infant mortality, followed by a decline in mortality after the second year of life.

The distribution by age group of the five major causes of death for children, 1807–1826, is shown in Figure 4.3. Convulsions were the major cause of death for infants less than a year old; the high incidence may be associated with a variety of disorders and fevers. There is also a possibility that the etiology of these convulsions was neonatal tetany (caused by the same bacteria as adult lockjaw due to an infected umbilical cord), as proposed by McMillen (1988). Although considered primarily a slave disease by southern doctors, infants of Euro-American immigrants in the Northeast also suffered and died from neonatal tetany, according to McMillen.

Cholera was the second highest cause of death for infants and children under the age of two (although lower than in the first year). When combined with dysentery, diarrheal diseases and inflammation of the stomach/bowel as causes of death, these bowel disorders account for 12.3 percent of all childhood deaths for the period. In addition, disorders such as marasmus, inanition, debility and decay, wasting away, and dropsy of the stomach attributable to mal-

Figure 4.3
Philadelphia Childhood Causes of Death, 1807–1826

Source: Emerson 1827.

Table 4.2
Child Mortality Rates

	1807–1826		1837–1840	
AGE	Number of Deaths	Percent	Number of Deaths	Percent
<1*	11,089	46.6	5,171	47.2
1–2	4,629	19.5	2,253	20.6
2–5	3,581	15.0	1,970	18.0
5–10	2,025	8.5	839	7.7
10–20	2,470	10.4	716	6.5
Totals	23,734	100.0	10,949**	100.0

*Stillborns excluded.
Sources: Emerson 1827, Table XI; Emerson 1848, Table K,** [summation error correction].

nutrition may actually have had diarrheal episodes as an underlying cause. Similar seasonal patterns have been observed for such causes of death as cholera and diarrheal diseases in the last quarter of the nineteenth century (Cheney 1984).

Consumption or tuberculosis, which accounted for less than 1 percent of deaths for children two and under, increased with age, especially when approaching adulthood. A similar pattern existed for the general category of deaths due to fevers, which included typhus, scarlet, and nonspecific fevers (e.g., remittent).

Seasonality and Infant Mortality

Cheney (1984) and Emerson (1848) observed a consistent seasonal pattern of summer infant mortality for infants and one year olds. This pattern, first observed in Philadelphia during the first half of the century, apparently continued through the last quarter of the nineteenth century. The winter months were the peak periods of mortality for children aged two and above.

This pattern corresponded with yearly summer epidemics of diarrheal disease in infants and toddlers. Although, limited to the summer months, cholera infantum or summer diarrhea was the leading reported cause of death for infants and toddlers in the city. By the early decades of the twentieth century this seasonal pattern disappeared. (Cheney 1984:561)

For one year olds, summer mortality, particularly in August, declined between 1865 and the early 1880s. (Cheney 1984: 565)

Similar seasonal patterns are found for all infantile diarrheal disease, including acute episodes of both enteric infections and undifferentiated diseases (e.g., weanling diarrhea). Acute enteric infections in normal well-nourished infants and young children led to death within a few days or weeks due to "wasting away" from dehydration. Specific isolated infections, such as bacillary dysentery and shigellosis, also displayed strong summer seasonality.

The majority of the infantile diarrheal deaths were associated with the ingestion of contaminated food, milk, water, or other matter infected by human feces, unclean hands, flies, or poor preservation/storage of food. These unsanitary conditions, found in Philadelphia, were also found throughout urbanized areas of nineteenth-century America (Cheney 1984, McMillen 1988, Swedlund 1993). Availability of water and contamination of the water supply were a particular problem in Philadelphia "water was drawn fairly directly from the Schuyllkill and Delaware rivers, which also received the untreated discharges of the city's sewage system...[and the] water supply was subject to seepage from ground saturated by privy pits" (Cheney 1984:565).

Declines in diahrreal diseases and infant mortality in the late nineteenth and early twentieth centuries can be partially attributed to Board of Health activities towards improving sanitary conditions. These included: (1) reduction of garbage, manure, and sewage; (2) the installation of iron water mains; (3) the availability and quality of ice, which affected household food supplies and food prices; (4) water closets in homes; (5) the decrease of horse drawn transportation; (6) the regulation of the milk supply (inspections, temperature controls and eventually pasteurization); and, (7) the creation of the Child Hygiene Bureau providing childcare education and aid to mothers (Cheney 1984).

The FABC cemetery interment records listed twenty-four children, with the month of interment recorded. The seasonality pattern associated with cholera infantum and diarrheal diseases can also be observed within this small sample.   Twelve of the twenty-four infant deaths occurred in the summer months, Six of these twelve were due to cholera or diarrhea. The remaining six causes of death included atrophy, pertussis (2), marasmus, measles, and heart disorder.

THE HEALTH OF PHILADELPHIA AFRO-AMERICANS

The classification of color was introduced into the bills of mortality in 1821. Therefore, the number of Afro-American deaths is available for 1821–1826 and from 1831–1840. Yet, much of what can be said about Afro-American mortality has to be extrapolated or inferred from the general populational information.

Afro-Americans constituted approximately 9 percent of the total population of Philadelphia and its adjoining districts between 1820 and 1840. Afro-Americans accounted for 10 percent of all deaths reported in the bills of mortality during the first six-year period and 11 percent during the following decade, thereby contributing proportionately more to mortality than did the general population. Emerson reported comparative proportional mortality rates as "one death in 50.8 of the white inhabitants, and that of the blacks to their population being as 1 death in 19" (1827:138) and calculated the mean age at death as 29.35. However, he did not report the age or sex distribution of Afro-American deaths; the greater mortality among Afro-American males was only alluded to in the discussion of the excess female-to-male sex ratio.

The seasonality of Afro-American deaths can only be examined for a four-year period (1837–1840) and compared to the seasonal mortality of the total population from 1831–1840, as illustrated in Figure 4.4. The summer months, June through August, were the peak mortality months for the overall population (Cheney 1984). Although Afro-American deaths did peak sharply during July, there was also an increase of deaths in April. This pattern of bimodal increased mortality may represent an adult peak mortality in the spring due to adult cholera, tuberculosis, and other related upper respiratory disorders, much as the summer peak was associated with cholera infantum and diarrheal diseases. A similar pattern of summer peak mortality was also observed for both FABC subadults and adults based on the partial interment records for the cemetery, as illustrated in Figure 4.5.

Emerson's comparison of Afro-American mortality for the two periods maintains that:

In the years 1821 to 1826, inclusive, the annual deaths of the coloured population of Philadelphia, averaged 1 to every 19.8 inhabitants, and during three years of the period 1 in 15, 1 in 16, and 1 in 17 of the coloured population were swept off. At present, instead of being double that of the whites, the average ratio of mortality between 1830 and 1840, is 1 in 31 of the coloured inhabitants, that of whites being 1 in 43. A very great amelioration in the condition of the coloured population is thus shown to have taken place. (1848:20)

Although underenumeration and methods of intercensal extrapolation for estimating population size may have had an effect on these conclusions, these trends are observable from crude death rates. The general decline in Afro-American mortality for 1821–1826 and 1831–1840, based on the proportion of Afro-American deaths to the number of deaths for the year, are illustrated in Figure 4.6. Afro-American mortality in 1821 accounted for 31.7 percent of all deaths, over three times their proportion of the general population. The following three years, during which cholera was at one of its epidemic peaks, Afro-American mortality declined by approximately 50 percent, but remained high (16.8%, 18.2%, 16.4% respectively). The explanation for this dramatic decline is not apparent from the literature of the day, but it may be associated with the spread of cholera into residential districts outside of the Afro-American community (Emerson 1831); and/or the survivors may have been

Figure 4.4
Philadelphia Total (1831–1840) and Afro-American Deaths (1837–1840)

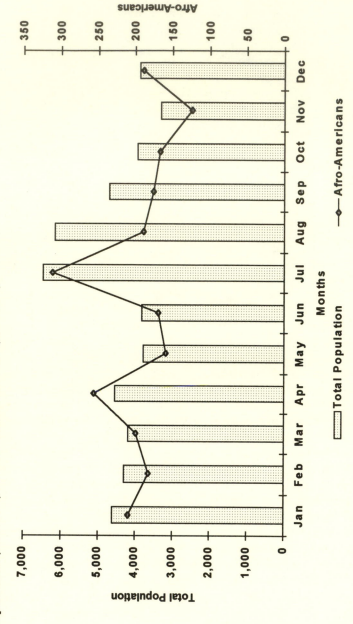

Source: Emerson 1848.

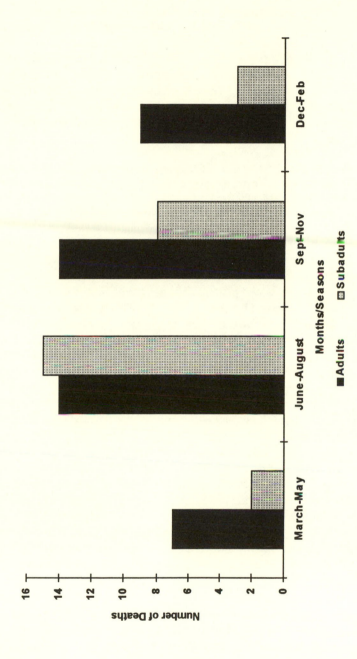

Figure 4.5
FABC Deaths by Seasonal Months, Adults and Subadults (1825–1842)

Source: Philadelphia Board of Health Cemetery Returns.

83

more resistant after exposure. There was a gradual reduction in the mortality rate with some degree of fluctuation from year to year in the succeeding years, reflected in a low of 9.6 percent in 1831.

Tuberculosis was a significant cause of death for adult Afro-Americans throughout the nineteenth century. Condran and Cheney (1982) observed that in 1870 Afro-Americans exhibited the highest death rates due to tuberculosis, with those aged 20–29 experiencing the highest mortality. Emerson also considered consumption, or "phthisis" to be a disease that affected Afro-Americans differentially:

The ratio of mortality from this direful scourge, though much lower than in some other of our cities, is increased by the greater prevalence of phthisis among the coloured population. Could the deaths from consumption of the whites be separately estimated, the ratio of mortality would be much less. (Emerson 1827:28)

Torchia (1977) in his analysis of tuberculosis as a "Negro" disease, agrees with Emerson and Condran and Cheney that Afro-Americans were affected differentially by the disease. He also concurs with Condran and Cheney that there was a "young adult" pattern. This pattern or type of tuberculosis had been classified and diagnosed by many physicians of the period as a distinct "Negro" disease. Torchia states that this was a "pattern of subacute infection, wherein individuals in apparent good health and strong physique would succumb within a few months. The difference between blacks and whites, though sharp, was one of degree rather than kind" (1977:266).

Epidemic typhoid was cited by Emerson as a major cause of death in 1818, "almost exclusively confined to the blacks inhabiting the narrow streets, courts, and alleys of the southwestern parts of the city and suburbs" (1827:123). This is an example of the nineteenth-century experience of Afro-Americans in Philadelphia, which was characterized by both high infant and adult mortality caused by infectious diseases. These infectious diseases were associated with both the general environmental conditions of the city and the specific socioeconomic and spatial conditions of the Afro-American community, which included poorer living conditions, residentially segregated neighborhoods, and further exposure to infectious disease through occupational roles. Socio-economic constraints limited the quality and diversity of the Afro-American diet, potentially increasing the possibility of episodic or ongoing marginal nutritional deficiency.

Philadelphians, in general, were at high risk of infection due to the frequent infectious disease epidemics (e.g., cholera, smallpox, tuberculosis) (Emerson 1827, 1848), the contamination of both water and milk supplies (Cheney 1984), unsanitary conditions (privies), and poor food storage methods (leading to, for example, botulism). Nineteenth-century Philadelphians experienced seasonal patterns of mortality, related to the environmental conditions of urban dwelling which produced increased incidence of cholera and diarrheal diseases during

Figure 4.6
Philadelphia Afro-American Deaths, 1821–1826 and 1831–1839

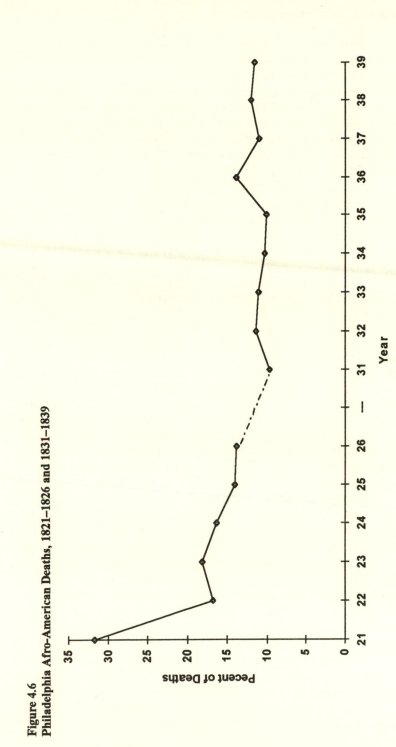

Source: Emerson 1848.

the summer. Throughout the nineteenth century, infant and early childhood mortality was high; reproductive age females were also at greater risk of dying due to childbirth complications.

The sociohistoric and demographic data presented in this chapter provide a basis for the interpretation and predication of health and disease patterns for nineteenth century Philadelphia Afro-Americans, as observed from skeletal remains. Afro-American skeletal series would be expected to exhibit: (1) high mortality rates for infants and reproductive age females; (2) high frequency of dental enamel defects indicating episodes of maternal, fetal, and early childhood stress; (3) high frequency of subadult systemic infection, especially infants; (4) little or no evidence of systemic infection in adults, due to the acute nature of epidemics; (5) low incidence of severe nutritional disorders, such as rickets and scurvy, and a moderate to high incidence of marginal nutrition, such as iron deficiency anemia; (6) high frequency of aggression-caused trauma due to prior slave status, mob attacks, and interpersonal strife; (7) low incidence of age-related trauma due to reduced longevity; and (8) high frequency of degenerative joint disease associated with strenuous physical labor for both sexes.

PALEODEMOGRAPHY

The historical demographic assessments of vital rates and population structure presented above provide a means of examining morbidity and mortality patterns in Antebellum Philadelphia during the period when the FABC congregation members lived and died. Studying the age-sex structure and populational patterns of mortality can provide relevant information concerning the health status of FABC congregation members. Paleodemographic analysis based on the skeletal aging and sexing of FABC burials (Angel, et al. 1987) provided an essential means of understanding the vital rates and population structure of this archeological population. Paleodemographic assessments focused on life expectancy, survivorship, and patterns of mortality. The impact of nutritional inadequacy and disease on differential mortality can be better assessed when the historical demographic and paleodemographic data are combined with skeletal evidence of physiological stress. FABC paleodemographic findings were also compared to the historical demographic data (see chapter 3) for Philadelphia Afro-Americans and paleodemographic data for other Afro-American skeletal series.

The excavation plan for the FABC cemetery was designed to retrieve the maximum amount of skeletal and cultural material possible. The 144 burials identified comprised all the graves that had not been destroyed by earlier construction and alteration of the site. The skeletal remains excavated represented interments throughout the twenty-year period that the cemetery was in use. The number of burials per year for a ten-year period, based on Board of Health partial interment records, averaged 6.6 per year, while the number of burials recovered for the twenty-year period averaged 7.2 per year. Therefore, the burials recovered should be considered to represent a significant proportion of the population interred in the cemetery.

To review, historical demographic data discussed in the previous chapter clearly indicated that although the First African Baptist Church congregation was small, its members included both the free-born and ex-slave Philadelphia Afro-Americans, although FABC households were more likely to have ex-slave household members than the general Afro-American population. Afro-Americans, in general, constituted the lower end of the Antebellum Philadelphia socioeconomic scale. FABC congregation members clearly represented the low socioeconomic status of Afro-Americans occupationally and in economic indicators. In addition, FABC congregation members were residentially distributed in a pattern consistent with the majority of Afro-American households. Therefore, FABC members were representative of the socioeconomic status, legal status, and residential patterns of the Philadelphia Afro-American population.

When the age-related pattern of mortality for Philadelphia (1807–1826) (Emerson 1827) was compared to that of FABC, the patterns were similar, with only minor differences. The most apparent deviations were the higher frequency of deaths in the 40–50 decade, slightly higher frequency of infant mortality (<1 year), and the slightly lower frequency in the 3–5 year age group for FABC (Figure 4.7).

Paleodemographic data can be analyzed by utilizing a life table that is a descriptive analytic model which "through a process of inference, is taken to represent the life processes of a local population and often forms the basis for further inference on the relationships between populational and cultural processes" (Moore, et al. 1975:57).

The major criticisms of the use of life tables for skeletal samples have been based on three problem areas (Angel 1969, Howell-Lee 1971; Weiss 1973): (1) populational growth, a contradiction to the fundamental assumption of stable population theory; (2) enumeration errors, especially infant underenumeration; and (3) the small population size of skeletal series.

More recently, Bocquet-Appel and Masset (1982) have stated that paleodemographic techniques are so flawed that the field should be abandoned, and they heralded their "farewell" to its "death." Their criticisms are based on two major points; they maintain that: (1) the age structures of skeletal samples reflect only the age structures of reference populations by which skeletal aging criteria have been established; and (2) age estimates of adults lack sufficient accuracy to allow for demographic analysis. Age estimates, then, are seen as mere "random fluctuations and errors of method" by these authors.

These authors reviewed and compared skeletal populational age data to reference populations based on two aging techniques: McKern and Stewart's

Figure 4.7
Philadelphia (1807–1826) [1] and FABC Mortality (ca.1822–1843)

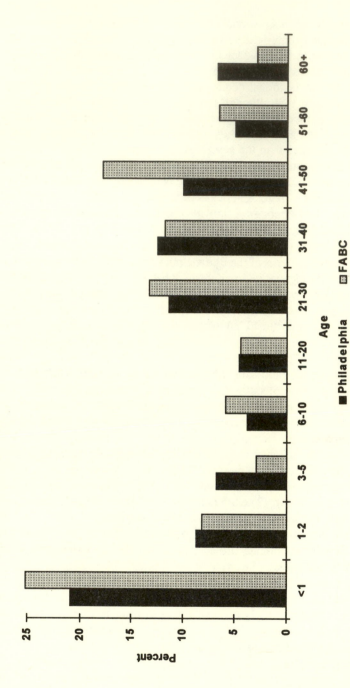

Source: 1 - Emerson 1827.

(1957) pubic symphysis aging system, and the cranial suture closure of Acsádi and Nemeskéri (1970); they refer to a third aging method, microscopic haversian system aging (Balthazard and Lebrun 1911). Interestingly, these authors disregarded the large body of recent literature on microscopic aging techniques. In each case they argued that the sample population age structure is a mirror image of the reference population. Although Bocquet-Appel and Masset admitted that age estimation error can be reduced by utilizing multiple aging techniques, they only allowed relevancy and accuracy to subadult aging methods.

Van Gerven and Armelagos (1983) responded to Bocquet-Appel and Masset (1982) on several critical points. Bocquet-Appel and Masset had mistakenly assigned the Wadi Haifa (Swedlund and Armelagos 1969) to the Mckern and Stewart system and not to the correct reference population. Regarding the relationship of skeletal samples to reference populations, the authors tested Bocquet-Appel and Masset's assertions by comparing the Wadi Haifa and Kulubnarti populations to the Todd (1920, 1921) reference population (modified by Brooks 1955). Van Gerven and Armelagos disproved the claim, showing that the Nubian samples differed significantly (99% confidence interval) from the reference population. In addition, the two Nubian samples were "strikingly different" from each other.

In response to the criticisms of determining age at death, Van Gerven and Armelagos cite the studies of age-dependent criteria, such as osteoporosis (Dewey, et al. 1969; Van Gerven 1969) and fracture rates (Lovejoy and Heiple 1981), which are independent of age determination and produce comparable patterns to age estimates. In addition, Van Gerven and Armelagos criticized Bocquet-Appel and Masset for ignoring the contribution of subadult remains to paleodemography and to the "modern florescence in paleopathology and growth and development [which] owe their current resurgence to a populational perspective provided by paleodemography" (1983:359).

The historical context of the FABC cemetery population indicates that population (membership) growth should not be a significant concern, since the schism with the mother church was based on this group's refusal to support or take in fugitive slaves. Therefore, the FABC congregation remained fairly stable, based on their exclusionary attitudes, throughout a period characterized by high infant mortality, high infectious disease rates, and limited in-migration into the group. Birth rates for the period are not available for Afro-Americans prior to 1850, and are extremely unreliable for the entire population until the twentieth century (Condran 1980, 1982).

FIRST AFRICAN BAPTIST CHURCH CEMETERY SAMPLE

The FABC cemetery sample presents the problem of small sample size (as do most archaeological populations), yet errors associated with infant underenumeration are relatively less significant than in other Afro-American and Amerindian skeletal series. The FABC infant (<1 year) mortality of 25.2 percent was higher than the reported 21 percent for all Philadelphians during the period of 1807–1826. The proportion of FABC infant deaths (56.7%) to childhood mortality rates was also significantly higher than those reported for Philadelphia for the 1807–1826 period (46.6%) and for the 1837–1840 period (47.1%). The true number of infant deaths was probably higher throughout the period in Antebellum Philadelphia since stillbirths were not included in reported figures and underreporting was common (Emerson 1827, 1848). In addition, Afro-American infant deaths were not reported separately and could not be assessed from the overall city rates.

Life table data, such as age-specific probability of dying and life expectancy, may be compared to other unsmoothed life table data for other regionally, temporally, and/or socioculturally comparable populations or to the patterns observed in model life tables. Examples of commonly used model life tables are those developed by Weiss (1973), based on both living and skeletal anthropological populations, and by Coale and Demeny (1966) for isolating abnormal characteristics in mortality profiles (Moore, et al. 1975). Through these demographic analyses, population parameters can be generated and long-term trends in adaptation, health, and disease examined. Therefore, life tables can be an effective assessment technique to ascertain mortality differences between or within segments of the population (age-specific or sex-specific mortality patterns).

Mortality

The FABC skeletal sample consisted of 135 skeletons available for analysis. These included 60 subadult and 75 adult skeletons of thirty-nine females and thirty-six males. The mean age at death for females was 38.9 years, and 44.8 years for males. This sex differential in mean age at death was also observed in the industrial slave population of Catoctin Furnace and post-Reconstruction period rural Afro-Americans from Cedar Grove. The reverse pattern, with males at greater risk, has been reported for colonial slave sites (Kelley and Angel 1987), South Carolinian plantation slaves (Rathbun 1987), and New Orleans urban slaves (Owsley, et al. 1987).

In general, FABC mortality was highest for infants under twelve months, who made up 25 percent of the total mortality of the population. Mortality declined during the second year of life to 8.1 percent, with a significant drop in mortality through the fifth year of life. Increased mortality in years six through ten was probably attributable to childhood epidemics, such as whooping cough and scarlet fever (as discussed in chapter 3). Mortality declined and remained low throughout the second decade of life. In the first half of the third decade of life (ages 20–25), mortality increased, most probably associated with the tuberculosis and epidemic fevers of the period, which affected this age group differentially, and female mortality associated with childbirth (Emerson 1827; Torchia 1977). Deaths then declined, rising again at ages 35–40, peaking during the first half of the fifth decade of life (ages 40–45), and then declining once more, as illustrated in Figure 4.8.

Differential patterns of mortality based on sex can be observed; adult female mortality peaked at ages 20–25 (26.4%), while adult male mortality peaked in the age range 45–50 (25%). In general, female mortality occurred bimodally in ages 20–30 and 35–45, with a combined mortality of 82 percent (41% each age group). Male mortality remained low until ages 30–35, with a slight increase to 13.9 percent, and then declined until peaking at ages 45–50, as illustrated in Figure 4.9, which compares male and female mortality by age group. This data is also summarized in Table 4.3.

Females accounted for 33 percent of all mortality by age forty, compared with only 16 percent for males; whereas, males accounted for 32 percent of mortality after age forty, but females only 18 percent. This earlier death of females may be related to reproduction, since mortality attributed to childbirth was very high in nineteenth century Philadelphia (Emerson 1827). During the third decade of life (20–30), female mortality peaked (20%), exceeding male mortality by 16 percent. In the following decade (30–40), male and female mortality was equal—yet, male mortality more than doubled from the previous decade. This is counterpoised to female mortality, which decreased by approximately 50 percent from the previous decade of life. In the following decade (40–49), mortality for both sexes increased, although proportionately higher

Table 4.3
FABC Adult Mortality by Age and Sex

Age	Adults		Males		Females	
	No.	Percent**	No.	Percent*	No.	Percent*
16–20	3	2.9	1	1.3	2	2.6
20–30	18	13.3	3	4.0	15	20.0
30–40	16	11.8	8	10.6	8	10.6
40–50	24	17.7	14	18.6	10	13.3
50–60	9	6.6	8	10.6	1	1.3
60+	5	3.0	2	2.6	3	4.0
	75	100.0	36		39	51.9

* % of adult mortality N=75.
** % of total mortality N=135, including subadults (n=60).

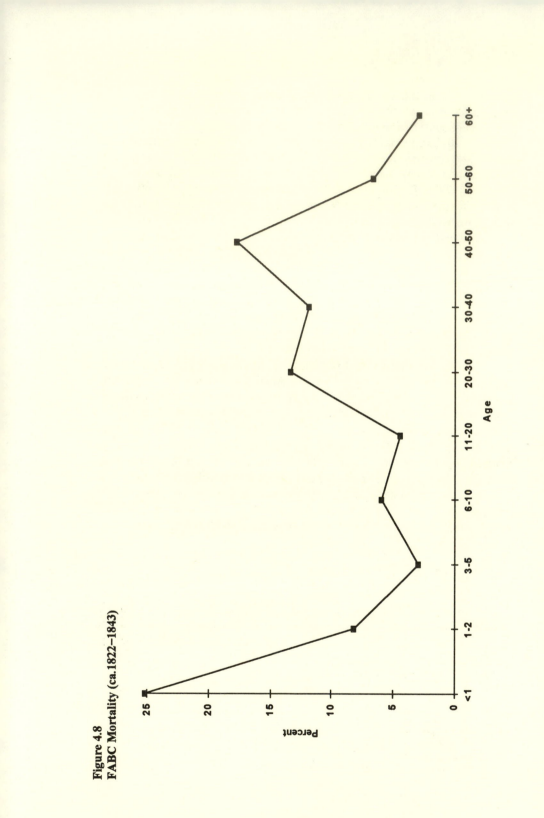

Figure 4.8
FABC Mortality (ca.1822–1843)

92

Figure 4.9
FABC Adult Males and Females (ca. 1822–1843)

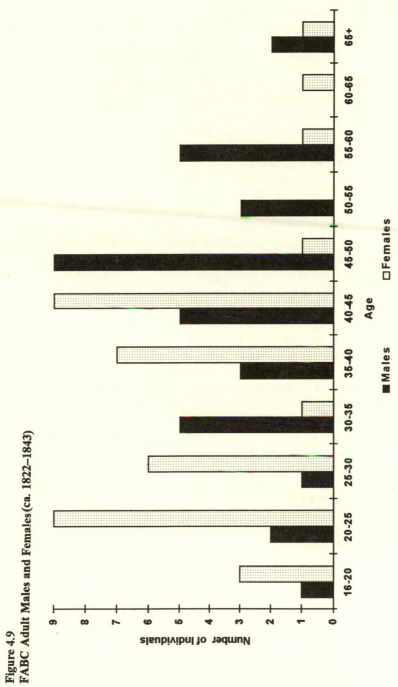

93

for males. For the succeeding decade (50–60), mortality declined gradually for males, and dramatically for females.

Infant and Subadult Mortality

Subadults, including infants (0–6 months), constituted 43 percent of the FABC cemetery population. The majority of subadult deaths (75%) occurred during the first two years of life, followed by a sharp decline between ages three and five, an increase again between ages six and ten, then the mortality apparently remained low until early adulthood (Table 4.4). If mortality of children is examined separately for those who died under age two, a differential pattern of mortality by age can be observed. Infants under one year of age (N=34) constituted 56.7% of all childhood deaths, while those aged one–two years accounted for 18.3 percent.   Mortality for children under two (twenty-four months) accounted for 75 percent of all childhood deaths and 32 percent of all deaths in the FABC population. Upon closer inspection, deaths under one year were primarily occurring during the first six months of life, accounting for 57.8 percent of deaths at under twenty-four months. Subadult mortality for those twenty-four months and under is summarized in Table 4.5, and illustrated in Figure 4.10.

If this group is further divided by fetal and/or newborn infants, it appears that stillbirths, and perhaps miscarriages, were a significant cause of the high infant mortality. High infant mortality had been reported by Emerson (1848), although not well documented as discussed earlier. Childhood mortality, in general, appeared to be operating bimodally, with 25 percent of FABC subadult deaths occurring during the first six months. This high infant mortality level was followed by a decline, and then an increase again during the sec ond year, which may have been associated with a weaning period. The increased second year pattern of mortality is also observed in the Cedar Grove post-Reconstruction Afro-American population (Rose 1985).

Table 4.4
FABC Subadult Mortality by Age Group

Age in Years	Number	Percent Child Deaths	Percent All Deaths
< 1	34	56.7	24.3
< 2	11	18.3	7.9
3–5	4	6.7	2.9
6–15	11	18.3	7.9
	60	100.00	43.0

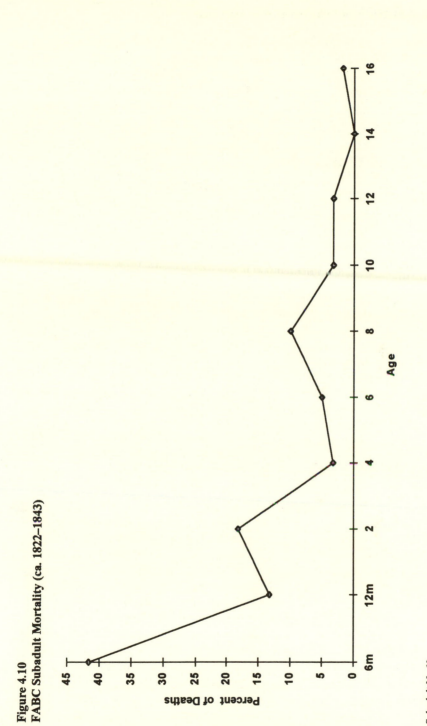

Figure 4.10
FABC Subadult Mortality (ca. 1822–1843)

Percent of Deaths

Age

Subadult N=60

Table 4.5
FABC Subadult Mortality—Under 24 Months

Months	No.	Percent <24	Percent All Children	Total Population
Fetus/newborn	14	31.1	23.3	10.0
1–6 months	12	26.7	20.0	8.6
7–12 months	8	17.8	13.3	5.7
13–18 months	4	8.9	6.7	2.9
19–24 months	7	15.5	11.7	5.0
	45	100.0	75.0	32.2

Survivorship

A life table using unsmoothed data was constructed for FABC using a Lotus 123 database computerized lifetable.   Survivorship (lx) for FABC, Cedar Grove (MT15.0–45.0), and MT30–60.0 clearly demonstrates the impact of infant mortality, with similar survivorship rates at one year.   The differences in mortality regimes between Cedar Grove and FABC can be observed, with lower survivorship for Cedar Grove from age five onward.   The FABC survivorship curve closely resembles Weiss's MT30.0–60.0 until age 45, at which point FABC survivorship declines at a faster rate, perhaps associated with the aging of older individuals (Figure 4.11).

Life Expectancy

Life expectancy (Eøx) at birth for FABC members was 26.59 years, significantly higher than the 14 years reported by Rose (1985) at Cedar Grove. FABC life expectancy was compared to Weiss's (1973:175) model life table MT30.0–60.0, the most comparable table, and to MT15.0–45.0 (1973:118), reported by Rose as the most comparable table to the Cedar Grove mortality experience.   The MT15.0–45.0 table exemplifies a highly stressed subadult population, although infant mortality was actually higher.   The FABC life expectancy curve fits closely to the Weiss MT30.0–60.0 until age 15.   FABC life expectancy for ages 20–40 was lower than MT30–60 and higher than that for Cedar Grove.   Similar life expectancy patterns for FABC and Cedar Grove are observed for ages 45–60, thus deviating from MT30–60.   After age 60, FABC life expectancy increases slightly, conforming to the MT30–60 curve.   The latter can be explained by the difficulty in correctly aging older individuals (Figure 4.12).   The differences between Cedar Grove and FABC life expectancy

Figure 4.11
FABC Survivorship (lx)

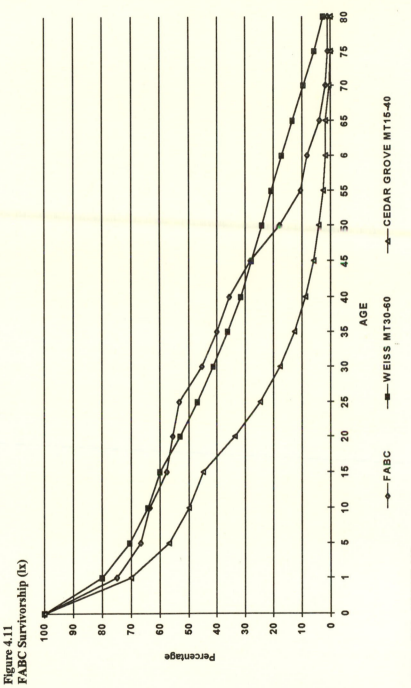

Sources: Weiss 1976:175, 118.

Figure 4.12
FABC Life Expectancy (ex)

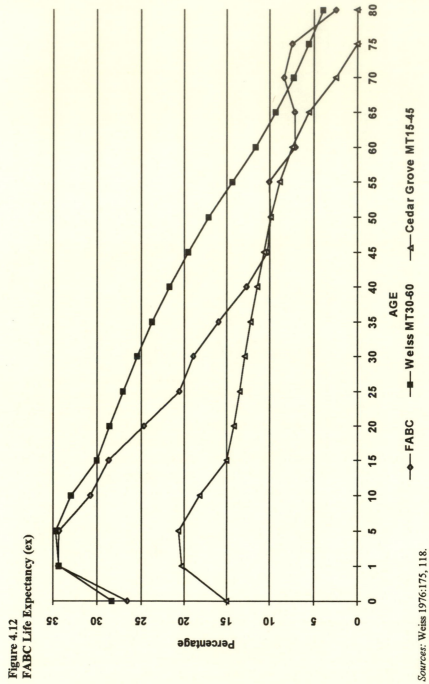

Sources: Weiss 1976:175, 118.

Figure 4.13
FABC Biocultural Model for Physiological Disruption

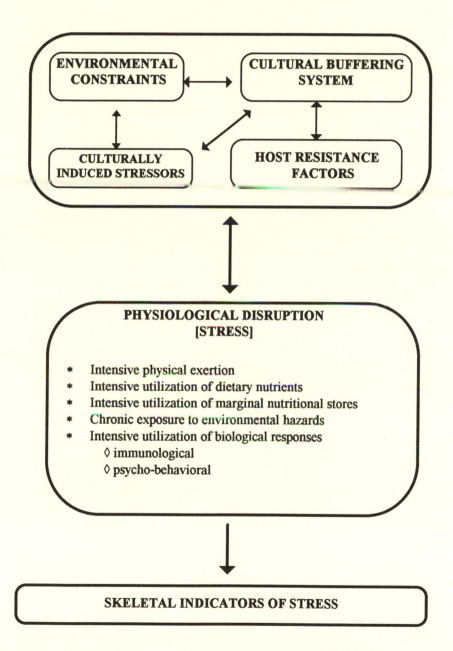

and mortality experience are significant. Clearly, Cedar Grove post-Reconstruction rural Arkansas Afro-Americans were at higher risk of dying earlier The factors that in interaction with host resistance factors cause physiological disruption are summarized in Figure 4.13.

Chapter 5

The Story the Skeletons Tell

INTRODUCTION

Skeletal material in the FABC cemetery site was differentially affected by the subsequent use and conditions of the site throughout the approximately 130 years that it remained forgotten. Several skeletons or portions of individuals were destroyed, either through the earlier construction of the homes (back yards and privies), the safe factory and other structures built on or adjacent to the site; or through the later excavation process that led to its discovery. Several burials were also affected by periodic wet and dry conditions related to their location near privies and water drainage on the site. Therefore, the preservation of the skeletal material varied greatly (see Tables 5.1 and 5.2).

A total of 135 skeletal remains were recovered, seventy-five adults and sixty subadults. The majority of the adult burials (66%) were available for more complete assessment. Only 53.3 percent (n=32) of subadult skeletons were available for study due to their fragmentary condition.

Paleopathological assessments provide the indicators to determine individual and general populational health status. In addition, these assessments allow for the identification of illness patterns that are utilized to study the interactions between environmental and sociocultural factors and biological processes.

NUTRITIONAL DEFICIENCIES

Nutritional disorders in the FABC population were primarily associated with iron deficiency anemia (porotic hyperostosis) rather than with more severe disorders such as rickets and scurvy, which are indicative of chronic or long-term nutritional stress and that were rare in the FABC skeletal remains. Porotic hyperostosis was observed in 53.3 percent (n=40) of FABC adults. Male

Table 5.1
Condition of FABC Adult Skeletal Remains

Status	Cranium		Skeleton	
	Number	Percent	Number	Percent
Missing	10	13.3	3	4.0
Present	65	86.7	72	96.0
Total Adult Burials	75	100.0	75	100.0
Condition	Number	Percent	Number	Percent
Fragmentary	9	13.8	8	11.1
Poor	7	10.8	14	19.4
Fair	16	24.6	24	33.4
Good	23	35.4	18	25.0
Excellent	10	15.4	8	11.1
Total Present	65	100.0	72	100.0

Table 5.2
Condition of FABC Subadult Skeletal Remains

Age Group	<1 year		<2 years		3–5 years		6–15 years		Totals	
Condition	No.	Percent	No.	Percent	No.	Percent	No.	Percent	No.	Percent
Fragmentary	12	35.3	8	72.7	3	75.0	5	45.4	28	46.7
Poor	5	14.7	0	0.0	1	25.0	2	18.2	8	13.3
Good	17	50.0	3	27.3	0	0.0	2	18.2	22	36.7
Excellent	0	0.0	0	0.0	0	0.0	2	18.2	2	3.3
	34		11		4		11		60	

incidence peaked at ages 40–50+, while the majority of females exhibiting porotic lesions were of reproductive age (18–40). This pattern correlated with the dental enamel defect analysis, that suggested which maternal nutritional and health status had been compromised in the FABC population.

Porotic Hyperostosis

Twenty-eight subadult remains were available for study (examined by Donald Ortner of Smithsonian Institution [Kelley 1988]). Three were diagnosed with porotic hyperostosis of these three, two were aged six months and one 10–12 years old; all three exhibited cribra orbitalia (lesions in the upper eye orbit). The two infants also exhibited periostitis, a generalized systemic infection similar to the synergistic patterns of infection and anemia reported in other archaeological populations (see Mensforth, et al. 1978 and Palkovich 1987).

Although it is primarily a childhood disease, porotic hyperostosis was observed in 53.3 percent (n=40) of the FABC adults; 55.6 percent of all males and 51.3 percent of females were diagnosed as having experienced iron deficiency anemia. The incidence between sexes was equal, but the distribution by age group revealed a diametrically opposed pattern. Male incidence of porotic hyperostosis was lower in the younger individuals aged 18–20 (5%), increased between ages 30 and 40 (20%), and then peaked at ages 40–50+ (75%). By comparison, the majority of females (60%) exhibiting porotic lesions were of reproductive age (18–40), a pattern observed in other archaeological populations (e.g., Palkovich 1987). In addition, this reproductive age female anemia pattern correlates with the subadult dental enamel defect data that suggests that maternal nutritional and health status had been compromised in the FABC population.

An important observation was the status of lesions; they revealed whether the anemia episode observed was active (unremodeled) at the time of death, or if it represents a previous episode from which the individual had recuperated and therefore the lesions appeared healed (remodeled).

The distribution of unremodeled and remodeled lesions was comparable for both sexes, with 60 percent remodeled and 40 percent unremodeled. Therefore, the indication is that the majority of adults had experienced earlier stress episode(s) prior to their demise. Statistical tests undertaken to ascertain whether there was a relationship between the status of anemia at the time of death and sex and/or age were significant only by sex and age group (20–40 and 41+) [Chi square analysis .10 level (x^2=3.43)]. This substantiates the hypothesis that the incidence of porotic hyperostosis was age related in reproductive age females (18–40) and related to the aging process in males 41 years and older. In most cases, older males with active lesions also exhibited expanded diploe of the crania as a corroborating indicator for anemia. The distribution of adult porotic hyperostosis by age and sex is summarized in Table 5.3 and by lesion status and sex in Table 5.4.

Among Afro-American skeletal series, reported frequencies of porotic hyperostosis have generally been high. Rose (1985) reported that 40.9 percent Cedar Grove subadults (n=18) exhibited cribra orbitalia (porotic hyperostosis of the eye orbit); of these, 84.3 percent of lesions were unremodeled. That is, the majority of Cedar Grove subadults (N=44) exhibited active iron deficiency at the time of death. Rathbun (1987) observed porotic hyperostosis (iron deficiency anemia) in 80 percent (n=4) of 38CH778 subadults. While only 5 percent of FABC subadults exhibited porotic hyperostosis of the eye orbit (cribra orbitalia), FABC had the highest overall frequency of adult porotic hyperostosis (53.3%), followed by 38CH778 (43%) and Cedar Grove (25%). The higher frequency for FABC may be due to methodological differences between observers. Rathbun reported only cribra orbitalia, while Rose reported "healed cribra orbitalia and healed cranial pitting." The distribution of porotic hyperostosis between the sexes for that South Carolina plantation population was almost equal, with a rate of 36 percent for males (n=5) and 33 percent for females (n=5). This pattern of slightly higher rates for porotic hyperostosis in males has been observed in both Cedar Grove (26.7% males and 23.8% females) and FABC (55.6% males and 51.3% females). Kelley and Angel (1983) reported that only two of thirty-one individuals (6.4%) from the Catoctin Furnace, Maryland, site exhibited porotic hyperostosis. The authors suggested that the low incidence of iron deficiency anemia was indicative of a generally higher quality diet and better treatment of industrial slaves compared to that of plantation slaves.

In general, evidence of inherited sickle cell anemia was not apparent from FABC skeletal remains. The occurrence of sickle cell anemia would have been expected in an Afro-American population, but the short life expectancy of sickle cell anemics prior to the late twentieth century and the poor preservation of subadult skeletons may have contributed to the lack of diagnosable pathology.

Table 5.3
FABC Porotic Hyperostosis by Age and Sex

	Males		Females	
Age	Number	Percent	Number	Percent
18–20	1	5.0	2	10.0
20–30	0	0.0	8	40.0
30–40	4	20.0	2	10.0
40–50	10	50.0	6	30.0
50+	5	25.0	2	10.0
	20		20	

Table 5.4
FABC Porotic Hyperostosis by Lesion Status and Sex

	Males		Females	
Lesion Status	Number	Percent	Number	Percent
Unremodeled	8	40.0	8	40.0
Remodeled	12	60.0	12	60.0
	20		20	

Rickets and Scurvy

The nutritional deficiencies of rickets and scurvy were diagnosed in only two subadult skeletons. Scurvy, a vitamin C deficiency, was observed in a child aged 10–12 (B39). A systemic hematogenous problem with diffuse periostitis on both humeri and tibiae was diagnosed (Kelley 1988). No enamel defects were observed in the dentition, therefore posing the possibility that the vitamin C deficiency developed after the dentition had formed, and that the deficiency was a more recent, albeit chronic, condition.

Vitamin D deficiency was diagnosed in an 8–10 year old child (B37); the skeleton was well preserved and almost complete. All long bones were severely bowed, indicating a well-developed case of rickets (Plate 5.1). In addition, the dentition exhibited several dental enamel defects (hypoplasias), indicating periods of stress with ages of onset between 4 and 5 years old; these probably were associated with the periods of nutritional deficiency.

In both of these cases nutritional deficiency may have contributed to childhood mortality by depressing resistance and increasing susceptibility, yet cause of death could not be determined from the remains.

Osteomalacia

Osteomalacia was diagnosed in a 20–25 year old female (B128). The left innominate of the pelvis was thinned and bulged around the acetabulum. The birth canal was somewhat flattened and narrow; no other pathologies were observed other than slight bowing of long bones, which also suggests malnutrition earlier in life. Osteomalacia in adults is the sequel to rickets in infants and adolescents. As in rickets, the chief factors are deficient dietary calcium, intestinal disease, inadequate sunlight, and, of significant importance for females, multiple pregnancies and prolonged lactation, which drain skeletal stores of calcium and phosphorus (Steinbock 1976). The majority of cases occur in reproductive age females, and especially among those who reproduce at young ages, because of maternal and fetal competition for nutrients. Differences be-

Plate 5.1
Femur and Tibia of Child Exhibiting Rickets
Burial 37, 8–10

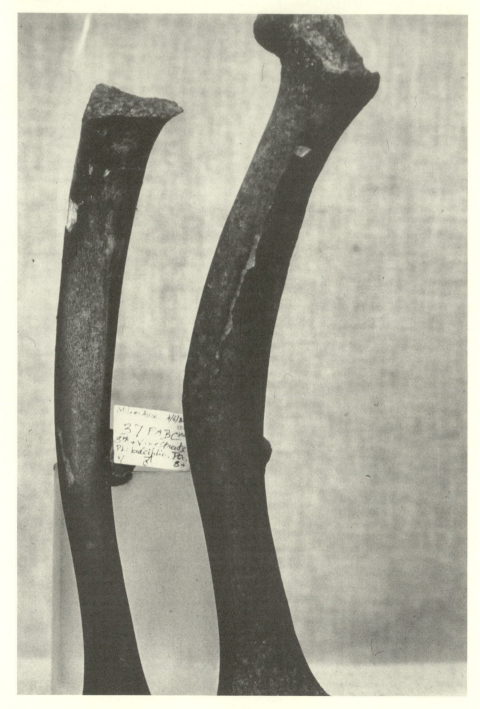

tween osteomalacia and rickets are primarily due to the underlying processes of growth at different ages.   Osteomalacia is usually diffused throughout the skeleton, with the most severe manifestations found in the flat bones and femurs of the postcranial skeleton, while rickets most actively affects the conjoining area between the shaft and the joint surface, where the majority of growth occurs (metaphyses), and the outer bone surface (periosteum) of long bones.

INFECTIOUS DISEASE

Nonspecific infectious disease rates were higher than expected, even taking into consideration the acute nature of epidemics of the period. Evidence of generalized infection was diagnosed in 25.3 percent (n=19) of adult skeletons. Yet, the incidence of tuberculosis was quite low (4%) in the FABC skeletal remains, considering the high prevalence in the Afro-American community. The FABC incidence of periostitis, both of general and specific etiology, was lower than in other Afro-American skeletal series.

Subadult

Evidence of infection (Kelley 1988) was observed in nine subadult skeletons exhibiting periostitis; five were infants (6 months or under), two aged 1–3 years, and two aged 8–12 years. The five infants duplicated the pattern of early or immediate onset after birth of infection associated with maternal nutritional status reported by Palkovich (1987).   Two of the infants (6 months) also showed evidence of porotic hyperostosis (iron deficiency anemia), and the 10–12-year-old was diagnosed as having suffered from scurvy (see section above). These three cases indicated a synergistic relationship between infectious disease and nutritional deficiency as observed in other archaeological populations (e.g., Mensforth, et. al 1978; Palkovich 1987). Two other children (6 months and 8 years) had severe ear infections (mastoiditis) that eventually were diffused systemically, affecting several bones.   One 8-year-old child exhibited tubercular meningitis of the pituitary fossa, an infection of the brain membranes that leads to coma and death if not treated appropriately. This child most probably died from the infection in a short period of time, leaving no further evidence of infection on the skeleton.   The distribution of periostitis and nutritional deficiency disorders and infections of specific etiology for subadults are summarized in Table 5.5.

Table 5.5
FABC Subadult Frequency of Periostitis/Nutritional Deficiency

Burial No.	Age	Periostitis	Infections (specific)	Nutritional Defect
21	6 mo.	+		
30a	4 mo.	+		
53	6 mo.	+	Mastoiditis	
141	6 mo.	+		Porotic hyperostosis
146	6 mo.	+		Porotic hyperostosis
108	14 mo.	+		
126	36 mo.	+		
58	8 yr.	+	Mastoiditis	
37	8 yr.	–		Rickets
60	8 yr.	–	Tubercular meningitis	
65	10 yr.	–		Porotic hyperostosis
39	12 yr.	+		Scurvy

+ = present.
– = absent.

Adults

Evidence of generalized infection, periostitis, was diagnosed in 25.3 percent of adult skeletons (n=19); three other adults also exhibited tubercular infections. Periostitis was observed in 36.1 percent of FABC males (n=13) and 15.4 percent of the females (n=6). The majority of the males (92.3%) exhibiting periostitis were aged 40 and older. These individuals represented 50 percent of all males in the age group. Females with periostitis were equally divided between the .ages of 20–40 and 40 and older, representing approximately 20 percent of all females in each age group. The majority (73.7%) of individuals with periostitis had slight conditions, and only one individual exhibited a severe lesion. The distribution of periostitis by sex and age group is summarized in Table 5.6, and distribution by bone and severity is detailed in Table 5.7.

Seventy-eight percent of FABC adults with iron deficiency anemia also exhibited periosteal lesions attributed to generalized infection. The association of infectious disease with porotic hyperostosis was found to be statistically significant at the .01 level using a chi square analysis (Table 5.8). To evaluate the etiological relationship between iron deficiency and infection, the distribution

Table 5.6
FABC Distribution of Periostitis by Sex

	Males		Females	
Status	Number	Percent	Number	Percent
Absent	23	63.9	33	84.6
Present	13	36.1	6	15.4

Table 5.7
FABC Periostitis by Number of Lesions and Severity

Number of Lesions	One		Two		Three		Four	
Severity	No.	Percent	No.	Percent	No.	Percent	No.	Percent
Slight	6	85.7	4	57.1	3	60.0	1	33.3
Moderate	0	00.0	2	28.6	1	20.0	1	33.3
Severe	1	14.3	1	14.3	1	20.0	1	33.3
	7		7		5		3	

Table 5.8
FABC Chi Square Analysis of Periostitis and Porotic Hyperostosis

Source	DF	X²	Significance
Porotic hyperostosis			
age (2 groups)	1	0.00000	n.s.
sex	1	0.41995	n.s.
*age (2 groups) and sex	1	3.43147	.10
Periostitis			
age (2 age groups)	1	7.99930	.005
sex	1	2.44766	.10
*age and sex	1	**	.07
Porotic hyperostosis and Periostitis	1	6.02780	.01

*Only diagnosed individuals.
**Fisher's Exact Test due to small sample size.

of porotic hyperostosis and periostitis by the status of lesions (unremodeled, being active at or near the time of death, or remodeled condition, healed/healing) was tested using a chi square analysis. Although statistical tests proved not to be significant, the majority (63.2%) of those with both anemia and infection had remodeled porotic hyperostotic lesions. This pattern points to periods of nutritional deficiency prior to episodes of infectious disease. Nutritional deficiency can compromise host resistance, causing physiological disruption that diminishes immunities and increases risk factors and susceptibilities. Therefore, members of FABC experienced episodes of malnutrition and/or undernutrition that affected their abilities to ward off infectious diseases. Those individuals experiencing infectious illnesses would have had a higher probability of developing/continuing episodes of anemia, thus continuing the feedback loop of infection and nutritional deficiency.

Cedar Grove, Arkansas, post-Reconstruction Afro-Americans exhibited a significantly higher rate of infection than FABC. Rose (1985) reported systemic active periostitis for 52.3 percent (n=23) of children aged 7 months in utero to 14 years old (n=44). When all periosteal lesions were combined, 77.3 percent of Cedar Grove children exhibited some form of periostitis, whether generalized (systemic) or localized (e.g., lower or upper limbs). The majority (91.3%) of subadult periosteal lesions were unremodeled at the time of death, indicating that infection may have contributed to death in Cedar Grove children. The greatest proportion (58.8%) of those affected were fetuses, infants, and children under 18 months of age. In addition, 47.1 percent of individuals exhibiting periostitis also were diagnosed as having porotic hyperostosis, thus duplicating the pattern of infectious disease and iron deficiency anemia interaction reported in other archaeological populations and observed in FABC.

The frequency of periostitis in Cedar Grove adults (80.5%) was also higher than in FABC adults. Similar to FABC, Cedar Grove male incidence (93.3%) was higher than female incidence (71.4%); and the majority of lesions were remodeled (healed). The percentage of Cedar Grove adults exhibiting both infection and iron deficiency anemia (27.6%) was dramatically lower than the 78.8 percent in FABC adults (Table 5.9). This different pattern between the two populations may be associated with dissimilar infectious disease etiologies.

Tuberculosis

Tuberculosis, an infectious disease caused by *mycobacterium tuberculosis*, may affect almost any tissue or organ of the body, but the lungs are the most common site affected (Stedman 1982). When tuberculosis affects bone, it is a secondary infection, since the lungs and lymph nodes are the primary sites of infection. Skeletally, the most common and characteristic tubercular lesions are found on the vertebral column, primarily affecting the lower thoracic and lumber vertebrae but rarely involving the cervical vertebrae and sacrum (Ortner and Putschar 1981; Steinbock 1976). This pattern has been observed in clinical, autopsy, and archaeological series. The organism's virulence and host resistance determine the degree of bone deformity and appearance. Severe conditions usually include the kyphosis or angulation of the spinal column, which occurs due to the collapse of the anterior portion of vertebral bodies. Tuberculosis usually begins in childhood, taking a chronic course; therefore, active and/or healed cases may be observed at any age.

Tuberculosis was the leading cause of death in Philadelphia throughout the nineteenth century, primarily affecting adults, according to the diagnoses of the period. During the period of 1807–1826, 15.04 percent (n=7,972) of deaths were due to tuberculosis; there was a slight decline for the years 1831–1840 to 14.23 percent (n=6,093). According to Torchia (1977), a high proportion of "consumption" deaths should be attributed to Afro-Americans, who were differentially affected by an acute fatal form of tuberculosis. In fact, for many years the medical community thought that Afro-Americans contracted a "different" and more virulent form of tuberculosis than Euro-Americans and Native Americans. Actual rates by race were not available for the period.

Four FABC individuals exhibited tubercular lesions (tubercular lesions were scored separately from generalized infectious lesions discussed above); all four were males aged between 33 and 55 years old. The most severe case was individual B66, a 50–60-year-old male whose fifth through eleventh thoracic and second and third lumbar vertebrae were fused together along with the right seventh rib (Plate 5.2). A 30–35-year-old male (B44) had a severe mycotic infection on the anterior surface of the sacrum along with periostitis and inflammation from the fifth lumbar to the first sacral joint (Plate 5.3).

Table 5.9
Adult Periostitis by Age and Sex for FABC and Cedar Grove

Age	FABC*				Cedar Grove**[1]			
	Males		Females		Males		Females	
	Number	Percent	Number	Percent	Number	Percent	Number	Percent
20–30	0	0.0	3	50.0	3	21.4	3	20.0
30–40	1	7.7	0	0.0	3	21.4	6	40.0
40–50	8	61.5	2	33.3	6	42.9	3	20.0
50+	4	30.8	1	16.7	2	14.3	3	20.0
	13		6		14		15	

*FABC N=19 with periostitis out of 75 adults
**Cedar Grove N=.29 with periostitis out of 36 adults.

Source: 1 - Rose 1985.

Plate 5.2
Tuberculosis of the Thoracic and Lumbar Vertebrae (Pott's Disease)
Burial 66, Male 50–60+

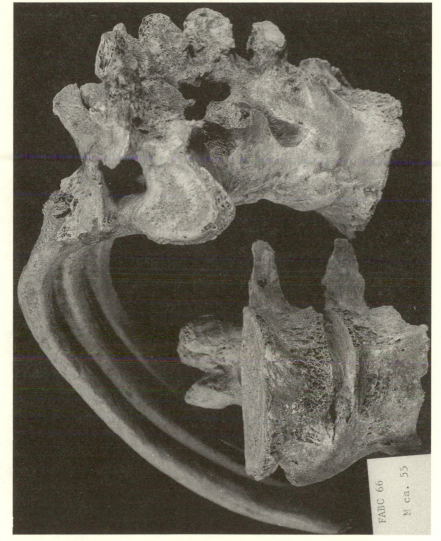

Plate 5.3
Mycotic Infection of Innominate and Sacrum
Burial 44, Male 30–35

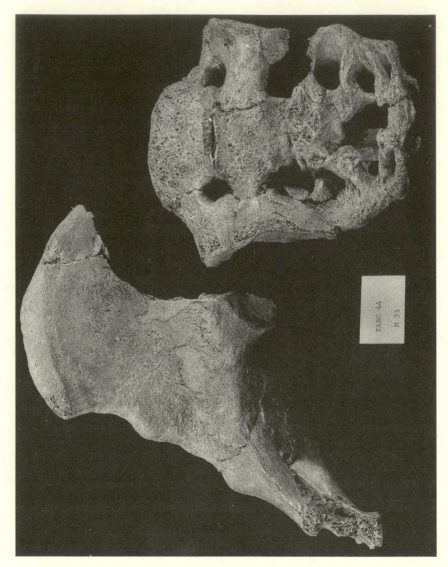

TRAUMA

Several factors led to an expectation of a high incidence of trauma for the FABC population: some members would have been ex-slaves, especially older individuals; the violence experienced by the Philadelphia Afro-American community throughout the period at the hands of rioting Euro-Americans; and accidental trauma associated with occupational risk. In actuality, FABC trauma incidence was low. Thirteen adults (17.3%), aged 35–80+ years, exhibited a total of twenty healed fractures distributed among seven bones, the vertebra, the hands (metacarpals and phalanges) and the feet (talus, phalanges).

The distribution of fractures in the FABC sample by age, sex, and bone appears to be primarily associated with occupational accidents. Therefore, the expected pattern of high incidence of trauma due to violence was not borne out, although several individuals (n=4) exhibited fractures that were most probably due to violence. The age-related frequency in males suggests a high probability of it being associated with their slave experience.

The majority (92.3%) of individuals with fractures were older than 40; only one individual, a female, was under 40 (Table 5.10). FABC males (n=10) had a higher incidence (13.6%) of fractures than females (7.7%). The majority of FABC fractures appear to be related to accidental trauma. Three individuals exhibited a colle's fracture (distal radius), which is usually associated with attempting to stop a fall forward.

Two individuals appear to have fractures caused by interpersonal violence (and there was possibly a third with multiple fractures): a 40–45-year-old female with a depression fracture of the left parietal; and a 40–45-year-old male with a well-healed fracture of the right clavicle. Significantly, strife-associated fractures were not observed for FABC children or young adults. One 55–60-year-old male (B82) did exhibit a well-healed greenstick fracture, which probably occurred in childhood. The majority of FABC fractures observed were well healed, with little or no angulation or distortion. Only one individual exhibited a midshaft fracture of the right femur that healed with a 2 centimeter override (anterior) that caused a shortening of the leg (Plate 5.4). Unlike the other FABC adults, this individual did not receive appropriate treatment for this fracture. Multiple fractures were observed in five older males, and the remaining nine individuals had one fracture each. The individual with the most fractures was a 45–50-year-old male (B14), with four well-healed fractures of the right distal radius (colle's), the right distal fibula, right fifth metacarpal, and the nasalia. The fracture to the nasal bones may be an indication of interpersonal violence or of a fall.

This age-related pattern of well-healed fractures points to the experiences of slavery for the majority of FABC individuals who would have been born prior to 1820; therefore, they were probably slave born rather than freeborn Afro-Americans. Some individuals born between 1790–1820 could have been freeborn due to the Gradual Abolition Act of 1790.

Table 5.10
Age and Sex Distribution of Fractures for FABC and Cedar Grove

Ages	FABC				Cedar Grove			
	Males		Females		Males		Females	
	Number	Percent	Number	Percent	Number	Percent	Number	Percent
17–20	0	0.0	0	0.0	1	6.6	0	0.0
20–30	0	0.0	0	0.0	0	0.0	1	4.8
30–40	0	0.0	1	2.6	1	6.6	1	4.8
41–50	7	19.4	2	5.1	5	33.3	2	9.5
50+	3	8.3	0	0.0	1	6.6	0	0.0
Totals	10	27.7	3	7.7	8	53.1	4	19.1

Source: 1 - Rose 1985.

116

Plate 5.4
Healed Femur Fracture with 2 cm. Overlap
Burial 47, Male 45–50 years old

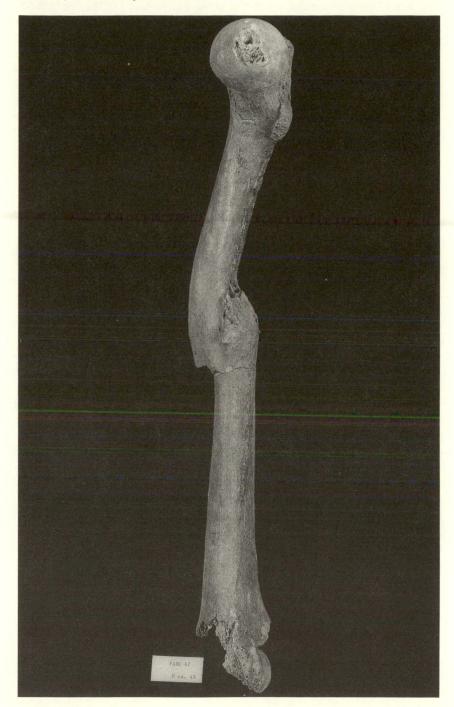

The Cedar Grove post-Reconstruction rural Arkansas skeletal sample was the only Afro-American skeletal series that could be compared to the fracture patterns of FABC. The distribution of fractures in this population was reported by general location rather than by individual bones (e.g., upper limbs, lower limbs). Fractures were observed in 33.3 percent (N=36) of the Cedar Grove adults, with seventeen healed fractures among twelve adult skeletons. Males (53.3%) also had a higher incidence of fractures than females (19%), as with FABC. The majority of those with fractures—as with FABC—were primarily older individuals aged between 40–50 years, including the five with two fractures each (four males and one female). Both Cedar Grove and FABC upper limb fractures had the highest frequency and were approximately equally distributed; fractures of the lower limbs followed; cranial fractures had the lowest frequency. Cedar Grove skeletons had a slightly higher frequency (17.6%) of cranial fractures than FABC (10.6%), most probably related to interpersonal violence. The distribution of FABC and Cedar Grove bone fractures by bone/location are summarized in Table 5.11.

DEGENERATIVE JOINT DISORDERS

Osteoarthritis

The majority of FABC adults (76%) exhibited osteoarthritis of slight severity, with the incidence slightly higher for males (77.7%) than for females (74.3%). The distribution of osteoarthritis by age and sex in FABC was somewhat different than would have been predicted. The expected age-related pattern was observed in FABC, but a significantly higher proportion of younger females, aged 18–30, were observed to have osteoarthritic changes (33.3%). In addition, 61.5 percent of these females also exhibited osteophytosis of slight severity. This pattern differs greatly from those reported in the literature and from those observed in Cedar Grove Afro-Americans (4.8%) and may be associated with the strenuous labor of Afro-American women. During this period there was a great demand for female domestic workers, thus establishing a pattern of female early entry into the work force, even as children (Emerson 1827; Hershberg 1975, 1981). The FABC females aged 18–30 exhibiting osteoarthritic changes (n=13) represented 76.5 percent of the females in their age group. Osteoarthritis was observed in 50 percent of the females aged 30–40, and by age 50, 100 percent of the females exhibited osteoarthritic changes.

The frequency of osteoarthritis for males increased with age, beginning at age 30–40. Early onset osteoarthritis was observed for only three males (ages 18–30) therefore lower than that observed for females. Osteoarthritic changes were observed in 62.5 percent of the males in the 30–40 age group; 71.4 percent of the males in the 40–50 age group exhibited osteoarthritic changes; and by age 50, 100 percent exhibited osteoarthritis. The majority of males (82.8%)

exhibiting osteoarthritis also exhibited vertebral osteophytosis (degeneration and bony proliferation of the vertebral bodies).

The overall incidence of osteoarthritis for FABC (76%) was much higher than for Cedar Grove (41.6%). The proportionate difference in the incidence of osteoarthritis between Cedar Grove and FABC was similar for both sexes. Cedar Grove males had a slightly higher frequency of osteoarthritis than females, with an age-related increase beginning at ages 30–40 for males. The distribution of osteoarthritis by age and sex for FABC and Cedar Grove is summarized in Table 5.12. Data for comparisons of severity were not available for any of the Afro-American skeletal series.

Osteoarthritis was observed in multiple joints for the majority of FABC adults (75.9%). In general, males had more joints affected by osteoarthritis than females; 24.1 percent of males and 13.8 percent of females exhibited osteoarthritic changes in four to six joints (only the eldest male B63, age 80+ had six joints affected). Both sexes had similar proportion of individuals with osteoarthritis with two to three joints affected (males 53.6%, females 51.7%). Only five males (17.8%) and nine (31%) females had only one joint exhibiting degeneration, although this may be associated with the preservation of the skeletal remains. The joints affected in three of the five males were the hip and the shoulder, and elbow for the other two. The joint affected in eight out of the nine females was the hip, including both the femoral head and the acetabulum. There was no significant age-related and/or sex-related pattern associated with the number of joints affected, although the two eldest males had the most joints affected. There was also no significant association between number of joints af-

Table 5.11
FABC and Cedar Grove Bone Fractures by Location

| Location | Bone | FABC | | Cedar Grove | | |
		Number	Percent	Location	Number	Percent
Cranial	Parietals	1	5.0	10.6	3	17.6
	Frontal	1	5.0			
Upper	Clavicle	1	5.0	47.3	8	47.1
	Vertebra	1	5.0			
	Radius	4	25.0			
	Hand	3	15.0			
Lower	Femur	2	10.0	42.1	6	35.3
	Fibula	3	15.0			
	Talus	1	5.0			
	Tibia	1	5.0			
	Foot	2	10.0			
All		*20	10.0		**17	

*FABC n=12.
**Cedar Grove n=12.
Source:** Rose 1985.

Table 5.12
Osteoarthritis by Age and Sex for FABC and Cedar Grove

| | FABC | | | | Cedar Grove[1] | | | |
| | Males | | Females | | Males | | Females | |
Ages	No.	Percent	No.	Percent	No.	Percent	No.	Percent
16–19	1	2.8	2	5.1	0	0.0	0	0.0
20–30	2	5.5	11	28.2	0	0.0	1	4.8
30–40	5	13.9	4	10.3	2	13.3	1	4.8
40–50	10	27.8	10	25.6	3	20.0	4	19.0
50–60	9	25.0	0	0.0	2	13.3	2	9.5
60+	2	5.5	2	5.1	0	0.0	0	0.0
Totals	29	80.5	29	74.3	7	46.6	8	38.1
Total No.	36		39		15		21	

Source: 1 - Rose 1985.
Note: Percentages based on total number of males and females for each site.

fected and evidence of periosteal infection, which is also an age-related disorder (Mensforth, et al. 1985).

When comparing the joints exhibiting osteoarthritic changes by sex, a differential pattern was observed, which may be related to different occupational activity patterns. Males had a higher prevalence of osteoarthritic degeneration in the shoulder (65.6%) and elbow (62.1%) than females (27.6% and 24.1%, respectively). This differential may be an indicator of the heavy manual labor and lifting involved in the main occupations of African Baptist men (laborers, porters, waiters, seamen, carters). Females had a higher prevalence of osteoarthritis in the hip (86.2%), knee (41.4%), and hand (20.7%) joints compared to males (82.7%, 31%, 6.9%, respectively). This pattern of joint degeneration may be associated with the predominant occupations of African Baptist females of washerwoman, laundress, domestic worker, and seamstress (see chapter 3). Osteoarthritis of the hip (affecting both the acetabulum and femoral head) had the highest frequency for both sexes, and may be associated with bending and lifting involved in the occupations of males and females, as well as childbearing and rearing for females. Only twelve individuals exhibited moderate or severe degeneration of the hip: seven males (one was B124, with a diagnosis of Legg-Calve-Perthes syndrome—discussed below) and five females. Three of the females were young adults (aged 18–21); one 18–20 year old (B107) had a cyst on the left femur and may have been compensating with the right leg if she experienced pain. The other two females were aged 40–45. The distribution of osteoarthritis by joint for those males and females exhibiting joint degeneration are summarized in Table 5.13.

The incidence of osteoarthritis for FABC was compared to that of 38CH778 (Rathbun 1987) and Cedar Grove (Rose 1985). Comparisons (Table 5.14) were limited to the major joints (combined), hands, and feet for Cedar Grove (Rose 1985). The highest frequency of osteoarthritis for both FABC and 38CH778 was found to be the hip for both sexes. However, 38CH778 males (100%) were significantly higher than females (77%), and FABC males and females were comparable. The highest incidence of osteoarthritis in the shoulder joint was reported for 38CH778 females who exhibited 85% of shoulder degeneration, followed by 38CH778 males (64%). FABC males were observed to have a higher incidence (52.8%) of shoulder osteoarthritis than females (20.5%), although lower than that observed in 38CH778 males and females.

This difference between FABC and 38CH778 females may be associated with types and levels of work associated with plantation slavery compared to urban domestic labor. Osteoarthritis of the elbow was higher for males in FABC (50%) and 38CH778 (45%), and lower for females (17.9% and 23%, respectively). The overall rate of FABC osteoarthritis of the major joints (74.7%) was significantly higher than that reported for Cedar Grove (39.3%). The frequency of osteoarthritis by sex was reversed when comparing FABC and Cedar Grove. FABC males (77.8%) had higher frequencies than FABC females

Table 5.13
FABC Osteoarthritis by Joint

Joint	Males *n=28		Females *n=29	
	Number	Percent	Number	Percent
Shoulder	19	67.8	8	27.6
Elbow	18	62.1	7	24.1
Hip	24	82.7	25	86.2
Knee	9	31.0	12	41.4
Hands	2	6.9	6	20.7
Feet	5	17.2	6	20.7

* Number of individuals with osteoarthritis.
N=75, Males=36, Females=39

(71.8%), while Cedar Grove females (28.6%) had higher frequencies compared to Cedar Grove males (23.9%).

Osteophytosis

Vertebral osteophytosis was found on 52% of FABC vertebrae, primarily of slight severity. Males had a higher incidence (69.4%) than females (35.9%). Thoracic vertebrae of males (55.5%) exhibited the highest frequency of osteophytic degeneration, followed by the lumbar vertebrae. The cervical vertebrae had the lowest incidence of osteophytosis for males (44.4%) and the highest for females (28.2%). The pattern for cervical vertebrae may be associated with axial loading due to carrying heavy loads on the top of the head or to other occupational activities requiring bending of the neck while lifting heavy objects (e.g., washing linens over a basin). The lowest osteophytosis incidence for female was observed for the thoracic vertebrae (20.5%). A total of nineteen (25.3%) individuals were observed to have all vertebrae affected by osteophytosis; males had the highest incidence with 33.3 percent (n=12) and females had only 17.9 percent (n=7). The differential pattern between males and females as to the type of vertebrae affected may have been associated with occupational activity patterns and biomechanics. The distribution of osteophytosis by vertebral type and sex for FABC is detailed in Table 5.15.

The overall incidence of osteophytosis in FABC (52%) was higher than that reported for Cedar Grove adults (38.9%). Osteophytosis was distributed somewhat differently for 38CH778 plantation slaves with the highest frequency observed for females (61%) in the cervical vertebrae. This was similar to FABC

Table 5.14
Osteoarthritis by Joint for FABC, 38CH778, and Cedar Grove

| Joints | FABC N=75 | | | | 38CH778[1] N=28 | | | | Cedar Grove[2] N=36 | | | |
| | Males | | Females | | Males | | Females | | Males | | Females | |
	No.	Percent	No.	Percent	No.	Percent	No.	Percent	No.	Percent	No.	Percent
Shoulder	19	52.8	8	20.5	7	64.0	11	85.0	-	-	-	-
Elbow	18	50.0	7	17.9	5	45.0	3	23.0	-	-	-	-
Hip	24	66.7	25	64.1	12	100.0	10	77.0	-	-	-	-
Knee	9	25.0	12	30.8	2	20.0	5	38.0	-	-	-	-
Hands	2	5.5	6	15.4	-	-	-	-	2	13.3	4	19.0
Feet	5	13.9	6	15.4	-	-	-	-	4	26.6	4	19.0
Major Joints	28	77.8	28	71.8	-	-	-	-	5	23.9	6	28.6
Total No. by Sex	36		39		13		15		15		21	
Percent all affected	74.7				82.1				30.5			

- = data not reported.

Source: 1 – Rathbun 1987.

2 – Rose 1985.

Table 5.15
FABC Osteophytosis by Vertebral Type and Sex

Sex	C1-7		T1-9		T10-12		L1-3		L4-5	
	No.	Percent	No.	Percent	No.	Percent	No.	Percent	No.	Percent
Males	16	44.4	18	50.0	19	52.8	19	52.8	16	44.4
Females	11	28.2	8	20.5	8	20.5	10	25.6	10	25.6
Adults	27	36.0	26	34.7	27	36.0	29	38.6	26	34.6

Table 5.16
Osteophytosis for FABC, 38CH778, and Cedar Grove

	FABC N=75				38CH778[1] N=28				Cedar Grove[2] N=36			
	Males		Females		Males		Females		Males		Females	
Vertebra	No.	Percent	No.	Percent	No.	Percent	No.	Percent	No.	Percent	No.	Percent
Cervical	16	44.4	11	28.2	3	30.0	8	61.0	–	–	–	–
Thoracic	20	55.5	8	20.5	4	40.0	5	38.0	–	–	–	–
Lumbar	19	52.7	10	25.6	3	30.0	4	31.0	–	–	–	–
Totals	25	69.4	14	35.9	–	–	–	–	7	46.6	7	33.3

– = no data available.

Sources: 1 – Rathbun 1987.

2 – Rose 1985.

females in that the cervical vertebrae were the most affected. The thoracic vertebrae were the most affected vertebrae for males. In general, 38CH778 males had lower incidence rates of osteophytosis for all vertebrae than did FABC. Osteophytosis of the thoracic and lumbar vertebrae for males and females were similarly affected for 38CH778 individuals. The distribution of osteophytosis for FABC, 38CH778, and Cedar Grove are presented in Table 5.16.

Several of these individuals were also diagnosed as having other degenerative disorders, such as schmorl's nodes and Leggs-Calves-Perthes syndrome.

Schmorl's Nodes

Schmorl's nodes, or cartilaginous nodes, develop when the tension of weight bearing causes the intervertebral disc to penetrate into the bony trabecular at points where there are gaps in the cartilaginous plate of the vertebral body These nodes usually occur in males, increase with age, and may also be associated with trauma (Clark 1985). Therefore, the frequency of schmorl's can be indicative of strenuous activity.

Schmorl's nodes were observed on 18.7 percent of FABC vertebrae (n=14), most often on the first through ninth thoracic and the lumbar vertebrae (L1–3=7, L4–5=6). Males (33.3%) had a significantly higher frequency of schmorl's nodes than females (5.1%). The majority (57.1%) of FABC skeletons with schmorl's nodes were older than 40 (n=8), and the remaining 42.9 percent were aged 25–40 (n=6). The distribution of schmorl's nodes by age, sex, and vertebral type are summarized in Table 5.17.

The incidence of schmorl's nodes in South Carolina plantation slaves from 38CH778 (39%) was higher than for FABC (18.7%), with substantially higher frequency in males (54%) than females (24%) (Table 5.18). Incidence of schmorl's nodes in Cedar Grove post-Reconstruction rural Arkansas male farmers (33.3%) was significantly lower than 38CH778 male slaves and similar to that found in FABC males. Distinct from the higher male incidence observed in FABC and 38CH778, schmorl's nodes were almost equally distributed by sex in Cedar Grove.

Table 5.17
Distribution of Schmorl's Nodes by Vertebral Type for FABC

	T1–9		T10–12		L1–3		L4–5	
Sex	No.	Percent	No.	Percent	No.	Percent	No.	Percent
Males	7	19.4	4	11.1	5	13.9	5	13.9
Females	0	0.0	0	0.0	2	5.1	1	2.5
Total*	7	9.3	4	5.3	7	9.3	6	8.0

*All FABC Adults N=75

Table 5.18
Distribution of Schmorl's Nodes for FABC, 38CH778, and Cedar Grove

	Males		Females		Total	
Site	No.	Percent	No.	Percent	No.	Percent
FABC	12	33.3	2	5.1	14	18.7
38CH778	7	54.0	4	24.0	11	39.0
Cedar Grove	5	33.3	4	25.0	8	25.0

Legg-Calve-Perthes Syndrome

One 55–60-year-old FABC male was diagnosed as having experienced Legg-Calve-Perthes syndrome in childhood (hip joint). According to Stedman (1982), Legg-Calve-Perthes syndrome entails the aseptic necrosis (tissue death not due to infection) of the femoral proximal epiphysis. It is also called pseudocoxalgia, coxaplana, osteochondritis deformans juvenilis, Perthes disease, Calve-Perthes disease, or quiet hip disease. During childhood, local circulatory disturbances to the metaphysis and epiphyseal cartilage of the femoral head lead to degenerative changes and the death of the outer layer of epiphyseal bone (avascular necrosis), but the exact etiology of the disorder is unknown. It occurs most commonly in boys between the ages of three and twelve years old, causing aching, deformity, shortening of the leg, and secondary osteoarthritis of the femur and innominate (Durham 1956; Ortner and Putschar 1981). The course of the disorder is self-limiting although it can last for several years, with revascularization and healing eventually occurring. Residual deformity, limitation of joint movement, and, in some cases, continued pain remain throughout adulthood. Legg-Calve-Perthes syndrome, according to Ortner and Putschar (1981), is an uncommon disorder that occurs unilaterally in 90 percent of cases. Therefore, the bilateral condition of Legg-Calve-Perthes syndrome observed in burial 124 is very rare (Plate 5.5). Paleopathologically, the femoral head will appear mushroom shaped, with an overhanging margin due to a combination of compression fracture and lack of enchondral bone growth, but without significant dislocation of the center of the femoral neck (an important characteristic for diagnostic differentiation with slipped femoral capital epiphysis). The head will be flattened, eburnated, and modified in appearance due to early severe degenerative arthritis.

There appears to be a conflict about the ancestry distribution of the Legg-Calve-Perthes syndrome reported in the literature. Ortner and Putschar (1981) maintain that the condition is rarely found in Afro-Americans, while Durham (1956) states that it is not an uncommon finding in patients with sickle cell anemia. There was no other pathological evidence that burial 124 could have suffered from sickle cell anemia (although radiographic analysis was not un-

Plate 5.5
Bilateral Legg-Calve-Perthes Disorder of the Femoral Head
Burial 124, Male 55–60

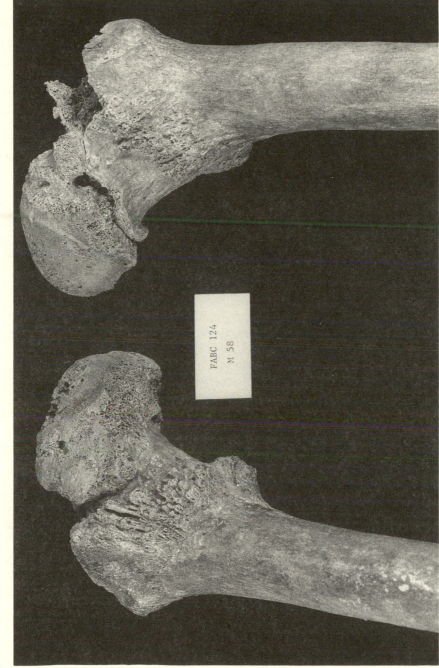

FABC 124
M 58

dertaken with the exception of the femurs). In addition, the advanced age of the individual also contraindicates sickle cell anemia. Nevertheless, the individual may have had sickle cell trait, since a disorder and/or lesion common to sickle cell anemia may be manifested in a trait carrier under stressful conditions (Diggs 1967:138).

Summary

Degenerative joint disorders were common in the FABC population. There was a high incidence of osteoarthritis observed for FABC adults (76%), but it was primarily of slight severity. An age-related pattern of osteoarthritis was observed, with an uncommon occurrence of early onset in females aged 18–30, which may have been associated with their early entry into the labor force and the type of domestic work in which they were employed. The majority of FABC adults exhibited osteoarthritis in multiple joints. A differential pattern of the joint affected was observed by sex, with males primarily exhibiting joint degeneration of the hip, shoulder, and elbow; and females exhibiting a pattern of hip, knee, shoulder, and hands.

Vertebral osteophytosis was found on 52 percent of FABC vertebrae, primarily of slight severity. Males had a higher incidence (69.4%) than females (35.9%). Females exhibited the highest frequency of osteophytosis in the cervical vertebrae and the lowest in the thoracic. Males exhibited the highest frequency in the thoracic and the lowest in the cervical vertebrae.

There appears to be a definite pattern of increasing incidence of osteoarthritis with age in the FABC population. Although there was early onset of osteoarthritis in females, the differential pattern of joints affected indicates that occupational activities of these urban laborers predisposed them to degenerative joint disorders at earlier ages.

GROWTH AND DEVELOPMENT: DENTAL ENAMEL DEFECTS, STATURE, AND BONE MORPHOMETRY

Dental Enamel Defects: Hypoplasias and Hypocalcifications

Dental enamel defects are indicators of nutritionally and/or disease-induced metabolic disruption of the dentition during its formation from the fifth prenatal month continuing to six years of age. Hypoplasias and hypocalcifications are enamel defects produced during different phases of tooth formation. Hypoplasias appear as transverse linear lesions (Plate 5.6 shows grooves and serial pitting can be seen in Plate 5.7). Hypocalcifications appear as transverse bands of opaque coloration (chalky white or yellow brown) and normal thickness.

Plate 5.6
Linear Enamel Hypoplasias, Mandible Exhibiting Multiple Defects

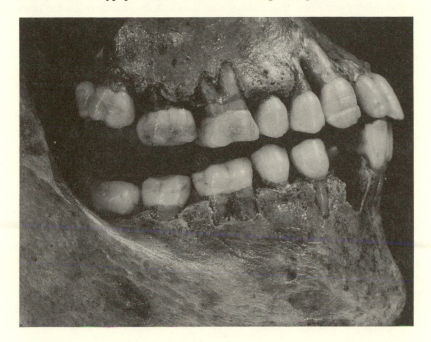

Plate 5.7
Pitted Enamel Hypoplasia

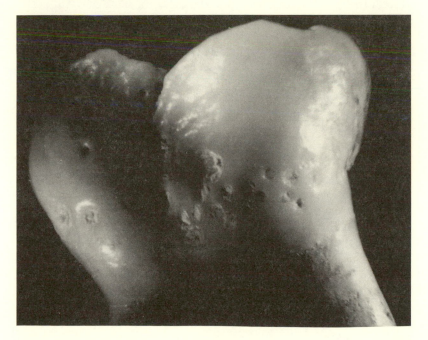

Subadult Dentition. The analyses of subadult deciduous dentition enamel defects included the observation of both hypocalcifications and hypoplasias. Deciduous dentition studied included maxillary and mandibular incisors and canines from twenty subadults (Table 5.19), representing 33.3 percent of the sixty subadult burials. Subadult sample ages ranged from three months to eight years old. Dental defects were observed on 92.5 percent (n=37) of the teeth, with only 7.5 percent exhibiting no defects. Individuals with enamel defects included: nine (45%) with hypocalcifications; four (20%) with only hypoplasias; and seven (35%) with both defects. Thirteen (55%) subadults exhibited multiple defects; the seven with only one defect also had only one tooth. Ten of the individuals with multiple defects had three to four defects, two had two defects each, and one had a total of five defects.

The majority of enamel defects identified (hypoplasias and hypocalcifications) had developed during the prenatal period, indicating that maternal health, as well as fetal health, had been compromised during the gestational period. The chronological distribution of enamel defects is illustrated in Figure 5.1. Primary onset of an enamel defect had developed in 25 percent (n=5) of the subadults by the fifth month in utero. By the ninth prenatal month, 70 percent (n=14) of all subadults had experienced the first onset of a defect, a pattern similar to a Native American population (Blakey and Armelagos 1985). No significant pattern in age at death was observed based on type of primary onset defect. A pattern of earlier mortality associated with prenatal primary onset was observed, similar to Dickson Mounds, although not as clearly delineated. Death occurred by age 3 years for 60 percent (n=12), and by ages 4–6 years for 15 percent (n=3) of subadults with prenatal onset; in subadults with postnatal primary onset of enamel defects, mortality occurred by ages 7–8 years for 15 percent and 1–2 years for 10 percent. Therefore, those children compromised in utero were at higher risk of dying during childhood.

Table 5.19
FABC Subadult Tooth Type and Number of Defects

Dentition	Deciduous		Permanent	
Tooth Type*	N=20	Number of Defects	N=4	Number of Defects
Maxillary Canine	9	12	1	1
Maxillary Incisor	12	16	3	9
Mandibular Canine	11	15	3	6
Mandibular Incisor	8	8	1	1
Totals	40	51	8	17

*Only 3 teeth had no defects.

Hypocalcifications had a higher incidence rate in the FABC deciduous dentition than hypoplasias, as found in other studies (Blakey and Armelagos 1985; Goodman, et al. 1980) where hypocalcifications occurred primarily in the deciduous dentition. A sharp distinction in onset patterns was exhibited in the FABC subadult dentition between hypocalcifications and hypoplasias (Figure 5.2). Hypocalcifications were primarily formed during the prenatal period, especially for primary onset episodes. Hypocalcification frequencies were the highest during the fifth, seventh, and eighth (respectively) prenatal months, indicating maternally related stress. A significant portion of this maternal stress occurred during the last trimester when fetal weight gain is critical and places a high demand on maternal stores (Beal 1980). These data point to the dietary marginality and, perhaps, the intensive physical labor these women experienced. Incidence declined gradually between the ninth prenatal month and the second postnatal month. Secondary and tertiary onset episodes occurred throughout the prenatal, birth, and seventh postnatal months (Figure 5.3).

The majority of subadult hypoplasias occurred postnatally during the first, third, and fourth postnatal months of life. Secondary onset of a hypoplasia peaked during the third postnatal month, while secondary and tertiary episodes were observed between the second and sixth postnatal months. Prenatally, hypoplasias occurred only during the eighth gestational month, corroborating the inference from the hypocalcification data that the critical fetal weight gain period may have been compromised (Figure 5.3).

The four subadults with permanent dentition all had multiple defects including hypocalcifications and hypoplasias. Two individuals aged 11–12 years had the greatest number of defects, including the subadult diagnosed with scurvy. The 12 year old with the highest number of defects (seven) had a primary onset of enamel defect by six months postnatal, while the other three subadults with permanent dentition had primary onsets during the second year of life.

Subadult enamel defects by age at death peaked at 14 months, gradually declining to age 36 months (3 years). The pattern may be indicative of the effect of the weaning process, with decline in dietary nutritional quality and increased exposure to environmental pollutants (e.g., contaminated water and milk, see chapter 4), diarrheal disorders, cholera, and other infectious diseases. Subadult enamel defects by age at death are presented in Figure 5.4.

Adult Permanent Dentition. Adult dentition studied included permanent maxillary and mandibular canines and central incisors. These teeth were selected based on two studies (El-Najjar, et al. 1978; Goodman, et al. 1980), which determined that the anterior dentition and, in particular, the maxillary central incisor and the mandibular canine, represent the most sensitive teeth in response to stress. A total of fifty adults had dentition available for study; these included: twenty-five maxillary canines, thirty-nine maxillary central incisors, thirty-five mandibular incisors, and thirty-nine mandibular canines. All FABC adults with teeth available for analysis exhibited an enamel defect: 15.7 percent had at least one defect and 84.3 percent had two or more. Only eight individuals had only one tooth each (of the four teeth studied), all with one defect; the remaining forty-three individuals had two or more teeth. All individuals were included in this analysis. Multiple defects were observed in 52 percent of maxillary canines, 69.2 percent of mandibular canines, 64.1 percent of maxillary incisors, and 37.1 percent mandibular incisors. The number of teeth available and the number of defects per tooth type are summarized in Table 5.20.

Hypoplasias had the greater frequency in FABC adults when compared to hypocalcifications. The peak age of onset for both enamel defects was between two and four years, corresponding to patterns observed in other archaeological populations (Corruccini et al. 1985; Goodman, et al. 1984; Huss-Ashmore, et al. 1982; Rose 1985; Schultz and McHenry 1975), and the Hammon-Todd (Goodman 1988) urban industrial sample. In general, hypocalcification frequencies were relatively low, as would be expected in permanent dentition (Blakey and Armelagos 1985). Hypocalcifications observed dated from the first six months through the sixth year of life, with the greatest occurrences in at six months and 2.5–4.0 years. Hypoplasia frequency was low for the first year and half, significantly increasing at 2.0 years, peaking at 3.0–3.5, and then decreasing (Figure 5.5). The high frequency of enamel defects during 2.0–4.0 years, which has also been observed in other populations discussed earlier, has been primarily attributed to weaning stress. Although this pattern may be related to weaning stress for FABC adults, it may also be associated with the high incidence of diarrheal diseases and cholera (in particular) experienced by children during the nineteenth century in Philadelphia, due to contaminated water and/or milk supply, poor sanitary conditions, and infectious disease episodes associated with childhood infectious disease epidemics (chapter 4).

The distribution of adult hypoplasias based on developmental age of the dentition (Blakey 1986; Goodman, et al. 1980; Rose 1985), when studied for each tooth, revealed different age related patterns of defect onset. These differ-

Table 5.20
FABC Adult Hypoplasias by Tooth and Number of Defects

Dentition	Teeth w/ Defects			Number of Defects		
Tooth Type	No.	Total Defects	Percent	0	1	2 +
Maxillary Canine	25	25	100.0	0	13	12
Maxillary Incisor	39	36	92.3	3	11	25
Mandibular Canine	39	37	94.9	2	10	27
Mandibular Incisor	35	28	80.0	7	15	13
Totals	138	126	—	12	49	77

Figure 5.1
Hypocalcifications and Hypoplasias (Subadults N=20)

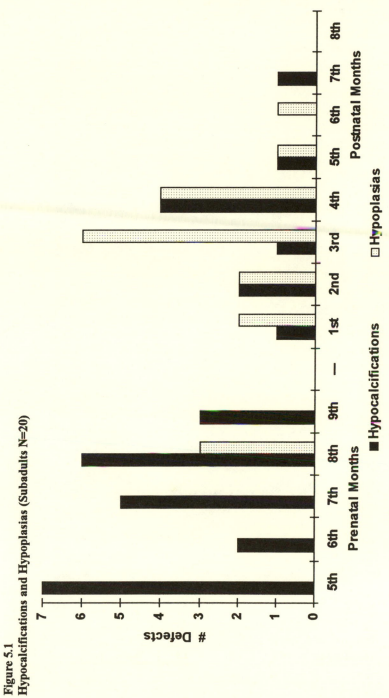

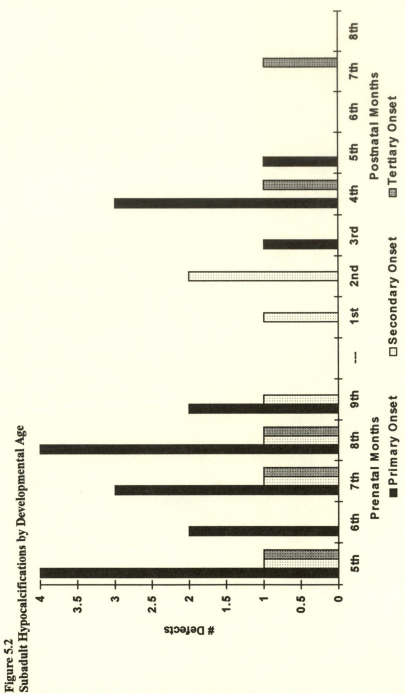

Figure 5.2
Subadult Hypocalcifications by Developmental Age

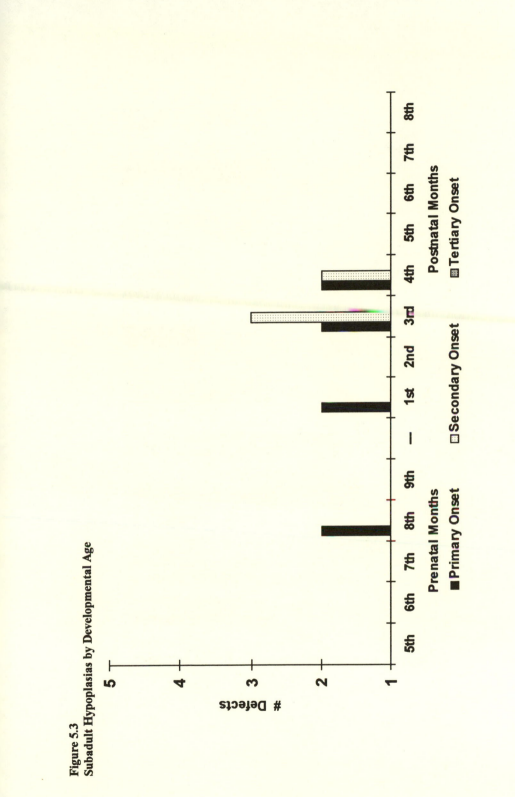

Figure 5.3
Subadult Hypoplasias by Developmental Age

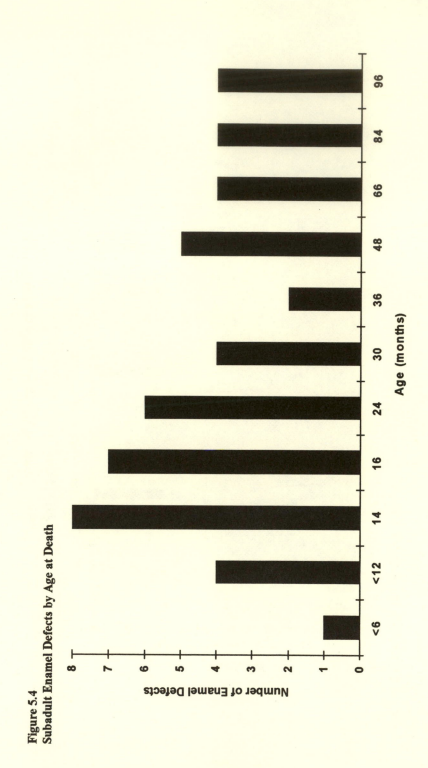

Figure 5.4
Subadult Enamel Defects by Age at Death

136

Figure 5.5
FABC Distribution of Enamel Defects: Hypoplasias and Hypocalcifications

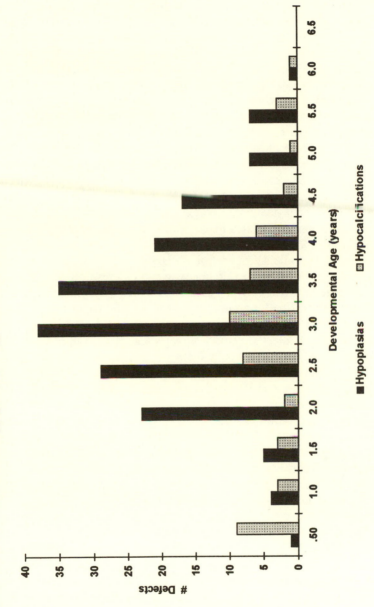

137

ential patterns by tooth and age of onset (primary, secondary, and tertiary) are summarized in Figure 5.6.

Despite different patterns of primary, secondary, and tertiary onset of enamel defects between tooth types, when total defects for each tooth are considered, the periods of peak defect formation overlap, thus indicating a period of nutritional and/or disease stress between ages 2.0 and 3.5 years. The distribution of adult hypoplasias by sex was not statistically significant. The distribution of enamel defects by sex and age are presented in Figure 5.7.

Hypoplasias for several Afro-American skeletal series have been reported, although measurement techniques and criteria have varied, thus limiting the scope of comparisons. Kelley and Angel (1983) reported hypoplastic frequencies of 71 percent for males (n=8) and 43 percent for females (n=7) from the Catoctin Furnace slave site. They concluded that these industrial slaves experienced childhood periods of nutritional/disease stress, despite being relatively healthy as adults. Angel, et al. (1987) in their preliminary analysis of the FABC permanent dentition reported that 68 percent of FABC males and 47 percent of females exhibited linear enamel hypoplasias; frequencies were comparable to Catoctin Furnace, but lower than that reported above, utilizing a multitooth, multiple defect analysis. Rathbun (1987) reported hypoplastic episodes for 38CH778 South Carolina plantation slaves utilizing Goodman, et al. (1980) criteria, whereby hypoplasias were scored only when a second tooth was affected. These South Carolina slaves had a high incidence of hypoplasias; 92 percent of the males and 50 percent of the females exhibited defects on two types of teeth, while 100 percent of males and 71 percent of females exhibited hypoplasias on one tooth (Figure 5.8).

Corruccini, et al. (1985) in their study of Newton Plantation slaves in Barbados undertook analysis of the permanent dentition of 103 individuals, focusing on the differential distribution of hypoplastic events by type/severity. Enamel defects were classified as: (1) linear enamel hypoplasias (LEH), observed as thin/shallow bands that typified the least number of defects possible; (2) major growth arrests (MGA), relatively wide and/or deep that typified the maximum defects possible without microscopic observation; and (3) transverse pitting (PIT) across the crown, the most severe and obvious defect.

Corruccini and coworkers reported that 54 percent of the individuals had hypoplastic defects for all tooth types. The majority of Newton slaves (60.7%) exhibited the more severe defects, major growth arrests (MGA) and pitting (PIT). The age-specific chronology of individual hypoplastic episodes indicated a peak occurrence of LEH at age 3.0–3.25 years, PIT at age 3.5, and MGA at age 4.0, with a combined peak of 3.5–3.75. The peak period is approximately a year later than other archaeological populations discussed above. On the basis of historical documents, it has been attributed to a later weaning period than in other populations (Corruccini, et al. 1985).

Utilizing similar criteria as Corruccini, et al. (1985), FABC hypoplasias were classified as LEH, MGA, and PIT. Pitting was rare in FABC dentitions

Figure 5.6
Enamel Defects by Tooth Type

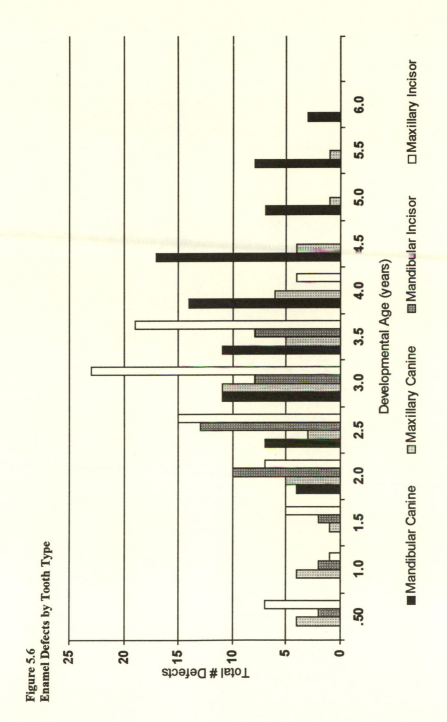

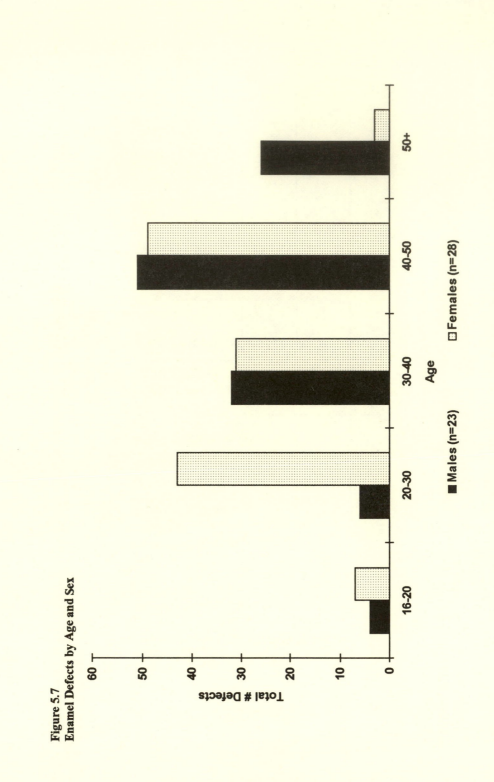

Figure 5.7
Enamel Defects by Age and Sex

140

Figure 5.8
Hypoplasias FABC and 38CH778 by Sex

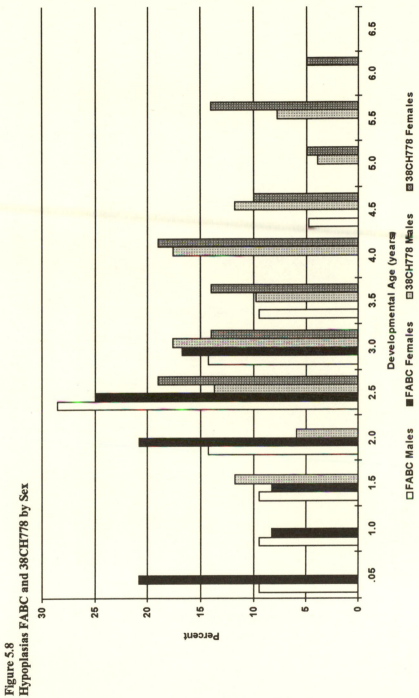

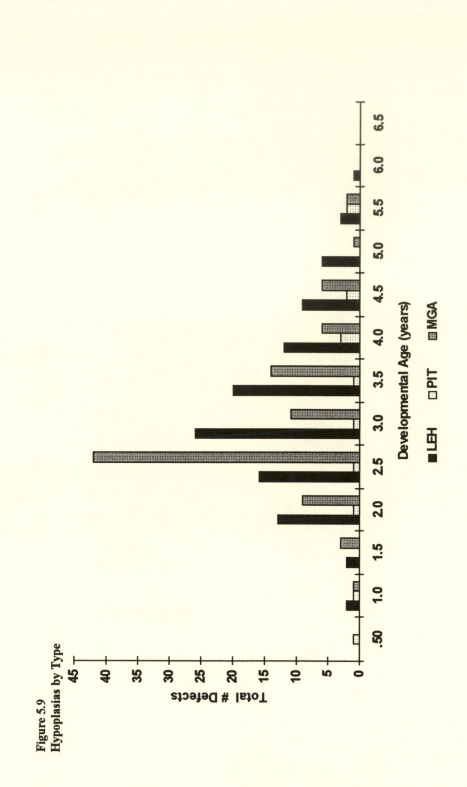

Figure 5.9
Hypoplasias by Type

with a combined frequency of MGA and PIT of 44 percent (based on primary onset only), significantly lower than the 60.7 percent of Newton Plantation slaves. Age-specific distribution of defects exhibited a marked peak at age 2.5 years for MGA and a lower peak for LEH at 3.0 years, while PIT was evenly distributed throughout all ages at minimal levels (Figure 5.9).   Therefore, FABC freedmen present a scenario opposite to that of Newton plantation slaves, among whom the least severe defects occurred earlier than the severe defects.   In FABC, MGA defects preceded the less severe defects and at an earlier age.   When primary onset by type of defect for FABC individuals was considered, LEH had a peak age of 2.5, MGA 2.0, and PIT 4.0.   These individual chronologies (rather than events) are also earlier than the event peaks seen in Newton, but with significantly lower differences than those at Newton.   These peaks in FABC were more distinctly delineated, with an earlier primary onset peak at ages 2.0–2.5.

Stature

Male mean stature was similar for the FABC urban freedmen, eighteenth century plantation/farm slaves, and Catoctin Furnace iron-working slaves. FABC had the highest male mean stature (172.2cm.); the mean statures for nineteenth century male plantation/farm slaves (167.8cm.) and South Carolina plantation slaves (167.4cm) were shorter and may be indicative of a poorer health status for these two populations.

Female mean stature was lower than that of males in all populations, as would be expected based on sexual dimorphism.   Catoctin Furnace females had the lowest stature (156.4cm.), corresponding with the overall indicators that females in this "healthy" population fared worse than their male counterparts. The high value placed on male labor in the iron- working industry most probably led to the economic devaluation of females.   Therefore, the combined effects of differential treatment by sex, intense strenuous labor, and the strains of the reproductive process contributed to lowered health status and depressed growth in Catoctin Furnace women.   FABC (159.1cm.), 38CH778 (160.6cm.) and eighteenth century plantation/farm female slaves (159.7cm.) had similar higher mean statures, with 38CH778 females having a slightly higher mean.   Stature comparisons by site and sex are summarized in Table 5.21.

Significantly, there was a wide range of variation (standard deviations of 8.7 males/6.75 females) in FABC stature within each sex.   There were FABC females who were close in stature (178.7cm.) to the tallest males (180.3cm). The shortest stature for both sexes was 147.3cm.   In general, FABC stature is indicative of the heterogeneous nature of this urban population—composed of ex-slaves and freeborn Afro-Americans—and their overall good health status when compared to enslaved counterparts.

Table 5.21
Mean Stature by Afro-American Skeletal Populations

Skeletal Population	Males		Females	
	N	Mean	N	Mean
FABC	34	172.2	37	159.1
18th century[1]	13	171.0	8	159.7
Catoctin Furnace[1]	7	171.6	8	156.4
19th century[1]	14	167.8	15	157.4
38CH778[2]	13	167.4	15	160.6

Sources: 1- Kelley and Angel 1987.
          2- Rathbun 1987.

Bone Morphometrics and Bone Maintenance: Cortical Thickness

Femoral cross-sections of fifty-four adults (twenty-eight males and twenty-six females) and seven subadult skeletons were measured for both mean cortical thickness and total cortical area. There were no significant differences in the average cortical thickness between males and females. Comparisons of cortical thickness by age group revealed that the two younger males, aged 19 and 29, had lower cortical thicknesses than females aged 16–40; and that younger males aged 19–39 (n=9) had lower thicknesses than the older males (40 and above).   This differential pattern in cortical thickness suggested that the younger males had experienced periods of disrupted childhood bone growth and development, a pattern also observed in the younger Cedar Grove males (Martin, et al. 1987). Females aged 19–30, representing 50 percent of the females (n=13), had lower cortical thickness values than the females in the succeeding decade (30–40). These lower values probably reflected the combined effect of childhood growth disruption and reproductive and/or lactational demands. Female mean cortical thicknesses decreased from age 40, with bone loss of 4.3 percent for those aged 40–50, and 17.1 percent for those aged 50 and above. Total loss of cortical thickness for males was 22.2 percent after age 40, and 7.8 percent for males after age 50. Therefore, as females decreased in mean cortical thickness in the fifth decade, males increased mean cortical thickness until finally declining in the sixth (50+) decade (Figure 5.10). Mean cortical thickness and percent change for FABC males and females by age group are summarized in Table 5.22.

Differences between sexes in cortical thickness were statistically significant using two-way ANOVA (Analysis of Variance), whether two (p<.01) or five (p<.05) age categories were used. Femoral length was held constant for this analysis as a means of controlling variation due to stature. Differences due to age were not statistically significant even when age groups were combined into two (16–40 and 40–50+) age categories because of small sample size (as

Table 5.22
FABC Mean Cortical Thickness by Age and Sex

Age Group	Males			Females		
	No.	Cortical Thickness	Percent Change	No.	Cortical Thickness	Percent Change
16–30	2	6.15	—	13	6.22	—
30–40	7	6.53	+4.2	5	6.53	+4.2
40–50	11	6.86	+5.8	6	6.13	minus 4.3
51+	8	6.74	minus 7.8	2	5.08	minus 17.1
	28			26		

listed in Table 5.23. A multiple regression analysis of cortical thickness by sex, age, and femoral length found that only sex was statistically significant (p=.07). Sex was an important predictor of cortical thickness but was not clearly confirmed.

FABC mean cortical thickness measures were comparable to, or exceeded, published values for archaeological populations (Carlson, et al. 1976; Gunness-Hey 1980; Martin and Armelagos 1979) and standardized values (using femoral length to control for variability due to stature differences), as reported by Dewey, et al. (1969) and Ericksen (1976). FABC female mean cortical thicknesses were consistently higher than those of other skeletal series, including Cedar Grove Afro-American females aged 20–40 (Figure 5.11), while male values were somewhat lower. A similar increased mean cortical thickness in third decade females was also observed in a Nubian population (Martin and Armelagos 1979, Martin, et al. 1981).

Bone Morphometrics and Bone Maintenance: Cortical Area

Total cortical area should be considered a relative measure of the cortical bone present compared to the size of the medullary cavity. It is a more accurate measure of the total amount of cortical bone present than cortical thickness, although it does not account for intracortical porosity, as does percent cortical area (Sedlin, et al. 1963). This measurement also provides a means of determining the relationship of cortical thickness to cortical area, since cortical area can increase even if cortical thickness decreases. Computerized image analysis programs, for example the Bioquant bone morphometrics software package utilized for this analysis, are recent additions to the histological techniques used to study archaeological populations. Therefore, comparability of techniques and data generated by these different methods will have to be tested in the future.

In general, FABC male cortical area duplicated the cortical thickness patterns of bone increase and loss by age. While female values differed for fe-

males aged 30–40 and 50+, the increase of cortical bone was less for cortical
area (+.34) than for cortical thickness (+4.2) for females aged 30–40. The loss
of cortical bone in older females (50+) indicated by cortical area (minus 9.6%)
was significantly less than by cortical thickness (minus 17.1%). This difference
may be due to the amount of endosteal porosity observed upon gross examination. FABC younger males had lower cortical area than females, as was observed for cortical thickness measures. Both younger males and females had
less cortical area than those aged 30–40, indicating arrested growth and development in younger individuals. Males had increased cortical area with age, yet
males aged 19–40 had lower cortical area values than females 19–50; males
exceeded females only in the two oldest age categories (40–50 and 51+), where
significant bone loss occurred. Total cortical area loss for males was 7.8 percent (equal to cortical thickness loss) and 13.5 percent for females. Cortical
area values and percent change for sex and age group are summarized in Table
5.23.

Differences in cortical area were found to be statistically significant in a
two-way ANOVA test (p<.05) due to the interaction of sex and age when two
age categories (16–40 and 40–50+) were considered; femoral length was held
constant as a means of controlling variation due to stature. Differences due to
age or sex alone were not significant (see Table 5.24 for the Analysis of variance tests results for cortical area. These patterns are illustrated in Figure
5.12). A multiple regression analysis of cortical area by sex, age, and femoral
length found no statistically significant relationships.

In summary, FABC females had higher cortical bone values, as indicated by
cortical thickness, than did females in other archaeological populations, while male
values appear to have been somewhat lower. Generally, the differences between
FABC male and female cortical bone are not distinctly divergent, as observed in the
majority of archeological populations. In addition, based on the lower values of both
mean cortical thickness and cortical area, the younger FABC individuals appear to
have experienced some degree of growth disruption compared to those dying at

Table 5.23
Cortical Area by Age and Sex

	Males			Females		
Age Group	No.	Cortical Area	Percent Change	No.	Cortical Area	Percent Change
16–30	2	67.15	—	13	73.82	—
30–40	7	70.08	+4.2	5	74.07	+0.34
40–50	11	74.39	+5.8	6	70.90	minus 4.4
51+	8	68.60	minus 7.8	2	64.11	minus 9.6
	28			26		

Table 5.24
Analysis of Variance—Cortical Thickness and Cortical Area

| | Cortical Thickness | | | | | | Cortical Area | | | | | |
| | Two age groups | | | Four age groups | | | Two age groups | | | Four age groups | | |
Significance	DF	F-Ratio	Level[1]	DF	F-Ratio	Level[1]	DF	F-Ratio	Level[1]	DF	F-Ratio	Level[1]
Femur Length	1	0.520	n.s.	1	0.284	n.s.	1	1.083	n.s.	1	2.012	n.s.
Age	1	0.014	n.s.	3	1.229	n.s.	1	0.592	n.s.	3	0.409	n.s
Sex	1	4.094	.05*	1	4.023	.05*	1	0.255	n.s.	1	1.888	n.s.
Interaction	1	2.671	.10*	3	2.114	n.s.	1	3.401	.10*	3	1.623	n.s

1 = Level of.
n.s. = statistically not significant.
* = statistically significant.

Figure 5.10
Mean Cortical Thickness by Age and Sex

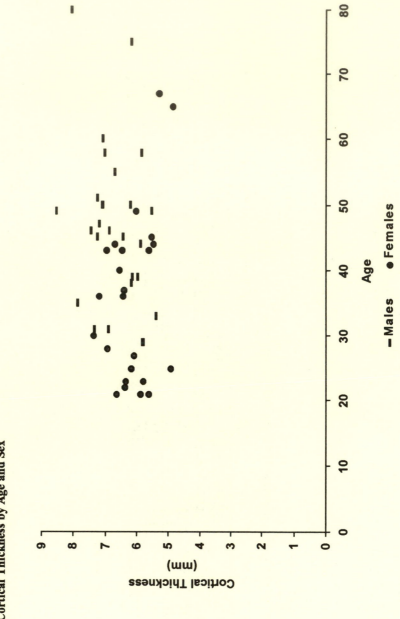

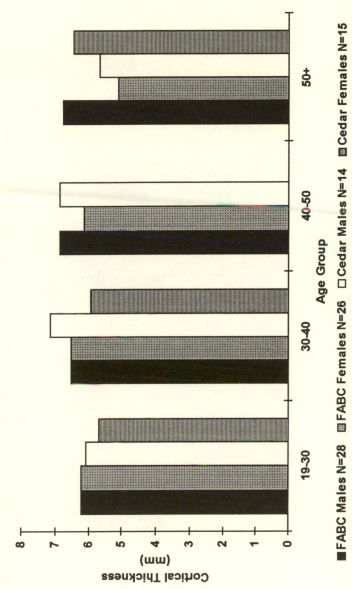

Figure 5.11
Mean Cortical Thickness, FABC and Cedar Grove

■ FABC Males N=28   ▤ FABC Females N=26   □ Cedar Males N=14   ▥ Cedar Females N=15

Figure 5.12
Mean Cortical Area by Age and Sex

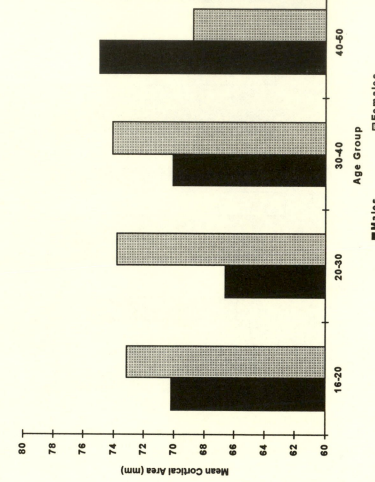

older ages. Cortical thickness and cortical area are macromeasurements that provide gross indicators of cortical bone maintenance within a population. Neither takes into account intracortical porosity, which would not necessarily affect the morphometrics of the femur significantly at the macroscopic level. This is particularly important with regard to the increased cortical measurements in the older men in this population and the discrepancy of bone loss measures between thickness and area in females. Therefore, microstructural studies measuring intracortical porosity (resorption spaces), bone turnover rates, and morphometrics would provide a clearer understanding of bone maintenance and loss in the FABC population between sexes and age groups.

OCCUPATIONAL STRESS MARKERS AND ANOMALIES

There are numerous indicators of occupational stress on the skeletons; several have been discussed above, such as schmorl's nodes and other degenerative disorders. Several skeletal markers associated with the utilization of specific muscles become evident due to the bony hypertrophy of muscle attachment areas. These "enthesopathies," as they are called, can vary from slight elevations or enlargements to very large protrusions or fossae along attachment surfaces (Kennedy 1983, 1989). These are not easily quantified and are best identified by seriating within populations, since it is a relative assessment. In addition, other anomalies found in the FABC population included: os acromiale, hyperostosis interna frontalis, hydrocephaly, and a bone cyst. Os acromiale appears to also be a work-related anomaly (Hill 1995 personal communication; Stirland 1985 personal communication, 1991).

Enthesopathies

Two occupational stress markers were selected for discussion because of their high frequency in the FABC population. These include the deltoid crest of the humerus and the supinator crest of the radius. Both muscles of the arm are involved in the process of lifting and carrying heavy loads and in rotational movement of the shoulder and arm. Enlarged deltoid crests were observed on 69.4 percent of all FABC males (N=36) and 56.4 percent of all FABC females (N=39). Supinator crest enlargement was observed on 58.3 percent of all males and 38.5 percent of all females. Between 15 and 20 percent of adults had either arm bones missing or ones that were too fragmentary to assess. In the majority of these individuals, both arms (when present) exhibited comparable enlargement. Handedness or repeated performance of a specialized task would account for greater development of muscle attachments of a single arm in an individual.

Os Acromiale

A partial fusion or nonfusion of the acromion, called os acromiale, was observed in 20 percent of FABC adults (n=15). Os acromiale has been observed in both clinical (radiographic) and forensic settings and has been called os acromiale, bipartite acromion, and meta-acromion (Chang and Nissenbaum 1975, Mudge, et al. 1984). The acromion has three separate ossification centers that unite with the spine of the scapula around age twelve, and then fuse to each other between 15–18 years. These ossification centers and the common sites of nonunion are illustrated in Figure 5.13. Mudge and coworkers (1984) proposed that os acromiale contributes to an impingement mechanism involving the rotator cuff, which results in a tear.

The incidence of os acromiale is relatively low, occurring in only 7 percent of the general U.S. population (Grant 1982). In contrast, os acromiale was found in 25 percent (n=9) of FABC males and 12.8 percent (n=5) of females. Bilateral os acromiale was observed in the majority (78.6%) of FABC adults, a higher frequency than the 62 percent reported clinically (Chang and Nissenbaum 1975; Mudge, et al. 1984). The majority (85.7%) of those with os acromiale were older individuals (n=11) aged between 30 and 50+. Angel, et al. (1987) have proposed that the high incidence of this anomaly in FABC may have a genetic etiology, although the etiology and high incidence of os acromiale in the FABC sample are not clearly indicated. It could be hypothesized that the majority of FABC congregation members were involved in strenuous labor as children and/or adolescents, a common practice for both slave and free Afro-Americans. It appears that strenuous lifting and carrying during growth and development affects the process of bone fusion. High frequencies of os acromiale have been observed in other populations where children were part of the work force (Hill 1995 personal communication, African Burial Ground Project; Stirland 1991).

Hyperostosis Interna Frontalis

A 27-year-old female exhibited bony swellings of the frontal portion of the endocranium (internal cranial surface; see Plate 5.8). These lesions are indicative of hyperostosis interna frontalis or Morgaani-Stewart-Morel syndrome, a neuropsychiatric syndrome that has an endocrinological etiology. This uncommon disorder appears to be age related, with higher frequency in contemporary populations perhaps due to increased longevity (Armelagos and Chrisman 1988). These endocranial masses appear to be formed of benign-looking new bone and are distinguishable from other tumors that are more destructive and usually affect both endocranial and ectocranial tables. This individual had been autopsied, a rare occurrence during the early nineteenth century, which may indicate that antemortem symptoms required further investigations. Ar-

Plate 5.8
Hyperostosis Interna Frontalis
Burial 50, Female 25–30

Figure 5.13
Os Acromiale

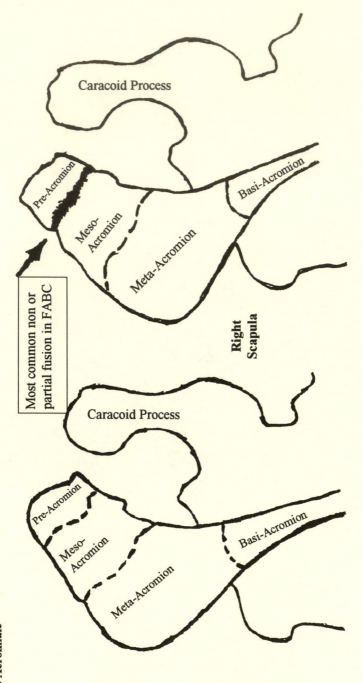

Caracoid Process

Pre-Acromion

Meso-
Acromion

Meta-Acromion

Basi-Acromion

Most common non or partial fusion in FABC

Right
Scapula

Caracoid Process

Pre-Acromion

Meso-
Acromion

Meta-Acromion

Basi-Acromion

Diagram represents the ossification centers of the acromion.
Illustration by Diane Ghalib, 1995.
Source: Mudge, Wood, and Frykman 1984.

melagos and Chrisman (1988) have also reported a case of this rare disorder in an archaeological series from ancient Nubia (40-year-old female).

Hydrocephaly

A 5-year-old FABC child (Burial 19) was diagnosed as having suffered hydrocephaly (Kelley 1988); in addition, dental hypocalcifications and hypoplasias on multiple teeth were observed. These are indicators that the child had experienced episodes of stress both in utero (seventh prenatal month) and childhood (3rd–6th month postnatal). Hydrocephaly is an abnormal increase in the amount of cerebrospinal fluid that circulates through the four ventricles of the brain and its surfaces, and then drains into the venous system (Zimmerman 1980). Obstruction of the cerebrospinal fluid outflow (from the ventricles), or its failure to reabsorb into the cerebral sinuses, results in an increased amount and pressure of the fluid. The fluid pressure in children prior to the fusion of cranial sutures produces an enlarged cranium and, may lead to severe brain damage at any age (Ortner and Putschar 1981; Zimmerman 1980). Hydrocephaly is commonly associated with spina bifida, a congenital anomaly characterized by the incomplete closure of the sacral bones. In addition, cerebrospinal meningitis (acute inflammation) caused by a virus, bacteria, protozoa, or fungi can also produce hydrocephaly. According to Emerson (1827, 1848), inflammation or "dropsy" of the brain was not an uncommon occurrence in nineteenth century Philadelphia.

Bone Cyst

A benign bone cyst was diagnosed in the left femur of an 18-year-old FABC female (Burial 107). Macroscopically, the femur appeared enlarged below the femoral head and greater trochanter, with no periosteal lesions present. When observed radiographically, the cyst appeared as a localized mass within the medullary cavity. The femur was also examined by Angel and Ortner, and both determined the etiology and type of cyst to be unknown.

SUMMARY

A pattern of health and illness had been predicted for the FABC skeletal sample based on the demographic and historical literature, which included: (1) a low incidence of severe gross pathology; (2) a higher incidence of pathologies associated with episodic, rather than chronic, nutritional deficiency, with episodic pathologies including porotic hyperostosis (iron deficiency) and dental enamel defects, while chronic nutritional problems would include rickets or scurvy;   (3) a high frequency of trauma due to interpersonal aggression (enslavement) or accident rather than age related fractures; (4) a high frequency of joint degeneration related to strenuous work and biomechanical stress; and (5) a high infant and early childhood mortality as a result of cholera and diarrheal diseases. It was also anticipated that FABC congregation members would exhibit better overall health status and lower incidence of trauma and nutritional deficiency than other Afro-American skeletal series from slave plantations. The paleopathological findings did indicate that some of these predicted patterns were present, but several differences were found in these indicators of health and illness.

Based on the biocultural model (Goodman, et. al 1984, chapter 1), indicators of stress are assessed within three broad categories: growth disruption, disease, and death. In general, the incidence of gross paleopathology was significantly low, as expected. Long-term chronic disorders were not common, and/or individuals died from acute episodes of illness, as was discussed in chapter 4.

Growth Disruption

Dental Enamel Defects. Dental enamel defects in the FABC population indicated periods of childhood growth disruption in both adult and subadult dentitions available for study. Most of the enamel defects found in subadults developed during the prenatal period, indicating that maternal and thus fetal health had been compromised during the gestational period. Primary onset of an enamel defect by the ninth prenatal month was indicated in 70 percent (n=14) of the subadults. In addition, a pattern of earlier mortality associated with prenatal primary onset was observed in subadults.

All FABC adults exhibited at least one enamel defect; the majority (84.3%) had two or more. The peak age of onset for enamel defects was between 2.0–4.0 years. The high frequency of enamel defects initiated during 2.0–4.0 years could be attributed to late weaning stress. According to Blakey, Leslie, and Reidy (1994), historical documentation does not support late weaning in enslaved Afro-American populations, since free Afro-American women were primarily employed in arduous labor outside the home. Therefore, the most probable etiology is the documented high risk of infection due to environmental conditions and high incidence of diarrheal diseases and cholera in Antebellum Philadelphia. The pattern of enamel defects leads to the conclusion that FABC members experienced both in utero and childhood episodes of undernutrition and/or disease stress.

Bone Maintenance. Bone maintenance assessments of cortical thickness and area indicate that FABC males and females formed and maintained similar amounts of cortical bone. Despite this overall pattern, males who died at younger ages appear to have experienced some degree of growth disruption, as they had lower values for cortical thickness and area than did older males and all females. FABC values for cortical thickness were somewhat higher than those reported for Cedar Grove Afro-Americans and Nubians. This is taken to indicate better overall health status for FABC.

Disease

Infectious Disease. Nonspecific infectious disease rates were higher than predicted, despite the acute nature of epidemics of the period. The incidence of tuberculosis was quite low (4%) in the FABC population, considering the high prevalence in the Afro-American community. Evidence of generalized infection was diagnosed in 25.3 percent (n=19) of adult skeletons. Periostitis was observed in 36.1 percent of FABC males (n=13) and 15.4 percent of the females (n=6); for 78 percent of those with generalized infection, iron deficiency anemia (porotic hyperostosis) was also present. The frequency of infection was associated with age in males. The FABC incidence of periostitis, both of general and specific etiology, was lower than in other Afro-American skeletal series.

Nutritional Disorders. Nutritional disorders in the FABC population were primarily associated with porotic hyperostosis, rather than with more severe disorders such as rickets and scurvy, which are indicative of chronic or long-term nutritional stress. These disorders were rare in the FABC skeletons. Porotic hyperostosis, from iron deficiency anemia, was observed in 53.3 percent (n=40) of FABC adults (55.6% of all males and 51.3% of females). Male incidence peaked at ages 40–50+ (75%), while the majority of females (60%) exhibiting porotic lesions were of reproductive age (18–40). This pattern correlated with the dental enamel defect analysis that suggested that maternal nutritional and health status had been compromised in the FABC population.

Degenerative Joint Disorders. The majority of FABC (76%) adults were observed to have some form of degenerative joint disease; most of these were diagnosed as slight osteoarthritis. The distribution of degenerative joint disease by age and sex in FABC was somewhat different than would have been predicted. The expected age-related pattern was observed in FABC, but a significantly higher proportion of younger females below age 30 were observed with degenerative joint changes (33.3%), and FABC females also exhibited higher frequencies of osteoarthritis than Cedar Grove females. This may be associated with female domestic labor beginning in adolescence.

The occurrence of vertebral osteophytosis in FABC skeletons was minimal, a pattern divergent from both Cedar Grove and 38CH778, which may be indicative of the varying biomechanical use between farm labor and the manual

Figure 5.14.
FABC Biocultural Model for Health and Skeletal Biology Synthesis

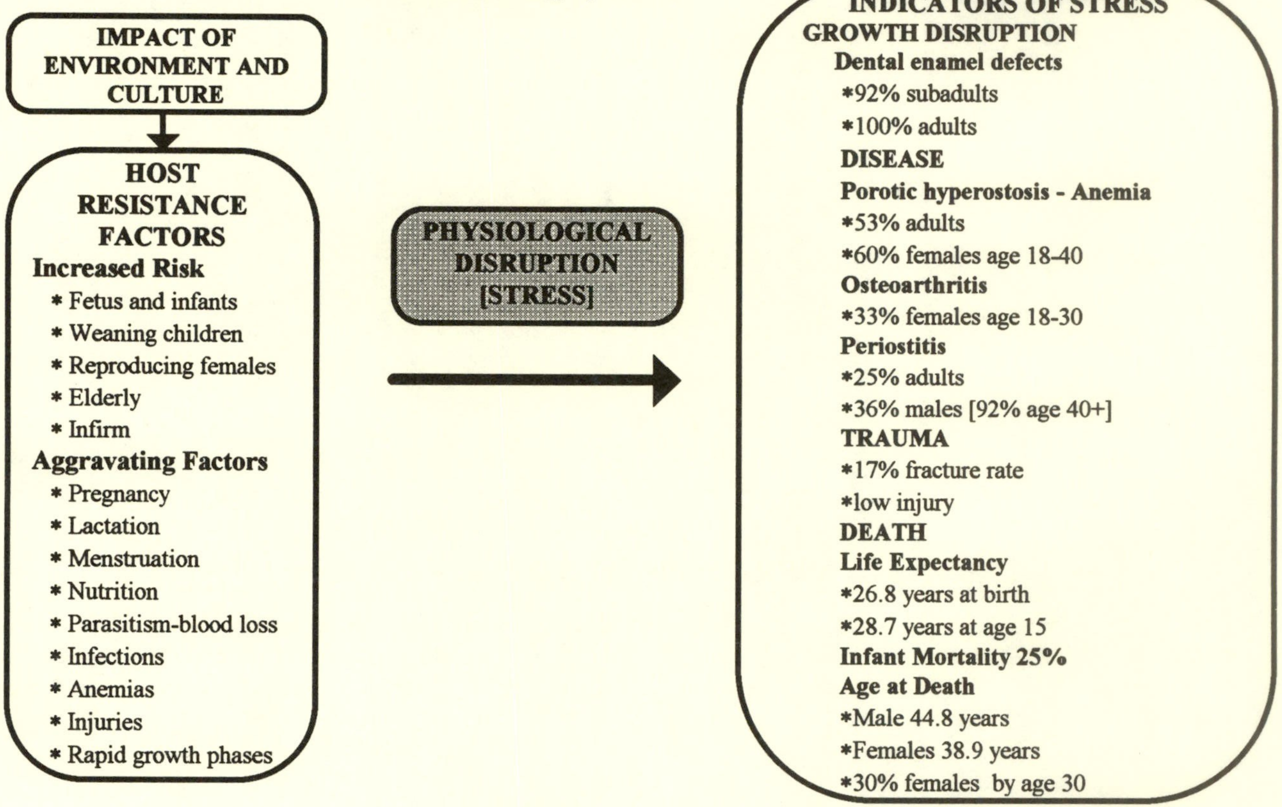

IMPACT OF
ENVIRONMENT AND
CULTURE

HOST
RESISTANCE
FACTORS

Increased Risk
* Fetus and infants
* Weaning children
* Reproducing females
* Elderly
* Infirm

Aggravating Factors
* Pregnancy
* Lactation
* Menstruation
* Nutrition
* Parasitism-blood loss
* Infections
* Anemias
* Injuries
* Rapid growth phases

PHYSIOLOGICAL
DISRUPTION
[STRESS]

INDICATORS OF STRESS

GROWTH DISRUPTION
Dental enamel defects
*92% subadults
*100% adults

DISEASE
Porotic hyperostosis – Anemia
*53% adults
*60% females age 18-40
Osteoarthritis
*33% females age 18-30
Periostitis
*25% adults
*36% males [92% age 40+]

TRAUMA
*17% fracture rate
*low injury

DEATH
Life Expectancy
*26.8 years at birth
*28.7 years at age 15
Infant Mortality 25%
Age at Death
*Male 44.8 years
*Females 38.9 years
*30% females by age 30

158

Table 5.25
Demographic Indicators of Stress for Afro–American Skeletal Populations

Demographic Indicators	FABC	Cedar Grove	Catoctin Furnace	38CH778	Newton
No. Burials	135	80	31	36	101
No. Males	36	15	7	13	*
No. Females	39	21	8	15	*
Subadults	60	44	16	8	9
Infant Mortality (%)	25.2	27.5	—	—	—
Mean age at Death -Males	44.8	41.2	41.7	35	*
Mean age at Death - Females	38.9	37.7	35.2	40	*
Life Expectancy at Birth	26.6	14.0	—	—	29

*Sexing not available due to poor preservation.
—Data not available.

Sources: 1 – Rathbun 1987.
2 – Rose 1985.
3 – Angel and Kelley 1983, 1987
4 – Corruccini, et al. 1982

159

Table 5.26
Skeletal Indicators of Stress for Afro–American Skeletal Populations

	FABC		Cedar Grove		Catoctin Furnace		38CH778		Newton
	Male	Female	Male	Female	Male	Female	Male	Female	Total
Stature (cm.) [std. dev.]	172.2 [4.4]	156.7 [20.4]	—	—	171.6 [7.5]	156.4 [5.5]	167.4 [4.6]	160.6 [6.1]	—
Periostitis	36.1	15.4	100.0	76.2	57	—	69.0	60.0	—
Porotic Hyperostosis	55.6	51.6	26.7	23.8	—	12.5	36.0	33.0	—
Enamel Defects	100.0	100.0	—	—	71.0	43.0	100.0	71.0	54.5
Osteoarthritis	77.7	74.3	46.7	38.1	—	—	100.0	77.0	—
Osteophytosis			46.7	33.3	—	—	30–48	30–48	—
Cortical Thickness (mm.)	6.56	5.99	6.43	6.02	—	—	—	—	—
Fractures	3.6	7.7	40.0	9.5	—	—	—	—	—

—Data unavailable.

Sources: 1 – Rathbun 1987.

    2 – Rose 1985.

    3 – Angel and Kelley 1987

    4 – Corruccini, et al. 1982

labor occupations of urban dwelling Philadelphia free Afro-Americans. Yet, the frequency of vertebral arthritis was similar to that of South Carolina plantation slaves (38CH778).

Trauma

The incidence of trauma in the FABC population was low. Fractures were found in 17.3 percent of the skeletons. FABC males (n=10) had a higher incidence (13.6%) of fractures than females (7.7%); and the majority (63.4%) of individuals with fractures were older than 40 years. The distribution of fractures in the FABC sample by age, sex, and bone appears to have been associated with occupational accidents. Therefore, the expected pattern of high incidence of trauma due to violence was not borne out, although several individuals (n=4) exhibited fractures that were most probably due to violence. The age-related frequency of well-healed fractures in males should be considered to have a high probability of being associated with enslavement.

Death

Despite disease stress and environmental risks, FABC free Afro-Americans had a reduced risk of dying compared to other Afro-Americans who were slaves or free (a synthesis of the health and skeletal biology data is presented in Figure 5.14). FABC mortality was highest for infants (25%), as was expected. Life expectancy (ex) at birth for FABC members was 26.59 years, a figure significantly higher than the 14 years reported by Rose (1985) at Cedar Grove. Thus, it appears that FABC members were likely to live longer than other Afro-Americans. The mean age at death for FABC females was 38.9 years and 44.8 years for males. This gender differential and similar mean ages at death have also been observed in the industrial slave population of Catoctin Furnace, which has been considered a generally healthy population. The reverse pattern, with males at greater risk, has been reported for colonial slave sites, South Carolina plantation slaves, and New Orleans urban slaves. Comparisons of demographic and skeletal indicators of stress in Afro-American skeletal populations are summarized in Tables 5.25 and 5.26.

In the concluding chapter, results from the sociohistoric and historical demographic analyses and the skeletal biological analyses are recast and jointly examined within the context of the biocultural model.

Chapter 6

The FABC Cemetery Population:
A Biocultural View

INTRODUCTION

Who the people buried in the First African Baptist Church Cemetery were, and what were the conditions and experiences of their lives has been the focus of this study. The search for these invisible people was predicated on two assumptions: (1) that the material lives of the poor and the powerless can be reconstructed by utilizing diverse sources; and (2) that the stories of people are written on the bones and teeth that are left behind. The material lives of nineteenth-century Philadelphia Afro-Americans were reconstructed through an extensive search of archives, documents, historical accounts, maps and drawings for the period. Health status assessment of this Afro-American community was accomplished through combining the archival research and the FABC skeletal analysis.

Names will never be linked to the individual skeletons. Nevertheless, through the data generated and a biocultural framework to guide the synthesis, who these invisible people were has been revealed. In fact, the characteristics of the Philadelphia Afro-American community as a whole and the identity of individual congregation members and some of the facets of their lives were ascertained. Therefore, the material lives of Afro-Americans and FABC congregation members and the impact on their health and mortality patterns could be determined. The biocultural model for the First African Baptist Church (Figure 6.1) synthesizes the most significant factors and their interactions in understanding the conditions and experiences of free nineteenth century Afro-Americans in Philadelphia.

Figure 6.1.
Synthesized FABC Biocultural Model

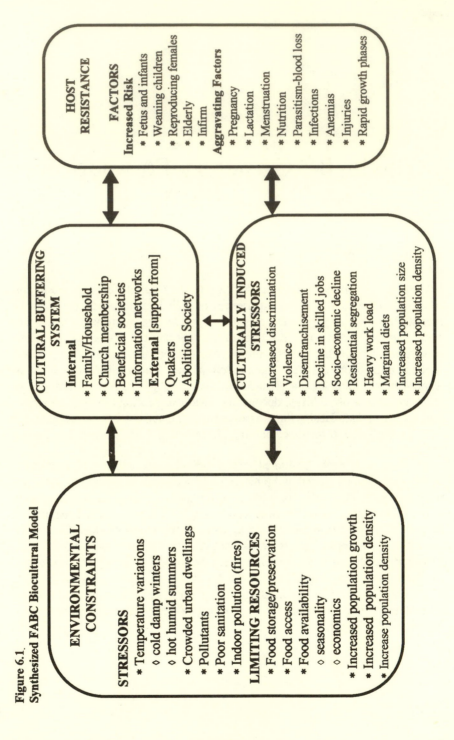

HOST RESISTANCE

FACTORS

Increased Risk
* Fetus and infants
* Weaning children
* Reproducing females
* Elderly
* Infirm

Aggravating Factors
* Pregnancy
* Lactation
* Menstruation
* Nutrition
* Parasitism-blood loss
* Infections
* Anemias
* Injuries
* Rapid growth phases

CULTURAL BUFFERING SYSTEM

Internal
* Family/Household
* Church membership
* Beneficial societies
* Information networks

External [support from]
* Quakers
* Abolition Society

CULTURALLY INDUCED STRESSORS
* Increased discrimination
* Violence
* Disenfranchisement
* Decline in skilled jobs
* Socio-economic decline
* Residential segregation
* Heavy work load
* Marginal diets
* Increased population size
* Increased population density

ENVIRONMENTAL CONSTRAINTS

STRESSORS
* Temperature variations
  ◊ cold damp winters
  ◊ hot humid summers
* Crowded urban dwellings
* Pollutants
* Poor sanitation
* Indoor pollution (fires)

LIMITING RESOURCES
* Food storage/preservation
* Food access
* Food availability
  ◊ seasonality
  ◊ economics
* Increased population growth
* Increased population density
* Increase population density

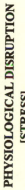

PHYSIOLOGICAL DISRUPTION
[STRESS]

* Intensive physical exertion
* Intensive utilization of dietary nutrients
* Intensive utilization of marginal nutritional stores
* Chronic exposure to environmental hazards
* Intensive utilization of biological responses
  ◊ immunological
  ◊ psycho-behavioral

INDICATORS OF STRESS
GROWTH DISRUPTION
Dental enamel defects
*92% subadults
*100% adults
DISEASE
Porotic hyperostosis – Anemia
*53% adults
*60% females age 18-40
Osteoarthritis
*33% females age 18-30
Periostitis
*25% adults
*36% males [92% age 40+]
TRAUMA
*17% fracture rate
*low injury
DEATH
Life Expectancy
*26.8 years at birth
*28.7 years at age 15
Infant Mortality 25%
Age at Death
*Male 44.8 years
*Females 38.9 years
*30% females by age 30

THE MATERIAL LIVES OF NINETEENTH CENTURY AFRO-AMERICAN PHILADELPHIANS

Environmental Constraints

The sociohistoric and historical demographic data from FABC suggests that urban dwelling was a stressful, unstable experience, which increased Afro-Americans' risk to disease, trauma, and mortality. Densely populated neighborhoods, small dwellings, and large households using common privies situated in dark alleyways were prime reservoirs for the proliferation and spread of pathogens in this residentially segregated city.

Philadelphians were exposed to environmental pollutants, such as contaminated drinking water from the nearby rivers and contaminated milk due to the lack of temperature control and sanitary codes for urban dairies (Cheney 1984). Also, occupational exposure of laundresses and domestic servants to contaminated water (river washing and low water temperatures), soiled clothing, and linens increased Afro-American women's risk of contracting infectious diseases. This is particularly relevant to FABC women, since 79 percent of African Baptist women were laundresses or domestics/day workers. Males were also at increased risk of contracting infectious diseases occupationally when working as laborers (coming into contact with contaminated water while digging ditches) or carters and stevedores (exposed to contaminated river water, rodents, and insects while unloading and carting cargo from ships).

Epidemics were a common problem throughout the eighteenth and nineteenth centuries in Philadelphia. Philadelphians experienced successive epidemics of cholera, scarlet and yellow fevers (Emerson 1827, 1837, 1848; Condran and Cheney 1982), as well as high frequencies of acute fatal tuberculosis (Condran and Cheney 1982). The impact of environmental conditions were documented in the causes of death and patterns of mortality and morbidity documented in the vital records of the period (Emerson 1827, 1837, 1848). The FABC partial interment records clearly corroborate the effects of infectious diseases on the congregation members based on the causes of death indicated on mortality bills.

In addition, inadequate methods of food preservation and storage limited the variety and quality of nutrients and increased the risk of food spoilage or contamination, thus increasing the risk of exposure to bacteria, toxins, and parasites. Seasonality of fresh foods (fruits and vegetables) limited the availability of vitamins and essential nutrients. Despite being situated within an animal and grain producing region, poorer Philadelphia households had limited access to food because of high prices generated by exportation (Smith 1981). Therefore, these Afro-American and immigrant households tended to have high carbohydrate (flour, cornmeal, rice), low protein, high fat diets. This diet provided sufficient calories but was marginal in other essential nutrients.

Population increases during the period created greater competition for un-skilled and skilled labor. Free Philadelphia Afro-Americans were competing for employment with immigrant Euro-Americans, Afro-Americans from the slaveholding states (runaways and freedmen), and freed rural Pennsylvanians. This growth in the lower socioeconomic sectors of nineteenth-century Philadel-phia also generated increased population density in residentially segregated areas inhabited by Afro-Americans and the poorest Euro-Americans.   The combination of Philadelphia being a seaport and the high in-migration (U.S. and foreign) provided a continuous source for infectious disease agents. In fact, the Board of Health Minutes (1818) document the acute concern with control-ling sea-borne entry of disease sources (contaminated supplies, rodents, ailing passengers and crews). The increase in population density also exacerbated the poor sanitary conditions and increased the potential for infectious diseases and epidemics.

Cultural Buffering System

The cultural buffering system for FABC congregation members should be viewed as a dual system comprised of internal and external buffering mecha-nisms. The Afro-American community and FABC congregation had estab-lished religious, economic, social, and familial internal buffering mechanisms. Philadelphia African Baptists had their church congregations and beneficial societies as sources of emotional, social, and economic support. They lived in large (mean 6.6), multiadult households, which may have functioned as domestic networks (Stack 1974) by linking households of relatives or church/society mem-bers. A substantial Afro-American information network appears to have been in place throughout the nineteenth century due to the interactions between Afro-American religious leaders, the publications of the Afro-American intelligent-sia, and residential segregation.

Euro-American associations like the Quakers, the Pennsylvania Abolition Society, and specific national church associations (e.g., National Baptist Asso-ciation)—which supported and, at times, aided Afro-American families, churches, and/or communities—served as external buffering mechanisms. In addition, these organizations were at the forefront of legislative and political reform movements for Afro-Americans. Euro-American households, which were the predominant employers of Afro-American females, are also included as an external buffering mechanism. In general, household servants tended to have better diets than other workers. Kitchen help and domestics, slave or free, tended to eat food served in their master's or employer's households. Some of these households were home to Afro-Americans, who lived in servants' quar-ters, kitchens, carriagehouses/stables, or nurseries. Conversely, these same households were also sources of environmental, biological, and psychosocial stressors.

Culturally Induced Stressors

FABC congregation members lived during a volatile period in Philadelphia, characterized by rising discrimination, violence (riots by Euro-Americans, kidnapping, and reenslavement), declining socioeconomic conditions, and disenfranchisement. Afro-Americans, already in the lowest socioeconomic strata, found themselves in a cycle of economic depression throughout the nineteenth century. Generally, Afro-Americans, and in particular African Baptist households, came up against a decrease in land ownership, personal property and total wealth. Afro-Americans not only experienced increasing employment discrimination in the skilled occupations but also growing underemployment that contributed to the socioeconomic decline.

The rapid population growth in Philadelphia throughout the nineteenth century, due to Euro-American immigrants and Afro-Americans migrants (runaway slaves and freedmen), had the long-term effect of decreasing Afro-Americans' access (economic, ecological, and political) to employment, quality nutrition, and housing. These limitations further increased Afro-Americans' risk of disease, trauma, and mortality due to increased exposure to occupational and environmental stressors and limiting resources.

Female and child labor, which was essential during this period for the economic survival of many households, should also be considered as contributory to both reproductive age female and childhood morbidity and mortality. The combination of heavy work-loads, long hours, and at best a marginal diet probably worked synergistically to further increase the risk of adult morbidity. In addition, the process of weaning was probably a significant factor in childhood mortality, as it hastened the exposure to environmental pollutants from contaminated water and inadequately stored foods and milk. The impact of socioculturally induced stressors on the psychosocial status of individuals, so difficult to assess in living populations, cannot be quantified in skeletal remains. It can only be conservatively assumed that the environmental, sociocultural, and economic conditions of Afro-Americans in nineteenth century Philadelphia were difficult to endure psychosocially, and would have had a significant impact on health status as they do in contemporary populations.

Host Resistance Factors

Host resistance encompasses the biochemical, genetic, immunological and physiological constitutions of individuals. Resistance or susceptibility to stressors are thus contingent upon the biological life-cycle stage and general health status. Based on the historical demographic evidence and the FABC skeletal biological indicators, groups at risk (predicted by life-cycle stage) were in fact differentially affected, especially fetuses, young children and reproductive age females. Parasitism, infections, and anemias—all aggravating factors compromising resistance—have been documented through the available literature, archival documents, or observed in skeletal analyses. Other aggravating factors such as marginal nutrition can be inferred, and potentially exacerbating biological processes (e.g., menstruation or lactation) can be assumed to be operational in the FABC population.

Physiological Disruption

Based on the environmental and sociocultural reconstructions and the risk and aggravating factors identified as affecting host resistance, it is apparent that Philadelphia Afro-Americans experienced, at minimum, episodes of physiological disruption. Many experienced repeated infections and/or undernutrition, which can increase individual susceptibility and decrease resistance to further insults. Despite recoveries from these physiological disruptions, many individuals may have remained less adaptive and resilient throughout their lifetime and manifested growth, behavioral, reproductive, or cognitive problems and/or earlier mortality. Growth disruption, pathology, and differential patterns of mortality as observed in the FABC remains are indicators of these physiological stressors.

Indicators of Stress

These indicators of physiological disruption provide a means of assessing the health, illness and mortality patterns of a skeletal population. FABC members experienced in utero, childhood, and adulthood episodes of undernutrition and/or disease stress, with subsequent growth disruption. FABC infectious disease rates were lowest among the Afro-American skeletal series. The majority of FABC adults with infection (78%) exhibited evidence of both generalized infection and iron deficiency anemia, which appeared to work synergistically.

The incidence of less severe nutritional disorders suggest a dietary regime that provided marginal to adequate calories, although nutrient content and bioavailibity apparently fluctuated. Despite disease stress and environmental risks, FABC free Afro-Americans had a reduced risk of dying when compared to other Afro-Americans, enslaved or free. Therefore, FABC members were more likely to live longer and die later than other Afro-American populations.

Thus, the FABC congregation members and free Philadelphia Afro-Americans, as represented by the FABC skeletal population, were generally healthier than their enslaved or emancipated counterparts.

The Material Lives of Afro-American and FABC Men

Afro-American male labor was important in the operation of nineteenth century Philadelphia as a major seaport, nascent industrial center, and burgeoning center of America's elites. Therefore, Afro-American workers, both skilled and unskilled, were needed to provide strenuous manual labor, services, and crafts for the Euro-American Philadelphia community. In addition, some Afro-Americans provided services to the Afro-American community due to the segregated nature and practices of the time. During enslavement and subsequent emancipation in the eighteenth century and the early part of the nineteenth century, skilled artisans and laborers were highly valued; by the 1830–1840s, however, many were losing their jobs and the opportunities for apprenticeships and journeymanships. Afro-American men worked 6 to 7 days a week, enduring long hours of physical labor and, for many, never utilizing their skills. Most significantly, they were systematically removed from accessing the growing opportunities of factory work.

FABC men worked primarily as laborers, waiters, and carters; a few worked as seamen, and a small number had a skilled trade (e.g., cooper, barber, blacksmith plasterer). The impact of the socioeconomic instability on their households is evident in that 97 percent of FABC wives worked outside the home. In addition, their households tended to be large, consisting of four to twelve people, primarily adults, both kin and nonkin. Apparently, these households (as well as those headed by females) were constituted so as to facilitate survival, either through cooperative living or as boarding houses. Socioeconomic indicators such as the value of real estate, property, and total wealth was at best minimal in FABC households with the exception of Reverend Henry Simmons, who was pastor, clothier, and property owner of the church's land (see chapter 3).

Solomon Bell, a FABC parishioner found in the 1834 FABC Penny Collection Book, was identified as a plasterer in the 1838 and 1847 censuses, one of the few skilled laborers in the congregation. Mrs. Bell "attended house" in a household that increased from two to seven in nine years; these additional members included three children and two adults. During this period, Solomon Bell's property value (not land) grew from $40 to $110.

John C. Carter appears in both censuses and in the FABC Penny Collection Book. The Carters remained at the same address throughout the period. Mr. Carter did change his occupation from a waiter in 1838 to a carman in 1847; his wife was a laundress. In 1847 the Carter household increased to three. Mr. Carter's real estate increased (from $210 in 1838 to $400 in 1847) between the two censuses. His property value ($200) remained the same, yet his encumbrances increased by $1950. Therefore, the Carters appeared to have deteriorated economically, since the encumbrance was substantial for the period. It may be that this debt was associated with his change in occupation.

Samuel George was a coachman and his wife worked as a domestic servant. The George household consisted of four members, including two other adults. Mr. George's total wealth was $200 in 1838; he died at the age of 50 from consumptive tuberculosis in 1841.

Daniel Burton, age 40, died of lung and heart disease in August 1841; he was a carter, an occupation that required intensive physical exertion, lifting, and carrying of heavy loads. Mr. Burton had one of the largest households among FABC congregation members; his wife remained at home, apparently running this household of twelve other adults, which may have been a boarding house.

Joshua Johnson, one of the oldest FABC congregation members interred in the cemetery, died at the age of 86 of "old age and general debility" in June of 1842, the last year that the cemetery was used as determined by the mortality bills and Board of Health minutes. In 1838 his household consisted of his wife and two other adults. Mr. Johnson had been a laborer and, based on his age, was either born enslaved or lived a portion of his life as an enslaved person.

The Material Lives of Afro-American and FABC Women

Afro-American women were in high demand as domestics and were recruited from outlying areas; manumitted, emancipated, freeborn, and runaway slaves came to Philadelphia for employment. Clearly, the population structure reflects this socioeconomic condition, since younger females were there in great numbers throughout the first half of the century.

Social status in general was derived from male spouses, as it was for Euro-American women. There were a few educated/entrepreneurial women in the Afro-American community, especially within the black elite (e.g., teachers, shopkeepers, musicians, midwives). In the Afro-American community, women had to work primarily outside of the home, and child labor was also essential to the survival of the family.

In 1838, a pattern of female-headed households was already becoming apparent in the Afro-American community. Twenty-eight percent of all Afro-American and African Baptist households were female headed, and 32 percent of these households were headed by widows. The remaining households were headed by single (42%) and married (26%) women, apparently without spouses present. Only three FABC congregation members' households were headed by females that were not widowed.

Female socioeconomic status was tenuous, as demonstrated by almshouse records and the existence and proliferation of beneficial societies, especially those for unmarried women. The Philadelphia Almshouse record book (1838—white residents were kept separate from residents of color) for colored women provides insight into their socioeconomic vulnerability. The almshouse apparently separated women by general medical categories (e.g., lying in for preg-

nant women, medical for the ill, lunatic asylum for the intemperate and in-
sane). Major life events such as widowhood and child-birth were some of the
"causes" of poverty for Afro-American women. "Increased family" was a significant cause of entry for many women, some of whose infants were then born
in the almshouse. Old age, illness, and causes such as debility, which may be
associated with aging, were also causes of poverty. Impairments such as
"blind, lame, deaf and dumb, idiocy, intemperance, vicious, and insanity"
(Almshouse record book 1838) all speak to a society ill-prepared to care for
people with special needs.

Homelessness appears to have been a problem, based on the proportion of
women who entered the almshouse who were actively working (38%); two-
thirds of these women were "incurable" (N=24) and working. This bears wit-
ness to the resilience and tenacity of these women, who were ill or in perilous
social circumstances yet continued to work and live in the almshouse (similar
to the contemporary phenomena of homeless shelters).

Socioeconomic, social, and spiritual support were integral to the survival
of the Afro-American community. Afro-American women were active in their
churches and beneficial societies. Many beneficial societies were self-help organizations and prototypes for the black insurance companies of later years.
Female members of the First African Baptist Church established such a society
for unmarried women ages 21–45 (joining age); First African Baptist Female
Union Society of Philadelphia was chartered on January 28, 1829. Members
paid 12½ cents a week. Duties and benefits included: visiting the sick and dis-
tressed members of the society; weekly payments ($1.00) to those too ill or old
to work; providing secured loans to members if the society was debt free and
had funds above $50.00; a decent, plain burial (not to exceed $20.00); and
members could bequeath to the society (e.g., real estate, chattel). In addition,
members could not be intemperate, be involved in criminal behavior, or con-
duct themselves in an immoral manner, clearly demonstrating the social control
role that many of these societies undertook.

The only female FABC congregation member that could be found in any
cross-checking was Mrs. Sylvia ("Sylvie") Dean, a founding member of the
society. Mrs. Dean was identified as a head of household in the 1838 census
and as a consistent contributor in the 1834 FABC Penny Collection Book. Mrs.
Dean was a widow whose occupation was listed as "washer." She lived in a
six-person household with at least four other adults and perhaps a child. Thus,
in many ways, being a woman, poor, and Afro-American intensified your invisibility in the historical record.

The skeletal remains of the FABC congregation members evidenced to
some extent the impact of their material lives on their health status and mortality.
Their arduous occupations that began early in adolescence (at least) left indeli-
ble marks of their overworked muscles on their bones and joints. The combination of physical exertion, marginal and fluctuating nutrition, and the rigors
of life in a segregated, environmentally stressful community demanded biologi-

cal and psychosocial responses beyond tolerance limits that led to chronic disease and eventual death for many. In addition, the material lives of women not only affected their own health and mortality patterns but also their unborn fetuses and compromised the viability of their children. Hence, women were at risk throughout their reproductive years due to impaired host resistance and subsequent/concomitant physiological disruption, which contributed to their early deaths.

Compared to other Afro-American skeletal series, the FABC skeletal population had better overall health status. FABC did repeat the three major patterns observed in other Afro-American skeletal populations of: (1) high infant and childhood mortality; (2) periodic malnutrition and infectious disease; and (3) high degenerative joint disease and muscle hypertrophy. These general patterns were present in FABC, yet distinctly different patterns also emerged associated with variation in environmental, occupational, and political-economic contexts.

The ubiquitous occurrence of enamel defects in the dentition of FABC subadults and adults indicated periods of in utero and childhood stress, which many survived into adulthood. The very high frequency of enamel defects, despite the heterogeneous nature of this population, points to the difficulty of nineteenth century Afro-American life, whether born enslaved or free. The difference in severity rates, low in FABC and high in the Newton sugar plantation population, illustrates the differential impact of political economic systems on growth disruption and overall health status. Therefore, the rigors of intensive sugar cane production slavery led to greater growth disruption and earlier death in Barbados compared to the urban-dwelling service and labor economy of enslaved and freeborn Afro-American Philadelphians.

In general, there were lower rates of nutritional defects and less severity in FABC congregation members' remains than in other Afro-American skeletal series. Bone maintenance data also attest to the periodicity and fluctuating nutritional resources for the majority of FABC individuals. In addition, the high variation of stature in the FABC population points to the heterogeneous nature of this population and improved health status of some individuals.

The evidence for the FABC higher rates of iron deficiency anemia in adults speaks to the more episodic nature and interaction of marginal nutrition, physical labor, and environmental stress characterizing urban dwelling when compared to their more rural counterparts. These other populations exhibited more prolonged chronic nutritional problems, such as rickets and growth disruption (e.g., adult mean stature).

FABC had lower generalized nonspecific infection disease rates than other populations. This is probably associated with the more acute nature of epidemics and seasonally driven infectious disease, despite the documented high rates of tuberculosis in urban environments.

In general, FABC had lower rates of osteoarthritis with less severity than other populations, yet with multiple joint involvement. The FABC remains had higher osteophytosis attributable to the carrying and lifting of very heavy loads. Other populations, especially the rural farming populations, had a higher rate of osteoarthritis with more severity and fewer joints involved; their rates of osteophytosis were lower but higher in severity. These differences may be associated with the more diverse or generalized biomechanical requirements for urban-dwelling populations counterpoised to the more specialized and intensive biomechanics of field work.

The nineteenth-century Philadelphia Afro-American community should be considered a population in transition from enslavement to freedom, although a very limited freedom fraught with the threat of reenslavement, economic instability, and sociocultural and environmental change. This was a heterogeneous population of Afro-Americans: some were born in the state of Pennsylvania; some were born in one of the surrounding states of Delaware, Maryland, and Virginia; and others as far away as Jamaica and Haiti (no one was identified as African born). This was a diverse population socially and biologically, based on diverse African provenience and possible admixture with Euro-Americans and/or Native Americans. The common threads that linked this Afro-American community were the hardship of their lives, their biological resilience, and their religious-social organizations. The First African Baptist Church and the First African Baptist Union Beneficial Society are examples of the organizations that provided social, economic, and psychological support for survival.

In the end, it is not critically important whether one Afro-American population was healthier than the other. The central issue becomes one of adaptability: how enslaved Africans and their descendants coped, survived, and persisted in the face of socioeconomic, sociopolitical, environmental, and biological adversity in the "New World."

The biocultural study of the FABC cemetery population has demonstrated how an Afro-American population responded to environmental and sociocultural stressors and the impact these stressors had on the population. In addition, it has illustrated how important it is to assume heterogeneity in these African diasporic populations in order to understand the range of variation in characteristics, biological impact, and sociocultural/psychosocial responses. Therefore, the diversity of these populations in terms of sociohistoric context, time, location, environment, and life styles must be considered in order to successfully undertake any biohistoric study of populations of African ancestry in the "New World" diaspora.

Epilogue

1. The FABC population was reinterred in July 1987 at the Eden Cemetery, Delaware County, Pennsylvania (where the current church inters many members). The ceremony was presided over by Reverend Elvis Turner, the current Pastor of the First African Baptist Church.

2. An archaeological data recovery project was undertaken (April and May 1990) by John Milner Associates under the auspices of Pennsylvania Department of Transportation and the Federal Highway Administration. The recovery project was undertaken as part of the Vine Street Expressway (I-676) construction project. The site included the former cemetery belonging to the founding congregation of the First African Baptist Church (ca.1810–1822), when it was at 10th and Vine Streets. Eighty-nine remains were recovered; fifty-six adults (thirty-eight females and eighteen males) and thirty-three infants/children. The 10th Street First African Baptist Church was the "mother" church of the 8th Street FABC population, which is the basis of this book, and of the 11th Street church, the direct antecedent to the contemporary church. This population was reinterred in May 1995 at the Eden Cemetery near the 8th Street congregation.

Appendix A

First African Baptist Church Cemetery Inventory as Prepared by J. O. Kelley 1988

Burial #	Sex	Age		Burial #	Sex	Age
1.	male	31		34.	female	25
2.	female	44		35.	infant	Fetus
3.	N/A	N/A		36.	N/A	N/A
4.	female	60		37.	child	8+
5.	female	27+		38.	N/A	N/A
6.	infant	newborn		39.	fem.?	11
7.	female	39+		40a.	infant	8 mos.
8.	male	49		40b.	infant	10 –11 mos.
9.	male	56		41.	child	2.5
10.	female	43		42.	female	23
11.	N/A	N/A		43.	male	35
12.	male	29		44.	male	33
13.	N/A	N/A		45.	male	24
14.	male	50		46.	fem.?	42
15.	infant	2 –3 mos.		47.	male	ca. 45
16.	male	39		48.	female	39+
17.	male	31		49.	female	21
18.	child	14 mos.		50.	female	27
19.	child	5.5		51.	N/A	N/A
20.	male	25		52.	female	37
21.	infant	0 –6 mos.		53.	infant	4 –6 mos.
22.	male	44		54.	infant	Newborn
23.	N/A	N/A		55.	female	19
24.	N/A	N/A		56.	infant	Fetus
25.	male	19		57.	infant	Newborn
26.	female	25		58.	male?	8
27.	male	49		59.	fem.?	5 –5.5
28.	child	6		60.	child	7 –8
29.	infant	Fetus		61.	female	67
30a.	infant	4 mos.		62.	female	22
30b.	infant	newborn		63.	male	80
31.	male	38		64.	female	43
32.	male	51		65.	child	6 –7
33.	male	31		66.	male	55

Burial #	Sex	Age
67.	N/A	N/A
68.	male	50
69.	infant	6 mos.
70.	infant	Newborn
71.	N/A	N/A
72.	N/A	N/A
73.	infant	6 mos.
74.	female	43
75a.	child	ca.12 mos.
75b.	child	20 –24 mos.
76.	infant	8 –10 mos.
77.	male	39
78.	infant	Newborn
79.	child	2
80.	male	48
81.	male	50
82.	male	45
83.	female	36
84.	child	2
85.	female	30
86.	female	45
87.	child	16 mos.
88.	infant	6 mos.
89.	child	16 mos.
90.	female	44
91.	female	21+
92.	infant	8 mos.
93a.	female	48
93b.	male	55
93c.	female	38
94.	male	42
95.	infant	10 mos.
96.	infant	Fetus
97.	male	46
98.	infant	Newborn
99.	female	44
100.	female	21
101.	male	46
102.	infant	4 mos.
103.	N/A	N/A
104.	female	25
105.	female	ca.65
106.	female	43
107.	female	18+
108.	child	14 mos.
109.	N/A	N/A
110.	child	2
111.	N/A	N/A
112.	male	60
113.	male	45
114.	female	40
115.	male	58

Burial #	Sex	Age
116.	male	58
117.	infant	8 mos.
118.	female	29
119.	N/A	N/A
120.	N/A	N/A`
121.	child	2
122a.	infant	8 mos.
122b.	infant	Newborn
123.	N/A	15
124.	male	58
125.	infant	Newborn
126.	child	3
127.	male	75
128.	N/A	N/A
129.	N/A	N/A
130.	female	36
131.	N/A	N/A
132.	male	47+
133.	fem.?	10
134.	female	23
135.	child	4
136.	child	6 –7
137.	infant	Newborn
138.	female	33
139.	female	28
140.	child	2.5
141.	infant	6 mos.
142.	female	30
143.	infant	4 mos.
144.	infant	4 mos.
145.	infant	6 mos.
146.	infant	6 mos.

Appendix B

Partial Interment Record, First African Baptist Church (ca. 1825–1842)

Date	Name	Age	Sex	Cause of Death
June 1825	Sara Johnson	6 mo.	F	Cholera infantus
	Nancy Johnson	40	F	Inflammation of Liver
February 1826	Margaret George	26	F	Inflammation of Lungs
	Isaac White	20	M	Catharral Fever
	Julia Johnson	32	F	Consumption
	George Cooper	3 days	M	Hemorrhage
March 1826	Amelia White	17	F	Consumption
April 1826	Amelia Lee	51	F	Inflammation of Lungs
	Ann Bullar	49	F	Mania a Patu
	Eliza Shields	45	F	Epilepsy
June 1826	Lewis Johnson	32	M	Consumption
	Emery Warren's Infant	5 mo.	F	Pertussis
July 1826	Mary Wood	53	F	Dropsey
	Maria Ferrel	34	F	Consumption/ Phthisis
	Helen Jane Johnston	3 mo.	F	Cholera
	Mary Keel	6 mo.	F	Cholera
August 1826	Mary Miliza Mitchell	3	F	Atrophy
October 1826	Peter Aberdeen	62	M	Scrofula
	Moses Bayard	30	M	Mania a Patu
	Louisa Napoleon's Infant	0	M	Stillborn
	Sarah Hagerman	49	F	Cholic/Crampcolic
December 1826	Clarissa Warmley	30	F	Consumption
	Henry Thompson	6 mo.	M	Debility

Date	Name	Age	Sex	Cause of Death
January 1828	Samuel Swan†	22	M	Enteritis
February 1828	Elizabeth McKell	3 mo.	F	Enteritis
March 1828	Joseph Poulson	90	M	Variola
June 1828	William Barger	2.5	M	Hydrocephalus
	Daniel Braxton's Infant	2 mo.	?	Marasmus
	Mrs. Scarber Harman	70	F	Smallpox
July 1828	Lucretia Johnson	8 mo.	F	Diarrhoea
	Albert Peter Daily	10 mo.	M	Measles
September 1828	Hesiah West	26	?	Bilious fever
October 1828	Annabella Burton	14	F	Hydsupalus interneus
July 1829	Benjamin Waters	75	M	Dropsey
November 1829	Charlotte Henry's Infant	5 days	?	Fits
	Asciela Brown	30	F	Unknown
October 1831	John Reynolds†	46	M	Dropsey or Ascites
October 1832	Daniel Bloxten's Infant	0	?	Stillborn
November 1832	Sarah Edwards	31	F	Smallpox
	John Edward's Infant	11 days	?	Smallpox
November 1832	James Holman's Child	2	?	Inflammation of Lungs
	Solomon Carter	29	M	Phthisis pulmonalis
August 1836	Eliza Buntick	32	F	Remitting fever
	Julianna Haines	6 mo.	F	Diarrhoe
February 1837	Samuel Longpoint	51	M	Pulmonary hemorrhage
August 1837	Cornelius Sinclair	56	M	Cholera morbus
	Roseanna Landerslay	40	F	Fever
October 1837	Michael Butler	65	M	Debility/Bladder Disease
	Sara Seaton	2	F	Measles
	Isaac Smith's Infant	6 mo.	F	Diarrhoea
	Jane Singleton	65	F	Inflammation of Lungs
January 1838	Mary Nutts	55	F	Remittent fever
August 1838	Martha Johnson	11 mo.	F	Disease of lungs
April 1839	Mary Douglass	3	F	Convulsions
June 1839	James Anderson	94	M	Infirmities of age
	Helen W. Keen	9	F	Disorder of heart
October 1841	Samuel George	50	M	Phthisis pulmonalis

Date	Name	Age	Sex	Cause of Death
	Phebe A. Peters	35	F	Habitual intemperance
November 1841	Mary Ann Prince	30	F	Consumption
	John Becket	18	M	Pulmonary consumption
January 1842	Mary A. Hurt	10 mo.	F	Pulmonary catarrh
	Sarah Miller	40	F	Carcinomic uteri
	Philip F. Power	48	M	Phthisis pulmonalis
March 1842	Sarah J. Fitterman	4	F	Marasmus
April 1842	Mr. Collins	56	M	Abdominal dropsey
May 1842	Mary Smith	68	F	Haemopthisis
June 1842	Joshua Johnson	86	M	Old age/General debility
	Pamala Jones	21	F	Phthisis pulmonalis
	Anna B. Johnson	10 mo.	F	Pertussis
July 1842	Elizabeth Thompson	2 mo.	F	Marasmus
	Robinette Harman	9 mo.	F	Whooping cough
	Phyllis Hart	85	F	Old age
August 1842	Daniel Burton	40	M	Disease of heart & lungs

From 1823 to 1824 there were twenty unidentified burials. *Desilver's Directory* for the city of Philadelphia 1824 lists ten burials for the First African Baptist Church "same as last year."

† These entries as well as all entries from 1836 on are from the City Archives of the City of Philadelphia. All other entries are from the collections of the Genealogical Society of Pennsylvania at the Historical Society of Pennsylvania.

This list was first compiled by Stephanie Pinter for Milner Associates, Philadelphia PA and subsequently by Lesley Rankin-Hill in 1991. All items are listed as they appear on the documents (e.g., misspellings).

Bibliography

Acsádi, G., and Nemeskéri, J. (1970). *History of Human Life and Mortality*. Budapest: Akademiai Kiado.

Aguirre Beltran, G. (1946). *La Población Negra de México (1519–1810)*. México D.F.: Ediciones Fuente Cultural.

——— (1958). *Cuijla, Esbozo Etnográfico de un Pueblo Negro*. México, D.F.: Fundo de Cultura Economica.

Ahlbom, A., and Norell, S. (1984). *Introduction to Modern Epidemiology*. Chestnut Hill, MA: Epidemiology Resources Inc.

Angel, J. L. (1966). Porotic Osteoporosis, Anemias, Malarias, and Marshes in Prehistoric Eastern Mediterranean. *Science, 153*, 760–763.

——— (1967). Porotic Hyperostosis or Osteoporosis Symmetrica. In Brothwell and Sandison (Eds.), *Diseases in Antiquity*. Springfield, Illinois: Charles C. Thomas.

——— (1969). The Bases of Paleodemography. *American Journal of Physical Anthropology, 48*, 493–533.

——— (1971). *The People of Lerna*. American School of Classical Studies at Athens and Washington, DC: Smithsonian Press.

——— (1976). Colonial to Modern Skeletal Change in the USA. *American Journal of Physical Anthropology, 45*, 723–736.

——— (1979). Osteoarthritis in Prehistoric Turkey and Medieval Byzantium. *Henry Ford Hospital Medical Journal, 27*, 38–43.

Angel, J. L., Kelley, J. O., Parrington, M., and Pinter, S. (1987). Life Stresses of the Free Black Community as Represented by the First African Baptist Church, Philadelphia, 1823–1841. *American Journal of Physical Anthropology, 74*, 213–229.

Armelagos, G. J., and Chrisman, O. D. (1988). Hyperostosis Frontalis Interna: A Nubian Case. *American Journal of Physical Anthropology, 76*, 25–28.

Armelagos, G. J., Goodman, A. H., and Jacobs, K. H. (1978). The Ecological Perspective in Disease. In Logan, J. and Hunt, (Eds.), *Health and Human Condition*. North Scituate, MA: Duxbury Press.

Armelagos, G. J., and Hill, M. C. (1990). An Evaluation of the Biological Consequences of the Mississippian Transformation. In Dye and Cox (Eds.), *Towns and Temples Along the Mississippi*. Birmingham: University of Alabama Press.

Audy, J. R., and Dunn, F. L. (1974). Health and Disease. In Sargent (Ed.), *Human Ecology*. New York: North Holland Publishing Company.

Bacon, B. C., and Gardiner, C. W. (1838) (enumerators—1837). Pennsylvania Abolition Society Census of Colored People for the City and County of Philadelphia. Ms. and microfilm on file, Historical Society of Pennsylvania.

Baker, V. G. (1982). Archaeological Visibility of Afro-American Culture: An Example from Black Lucy's Garden, Andover, Massachusetts. In Schuyler (Ed.), *Archaeological Perspectives on Ethnicity in America*. Baywood Press,N.Y.

Balthazard, and Lebrun (1911). *Les Canaux de Havers de L'os Humain aux Différents Âges*. Annales d'Hygiene Publique et Medecine Légale 114.

Bassett, V. H. (1940). Plantation Medicine. *Journal of the Medical Association of Georgia, 29*, 112–122.

Beal, V. A. (1980). *Nutrition in the Life Span*. New York: John Wiley and Sons.

Berreman, G. D. (1982). Race, Caste and Other Invidious Distinctions. In Cole (Ed.), *Anthropology for the Eighties*. New York: Free Press.

Blakey, M. L. (1981). An Analysis of Hypoplasia and Hypocalcification in Deciduous Dentition from Dickson Mound. In Martin and Bumsted (Eds.), *Biocultural Adaptation: Comprehensive Approaches to Skeletal Analysis*.

Blakey, M. L. (1986). Fetal and Childhood Health in Late 18th and Early 19th Century Afro-Americans: Enamel Hypoplasia and Hypocalcification in the FABC Skeletal Population. *American Journal of Physical Anthropology, 72*, 179.

——— (1988). Social Policy, Economics and Demographic Change in Nanticoke–Moor Ethnohistory. *American Journal of Physical Anthropology, 75*, 493–502.

Blakey, M. L., and Armelagos, G. J. (1985). Deciduous Enamel Defects in Prehistoric Americans from Dickson Mounds: Prenatal and Postnatal Stress. *American Journal of Physical Anthropology, 66*, 371–380.

Blakey, M. L., Jenkins, S. B., and Jamison, D. (1989). *Dental Indicators of Fetal and Childhood Health in the Archeological Remains of an Early 19th Century African American Community*. Unpublished manuscript.

Blakey, M. L., Leslie, T. E., and Reidy, J. R. (1994). Frequency and Chronological Distribution of Dental Enamel Hypoplasia in Enslaved African Americans: A Test of the Weaning Hypothesis. *American Journal of Physical Anthropology, 95*, 371–383.

Blakley, R., and Beck, L. A. (1982). Bioarcheology in the Urban Context. In Dickens (Ed.), *Archeology of Urban America*. New York: Academic Press.

Blauner, R. (1970). Black Culture: Myth or Reality? In Whitten and Szwed (Eds.), *Afro-American Anthropology*. New York: The Free Press.

——— (1972). *On Racial Oppression*. New York: Harper and Row.

Boas, F. (1906). Changing the Racial Attitudes of White Americans. In Stocking (Eds.), *The Shaping of American Anthropology, 1883–1911: A Franz Reader*. Chicago: University of Chicago Press (1974).

——— (1909). The Outlook for the American Negro. In Stocking (Ed.), *The Shaping of American Anthropology, 1883–1911: A Franz Boas Reader*. Chicago: University of Chicago Press (1974).

—— (1909). The Outlook for the American Negro. In Stocking (Ed.), *The Shaping of American Anthropology, 1883–1911: A Franz Boas Reader*. Chicago: University of Chicago Press (1974).

Bocquet-Appel, J. P., and Masset, C. (1982). Farewell to Paleodemography. *Journal of Human Evolution, 11*, 321–333.

Bohannan, P., and Curtain, P. (1988). *Africa and Africans*. Prospect Heights, IL: Waveland Press.

Bourguignon, E. (1970). Ritual Disassociation and Possession Belief in Caribbean Negro Religion. In Whitten and Szwed (Eds.), *Afro-American Anthropology*. New York: The Free Press.

Bowser, F. P. (1975). The Free Person of Color in Mexico City and Lima: Manumission and Opportunity, 1580–1650. In Engerman and Genovese (Eds.), *Race and Slavery in the Western Hemisphere: Quantitative Studies*.

Bracey, J. H., Meier, A., and Rudwick, E. (1972). *Free Blacks in America, 1800–1860*. Belmont, CA: Wadworth Publishing Company.

Bridges, S. T., and Salwen, B. (1982). Weeksville: The Archeology of A Black Urban Community. In Schuyler (Ed.), *Archeological Perspectives on Ethnicity in America*

Brooks, C. H. (1922). *Official History of the First African Baptist Church Philadelphia, PA*. Philadelphia, PA: First African Baptist Church.

Brooks, S.T. (1955). Skeletal Age at Death: the Reliability of Cranial and Pubic Age Indicators. *American Journal of Physical Anthropology, 13*, 567–598.

Buhr, A. J., and Cook, A. M. (1959). Fracture Patterns. *Lancet, 1*, 531–536.

Buikstra, J. E., and Konigsberg, L. W. (1985). Paleodemography: Critiques and Controversies. *American Anthropologists, 87*, 316–333.

Buikstra, J. E., and Cook, D. C.(1985). Paleopathology: An American Account. *Annual Review of Anthropology, 9*, 433–470.

Bumsted, P. M. (1981). The Potential of Stable Carbon Isotopes in Bioarcheological Anthropology. In Martin and Bumsted (Eds.), *Biocultural Adaptation Comprehensive Approaches to Skeletal Analysis*. Amherst, MA: University of Massachusetts, Department of Anthropology.

Cannon, W. (1939). *The Wisdom of the Body*. New York: W. W. Norton.

Cardell, N. S., and Hopkins, M. M. (1978). The Effect of Milk Intolerance on the Consumption of Milk by Slaves in 1860. *Journal of Interdisciplinary History, 8*, 507–513.

Carey, H. C., and Lea, I. (1824). *Philadelphia in 1824 or a Brief Account of the Various Institutions and Public Objects in This Metropolis: Being a Complete Guide for Strangers and a Useful Compendium for the Inhabitant*. Carey and Lea Publishers: Philadelphia

Carlson, D. S., Van Gerven, D. P., and Armelagos, G. J. (1974). Factors Influencing the Etiology of Cribra Orbitalia in Prehistoric Nubia. *Journal Human Evolution, 3*, 405–410.

—— (1976). Patterns of Age Related Cortical Bone Loss (Osteoporosis) within the Femoral Diaphysis. *Human Biology, 48*, 295–314.

Chang, S.M.K., and Nissenbaum, M. M. (1975). Congenital and Developmental Defects of the Shoulder. *Orthopedic Clinician of North America, 6*, 381–392.

Cheney, R. A. (1984). Seasonal Aspects of Infant and Childhood Mortality: Philadelphia, 1865–1920. *Journal of Interdisciplinary History, 14*, 561–585.

Clark, G. (1985). *Heterochrony, Allometry, and Canalization in the Human Vertebral Column*. Ph.D. dissertation, University of Massachusetts, Amherst.

Clark, G., and Delmond, J. (1979). Vertebral Osteophytosis in Dickson Mound Population: A Biochemical Interpretation. *Henry Ford Hospital Medical Journal, 27,* 54–58.

Coale, A. J., and Demeny, P. (1966). *Regional Model Life Tables and Stable Populations*. Princeton, NJ Princeton University Press.

Cobb, W. M. (1934). The Physical Constitution of the American Negro. *Journal of Negro Education, 3,* 340–388.

——— (1936). Race and Runners. *Journal of Health and Physical Education, 7,* 1–9.

——— (1939). The Negro as a Biological Element in the American Population. *Journal of Negro Education, 8,* 336–348.

Condran, G. A. (1984). An Evaluation of Estimates of Underenumeration in the Census, and the Age Pattern of Mortality, Philadelphia 1880. *Demography , 21:* 53–69.

Condran, G. and Cheney, R. (1982). Mortality Trends in Philadelphia: Age and Cause Specific Rates 1870–1930. *Demography, 19,* 97–123.

Condran, G. A., and Crimmins, E. (1979). A Description and Evaluation of Mortality data in the Federal Census: 1850–1900. *Historical Methods, 12,* 1–23.

Condran, G. A., and Crimmins, E. (1980). Mortality Differentials between Rural and Urban Areas of States in the Northeastern United States 1890–1900. *Journal of Historical Geography, 6,* 179–202.

Connah, G. (1987). *African Civilizations: Precolonial Cities and States in Tropical Africa: An Archeological Perspective*. Cambridge: Cambridge University Press.

Cook, D. C., and Buikstra, J. E. (1979). Health and Differential Survival in Prehistoric Populations: Prenatal Dental Defects. *American Journal of Physical Anthropology, 51,* 649–664.

Cooper, D. B. (1986). The New "Black Death": Cholera in Brazil. *Social Science History, 10,* 467–487.

Corruccini, R. S., Handler, J. S., and Jacobi, K. P. (1985). Chronological Distribution of Enamel Hypoplasias and Weaning in a Caribbean Slave Population. *Human Biology, 57,* 699–711.

Corruccini, R. S., Handler, J. S., Mutaw, R. J., and Lange, F. W. (1982). Osteology of a Slave Burial Population from Barbados, West Indies. *American Journal of Physical Anthropology, 59,* 443–459.

Craton, M. (1975). Jamaican Slavery. In Engerman and Genovese (Eds.), *Race and Slavery in the Western Hemisphere: Quantitative Studies*.

Craton, M. (1976). Death, Disease and Medicine on Jamaican Slave Plantations: the Example of Worthy Park, 1767–1838. *Histoire Sociale; Social History, 18,* 237–255.

Crawford, M. H. (1984). *Current Developments in Anthropological Genetics*. New York: Plenum Press.

Curry, L. P. (1981). *The Free Black in Urban America 1800–1850: The Shadow of the Dream*. Chicago: Chicago University Press.

Curtin, P. D. (1968). Epidemiology and the Slave Trade. *Political Science Quarterly, 83,* 190–216.

——— (1969). *The Atlantic Slave Trade: A Census*. Madison: University of Wisconsin Press.

———— (1975). Measuring the Atlantic Slave Trade. In Engerman and Genovese (Eds.), *Race and Slavery in the Western Hemisphere* Quantitative Studies.

———— (1983). Nutrition in African History. *Journal of Interdisciplinary History, 14,* 371–382.

Cutler, W.W.I., and Gillette, J. H. (1980). *The Divided Metropolis: Social and Spatial Dimensions of Philadelphia, 1800–1975.* Westport, CT: Greenwood Press.

David, P. A., Gutman, H. G., Sutch, R., and Temin, P. (1976). *Reckoning With Slavery: A Critical Study in the Quantitative History of American Negro Slavery.* New York: Oxford University Press.

Day, C. B. (1932). *A Study of Some Negro-White Families in the United States.* Cambridge: Harvard University Press.

Despres, L. (1970). Differential Adaptations and Microcultural Evolution in Guyana. In Whitten and Szwed (Eds.), *Afro-American Anthropology*

Dewey, J. R., Armelagos, G. J., and Bartley, M. H. (1969). Femoral Cortical Involution in Three Nubian Archeological Populations. *Human Biology, 41,* 13–28.

Diehl, L. R., (1992). Skeletons in the Closet: Uncovering the Rich History of the Slaves of New York. *New York, 25*(39), 78–86.

Diggs, L. W. (1967). Bone and Joint Lesions in Sickle Disease *Clinical Orthopaedics and Related Research., 52,* 119–143.

Dillard, J. L. (1970). Non-Standard Negro Dialects: Convergence or Divergence? In Whitten and Szwed (Eds.), *Afro-American Anthropology.*

Du Bois, W.E.B. (1899). *The Philadelphia Negro: A Social Study.* New York: Schocken Books.

———— (1970). *The Suppression of the African Slave-Trade to the United States of America, 1638–1870.* New York: Dover Publications.

Dubos, R. (1965). *Man Adapting.* New Haven: Yale University Press.

Duffy, J. (1968). A Note on Ante-Bellum Southern Nationalism and Medical Practice. *Journal of Social History, 34,* 266–276.

Durham, R. H. (1956). Encyclopedia of Medical Syndromes. New York: Hoeber.

Eblen, J. E. (1972). Growth of the Black Population in Antebellum America, 1820–1860. *Population Studies, 26,* 273–289.

———— (1974). New Estimates of the Vital Rates of the United States Black Population During the Nineteenth Century. *Demography, 11*(2): 301–319.

Elkins, S. (1968). *Slavery: A Problem in American Institutional and Intellectual Life.* Chicago: University of Chicago Press.

Ellison, Ralph. 1952. The Invisible Man. New York: Random House.

El-Najjar, M., DeSanti, M. V., and Ozebek, L. (1978). The Etiology of Porotic Hyperostosis among the Prehistoric and Historic Anasazi Indians of Southwestern United States. *American Journal of Physical Anthropology, 48,* 185–192.

Emerson, G. (1827). Medical Statistics: Being a Series of Tables, Showing the Mortality in Philadelphia, and the Immediate Counties, during a Period of Twenty Years. *American Journal of the Medical Sciences, Nov. 1827,* 116–155.

———— (1837). Statements of Death, with the Disease and Ages, in the City and Liberties of Philadelphia during the Year 1835. *American Journal of Medical Science, Nov. 1837,* 261–267.

———— (1848). Vital Statistics of Philadelphia, for the Decennial Period from 1830 to 1840. *American Journal of Medical Science, 31* (July), 13–33.

Engerman, S. (1975). Comments on the Study of Race and Slavery. In Engerman and Genovese (Eds.), *Race and Slavery in the Western Hemisphere: Quantitative Studies.*

——— (1976). The Height of Slavery in the United States. *Local Population Studies, 16,* 45–50.

Engerman, S., and Genovese, E. D. (1975). *Race and Slavery in the Western Hemisphere: Quantitative Studies.* Princeton, NJ: Princeton University Press.

Ericksen, M. F. (1976). Cortical Bone Loss in Three Native American Populations. *American Journal of Physical Anthropology, 45,* 443–452.

Evans, R. J. (1962). The Economics of American Negro Slavery, 1830–1860. In Aspects of. Legal Economics. National Bureau of Economic Research (Eds.), Princeton University Press.

Farley, R. (1965). The Demographic Rates and Social Institutions of the Nineteenth Century Negro Population: A Stable Population Analysis. *Demography, 2,* 386–398.

Federal Writers Project. (1941). *Slave Narratives.*

Fisher, W. (1968). Physicians and Slavery in the Antebellum Southern Medical Journal. *Journal of History of Medicine and Allied Sciences, 23,* 36–49.

Fogel, R. W., and Engerman, S. L. (1971). The Relative Efficiency of Slavery: A Comparison of Northern and Southern Agriculture in 1860. *Explorations in Economic History, 8,* 353–367.

——— (1974). *Time on the Cross: The Economics of American Negro Slavery.* Boston: Little Brown and Company.

Fox-Genovese, E., and Genovese, E. D. (1983). *Fruits of Merchant Capital: Slavery and Bourgeois Property in the Rise and Expansion of Capitalism.* New York: Oxford University Press.

Fraginals, M. M. (1977). Africa in Cuba: A Quantitative Analysis of the African Population in the Island of Cuba. In Rubin and Tuden (Eds.), *Comparative Perspectives on Slavery in the New World Plantation Societies.* Annals of the New York Academy of Sciences.

Friends, Society of Friends. (1847). *Statistical Inquiry into the Condition of the People of Colour of the City and District of Philadelphia.*

Frost, H. M. (1966). *The Bone Dynamics in Osteoporosis and Osteomalacia.* Springfield, IL: Charles C. Thomas.

——— (1985). The "New Bone": Some Anthropological Potentials. *Yearbook of Physical Anthropology, 28,* 211–226.

Frucht, R. (1971). *Black Society in the New World.* New York: Random House.

Geffen, E. M. (1982). Industrial Development and Social Crisis, 1841–1854. In *Philadelphia History.* Philadelphia: City History Society.

Genovese, E. D. (1965). *The Political Economy of Slavery: Studies in the Economy and Society of the Slave South.* New York: Vintage Books.

——— (1969). The Treatment of Slaves in Different Countries: Problems in the Applications of the Comparative Method. In Foner and Genovese (Eds.), *Slavery in the New World.* Englewood Cliffs, NJ: Prentice–Hall.

——— (1972). The Slave States of North America. In Cohen and Greene (Eds.), *Neither Slave Nor Free.* Baltimore: John Hopkins University Press.

Gibbs, T., Cargill, K., Lieberman, L. S., and Reitz, E. (1980). Nutrition in a Slave Population: An Anthropological Examination. *Medical Anthropology, 4,* 175–262.

Gillette, Albert D. (Ed) (1851). *Minutes of the Philadelphia Baptist Association from A.D. 1707 to A.D. 1807; Being the First One Hundred Years of Its Existence.* Philadelphia: American Baptist Publication Society

Gonzalez, N. L. (1970). Toward a Definition of Matrifocality. In Whitten and Szwed (Eds.), *Afro-American Anthropology.*

Goodman, A. H. (1988). The Chronology of Enamel Hypoplasias in an Industrial Population: A Reappraisal of Sarnat and Schour (1941, 1942). *Human Biology, 60,* 781–791.

Goodman, A. H., and Armelagos, G. J. (1985). Factors Affecting the Distribution of Enamel Hypoplasias within the Human Permanent Dentition. *American Journal of Physical Anthropology, 68,* 479–493.

Goodman, A. H., Armelagos, G. J., and Rose, J. C. (1980). Enamel Hypoplasias as Indicators of Stress in Three Prehistoric Populations from Illinois. *Human Biology, 52,* 515–528.

Goodman, A. H., Martin, D. L., Armelagos, G. J., and Clark, G. (1984). Indicators of Stress from Bone and Teeth. In Cohen and Armelagos (Eds.), *Paleopathology at the Origins of Agriculture.* Orlando: Academic Press

Goodyear, J. D. (1978). *Agents of Empire; Portuguese Doctors in Colonial Brazil and the Idea of Tropical Disease.* Ph.D. dissertation, Johns Hopkins University.

Gough, K. (1968). The New Proposals for Anthropologists. *Current Anthropology, 9,* 403–407.

Grant, JCB. (1982). *An Atlas of Anatomy.* Baltimore: The Williams and Wilkins Company.

Greene, D., Van Gerven, D. P., and Armelagos, G. J. (1986). Life and Death in Ancient Populations: Bones of Contention in Paleodemography. *Human Evolution, 1,* 193–207.

Gunness-Hey, M. (1980). *Bone Mineral and Histological Variation with Age and Vertebral Pathology in Two Human Skeletal Populations.* Ph.d. dissertation, University of Connecticut, Storrs.

Gutman, H. G. (1975). The World Two Cliometricians Made. *Journal of Negro History, 60,* 54–227.

Handler, J. S., Aufderheide, A. C., Corruccini, R. S., Brandon, E. M., and Wittmer, L. E., Jr. (1986). Lead Contact and Poisoning in Barbados Slaves: Historical, Chemical and Biological Evidence. *Social Science History, 10,* 399–425.

Handler, J. S., and Corrucini, R. S. (1986). Weaning among West Indian Slaves: Historical and Bioanthropological Evidence from Barbados. *William and Mary Quarterly, 43,* 111–117.

Handler, J. S., and Lange, F. W. (1978). *Plantation Slavery in Barbados: An Archaeological and Historical Investigation.* Cambridge: Harvard University Press.

Harris, M. (1964). *Patterns of Race in America.* New York: Walker Press.

Hartwig, G. W., and Patterson, K. D. (1978). *Disease in African History: An Introductory Survey and Case Studies.* Durham, NC: Duke University Press.

Hastings, W. S. (1967). Philadelphia Microcosm. *Pennsylvania Magazine, 91,* 164–180.

Hershberg, T. (1971). Free Blacks in Antebellum Philadelphia: A Study of Ex-Slaves, Free-Born, and Socioeconomic Decline. *Journal of Social History, 5,* 183–209.

——— (1973) *The Philadelphia Social History Project: A Methodological History.* Ph.D. dissertation, Stanford University, Stanford CA.

———— (1975). Free-Born and Slave-Born Blacks in Antebellum Philadelphia. In Engerman and Genovese (Eds.), *Race and Slavery in the Western Hemisphere: Quantitative Studies*.

———— (1976a). The Philadelphia Social History Project: An Overview and Progress Report. *Review of Public Data Use, 4*, 29–36.

———— (1976b). Making it in 19th Century Urban America...Another Philadelphia Story, New Dimensions in Mental Health. *Department of Health, Education and Welfare* (July).

Hershberg, T. (1981). *Philadelphia: Work, Space, Family and Group Experience in the Nineteenth Century: Essays Toward an Interdisciplinary History of the City*. New York: Oxford University Press.

Herskovits, M. J. (1930). *The Anthropometry of the American Negro*. New York: Columbia University Press.

———— (1958). *The Myth of the Negro Past*. Boston: Beacon Press.

Higman, B. W. (1979). Growth in Afro–Caribbean Slave Populations. *American Journal of Physical Anthropology, 50*, 373–386.

Hill, M. C., and Armelagos, G. J. (1987). Porotic Hyperostosis in Past and Present Perspective. In Buikstra (Ed.), *A Life in Science: Papers in Honor of J. Lawrence Angel*. Scientific Papers No.6, Center for American Archeology.

Hilliard, S. B. (1972). *Hog Meat and Hoecake: Food Supply in the Old South 1840–1860*. Carbondale: Southern Illinois University Press.

Hoetnik, H. (1967). *The Two Variants in Caribbean Race Relations*. London: Oxford University Press.

Holcombe, D. D. (1818). *Misrepresentation Exposed: A Statement by the First Baptist Church of Philadelphia Exhibiting the Grounds on Which She Withdrew from the Philadelphia Baptist Association*. Philadelphia: Carey and Son.

———— (1820). The Whole Truth, Relative to the Controversy Betwixt the American Baptists. Philadelphia: Printed for the author by John H. Cunningham.

Howell-Lee, N. (1971). The Feasibility of Demographic Studies in Small and Remote Populations. In *Ecology Seminar, December*. Paper presented at Columbia University.

Hunt, E. E. (1978). Ecological Frameworks and Hypothesis Testing in Medical Anthropology. In Logan and Hunt (Eds.), *Health and Human Condition*. North Scituate, MA: Duxbury Press.

Huss-Ashmore, R., Goodman, A. H., and Armelagos, G. J. (1982). Nutritional Inference from Paleopathology. In Schiffer (Ed.), *Advances in Archaeological Method and Theory*. New York: Academic Press.

Hutchinson, D. L., and Larsen, C. S. (1988). Determination of Stress Episode Duration from Linear Enamel Hypoplasias: A Case Study from St. Catharines Island, Georgia. *Human Biology, 60*, 93–110.

Hutchinson, J. (1987). The Age-Sex Structure of the Slave Population in Harris County, Texas: 1850–1860. *American Journal of Physical Anthropology, 74*, 231–238.

Johansson, S. R., and Horowitz, S. (1986). Estimating Mortality in Skeletal Populations: Influences of the Growth Rate on the Interpretations of Levels and Trends. *American Journal of Physical Anthropology, 71*, 233–250.

Jones, D. (1970). Towards a Native Anthropology. *Human Organization, 29*, 251–259.

Jordan, W. T. (1950). Plantation Medicine in the Old South. *Alabama Review, 31*, 83–107.

Jurmain, R. D. (1977). Stress and the Etiology of Osteoarthritis. *American Journal of Physical Anthropology, 46,* 353–365.

Karasch, M. (1975). From Porterage to Proprietorship: African Occupations in Rio de Janeiro, 369–394. In Engerman and Genovese (Eds.), *Race and Slaver in the Western Hemisphere Quantitative Studies.*

Kelley, J. O. (1988). *The First African Baptist Church Community.* Report to John Milner Associates. Philadelphia, PA. Unpublished manuscript.

Kelley, J. O., and Angel, L. J. (1983). Workers of Catoctin Furnace. *Maryland Archeology, 19,* 2–17.

—— (1987). Life Stresses of Slavery. *American Journal of Physical Anthropology, 74,* 199–211.

Kelley, M. A. (1979). A Survey of Joint Disease at the Libben Site, Ottawa County, Ohio. *Henry Ford Hospital Medical Journal, 27,* 64–67.

Kennedy, KAR, (1989). Skeletal Markers of Occupational Stress. In Kennedy and Iscan (Eds.), *Reconstruction of Life From the Skeleton.* New York: A. R. Liss.

—— (1983). Morphological Variations in Ulnar Supinator Crests and Fossae, as Identifying Markers of Occupational Stress. *Journal of Forensic Science, 28* (4), 871–876.

Kerri, J. N. (1980). Black Progress: Myths and Realities. *Journal of Anthropological Research, 36,* 431–436.

Kiple, K. F. (1984). *The Caribbean Slave: A Biological History.* Cambridge: Cambridge University Press.

—— (1986). Future Studies of the Biological Past of the Black. *Social Science History, 10,* 501–506.

Kiple, K. F., and King, V. H. (1981). *Another Dimension of the Black Diaspora: Diet, Disease and Racism.* Cambridge: Cambridge University Press.

Kiple, K. F., and Kiple, V. H. (1977a). Black Tongue and Black Men: Pellagra and Slavery in the Antebellum South. *Journal of Southern History, 43,* 411–428.

—— (1977b). Slave Child Mortality: Some Nutritional Answers to a Perennial Puzzle. *Journal of Social History, 10,* 284–309.

—— (1980a). The African Connection: Slavery, Disease and Racism. *Phylon, 41,* 211–222.

—— (1980b). Deficiency Diseases in the Caribbean. *Journal of Interdisciplinary History, 11,* 197–215.

Klein, H. S. (1967). *Slavery in the Americas: A Comparative Study of Virginia and Cuba.* Chicago: University of Chicago Press.

Klein, H. S., and Engerman, S. L. (1978). Fertility Differences Between Slaves in the United States and the British West Indies: A note on Lactation Practices and their Possible Implications. *William and Mary Quarterly, 35,* 357–374.

Klumpp, K. (1970). Black Traders of North Highland Ecuador. In Whitten and Szwed (Eds.), *Afro-American Anthropology*

Kunitz, S. J. (1984). Mortality Change in America, 1620–1920. *Human Biology, 56,* 559–582.

Lallo, J., Armelagos, G. J., and Mensforth, R. P. (1977). The Role of Diet, Disease, and Physiology in the Origin of Porotic Hyperostosis. *Human Biology, 49,* 471–483.

Lapsansky, E. J. (1980). "Since They Got Those Separate Churches": Afro-Americans and Racism in Jacksonian Philadelphia. *American Quarterly, 32(1),* 54–78.

Laurie, B. (1980). *Working People of Philadelphia, 1800–1850*. Philadelphia: Temple University Press.

Lewis, D. (1973). Anthropology and Colonialism. *Current Anthropology, 14*, 581–602.

Lewis, H. (1967). Culture, Class and Family Life Among Low-Income Urban Negroes. In Ross and Hill (Eds.), *Employment, Race and Poverty* New York: Harcourt, Brace and Ward.

Lomax, A. (1970). The Homogeneity of African-Afro-American Musical Style. In Whitten and Szwed (Eds.), *Afro-American Anthropology*.

Lovejoy, C. O., and Heiple, K. G. (1981). The Analysis of Fractures in Skeletal Populations with an Example from the Libben Site, Ottowa County, Ohio. *American Journal of Physical Anthropology, 55*, 529–541.

Lovejoy, P. E. (1983). *Transformations in Slavery: A History of Slavery in Africa*. Cambridge: Cambridge University Press.

Mangaroo, J., Glasser, J. H., Roht, L. H., and Kapadia, A. S. (1985). Prevalence of Bone Demineralization in the United States. *Bone, 6*, 135–139.

Magennis, A. L. (1986). The Physical Anthropology of the Indian Neck Ossuary. In McManamon, Bradley and Magennis, *The Indian Neck Ossuary: Chapters in the Archeology of Cape Cod, V*. Cultural Resources Management Study No.17. Boston: U.S. Department of the Interior.

Margo, R. A., and Steckel, R. H. (1982). The Heights of American Slaves: New Evidence on Slave Nutrition and Health. *Social Science History, 6*, 516–538.

Martin, D. L., and Armelagos, G. J. (1979). Morphometrics of Compact Bone: An Example from Sudanese Nubia. *American Journal of Physical Anthropology, 51*, 571–578.

——— (1985). Skeletal Remodeling and Mineralization as Indicators of Health: An Example from Prehistoric Sudanese Nubia. *Journal of Human Evolution, 14*, 527–537.

Martin, D. L., Armelagos, G. J., and King, J. R. (1979). Degenerative Joint Disease of the Long Bones in Dickson Mounds. *Henry Ford Hospital Medical Journal, 27*, 60–63.

Martin, D. L., Armelagos, G. J., Mielke, J. H., and Meindl, R. S. (1981). Bone Loss and Dietary Stress in an Adult Skeletal Population from Sudanese Nubia. *Bull. et Mem. de la Soc. d'Anthrop. de Paris, 8*, 307–319.

Martin, D. L., and Bumsted, M. P. (1981). *Biocultural Adaptation Comprehensive Approaches to Skeletal Analysis* (Research Reports, No. #20). Department of Anthropology University of Massachusetts, Amherst.

Martin, D. L., Goodman, A. H., and Armelagos, G. J. (1985). Skeletal Pathologies as Indicators of Quality and Quantity of Diet. In Gilbert and Mielke (Eds.), *The Analysis of Prehistoric Diets*. Orlando: Academic Press.

Martin, D. L., Magennis, A. L., and Rose, J. C. (1987). Cortical Bone Maintenance in an Historic Afro-American Cemetery Sample from Cedar Grove, Arkansas. *American Journal of Physical Anthropology, 74*, 255–264.

Mazees, R. B. (1975). Biological Adaptation: Aptitudes and Acclimatization. In Watts, Johnston, and Lasker (Eds.), *Biosocial Interrelations in Population Adaptation*. Paris: Mouton Publishers.

McKern, T. W., and Stewart, T. D. (1957). *Skeletal Age Changes in Young American Males* (Technical Report No. EP–45). Natick, Massachusetts Headquarters, Quantitative Research and Development Command.

McMillen, S. (1985). Mother's Sacred Duty: Breast Feeding Patterns among Middle–and Upper–Class Women in the Antebellum South. *Journal of Southern History*, *51*, 333–356.

——— (1988). No Uncommon Disease. In *Papers Presented at the Annual Meeting of the American Medical Historical Association*.

Meeker, E. (1972). The Improving Health of the United States, 1850–1915. *Explorations in Economic History*, *9*, 353–373.

Mensforth, R. P., Lovejoy, C. O., Lallo, J., and Armelagos, G. J. (1978). The Role of Constitutional Factors, Diet, and Infectious Disease in the Etiology of Porotic Hyperostosis and Periosteal Reactions in Prehistoric Infants and Children. *Medical Anthropology*, *2*, 1–59.

Mensforth, R. P., and Lovejoy, C. O. (1985). Anatomical, Physiological and Epidemiological Correlates of the Aging Process: A Confirmation of Multifactorial Age Determination in the Libben Skeletal Population. *American Journal of Physical Anthropology*, *68*, 87–106.

Merbs, C. F. (1983). *Patterns of Activity-Induced Pathology in a Canadian Inuit Population*. Ottawa, Canada: National Museum of Canada.

Milner, J. A. (1981). *Professional Services Proposal for Provision of Archeological and Osteological Investigations of an Early 19th Century Cemetery Adjacent to Construction Section Number 5 of the Center City Commuter Connection Philadelphia, Pennsylvania*. Unpublished manuscript.

——— (1985). *Management Summary: Human Remains Unearthed during Archaeological Data Recovery, Philadelphia-Block 20*. Unpublished manuscript.

Mintz, S. W. (1951). The Role of Forced Labor in Nineteenth Century Puerto Rico. *Caribbean History Review*, *2*, 134–141.

——— (1961). Slavery and Emigrant Capitalisms. *American Anthropologists*, *63*, 579–587.

——— (1974). *Slavery, Colonialism and Racism*. New York: W.W. Norton.

——— (1975). History and Anthropology: A Brief Reprise. In Genovese and Engerman (Eds.), *Race and Slavery in the Western Hemisphere: Quantitative Studies*.

Mintz, S. W., and Price, R. (1976). *An Anthropological Approach to the Afro-American Past: A Caribbean Perspective*. Philadelphia: Institute for the Study of Human Issues.

Mitchell, M. C. (1944). Health and the Medical Profession in the Lower South, 1845–1860. *Journal of Social History*, *10*, 424–446.

Minton, H. M. (1913). Early History of Negroes in Business in Philadelphia. Read before the American Negro Historical Society, March 1913. Manuscript on file, Historical Society of Pennsylvania.

Moore, J. A., Swedlund, A. C., and Armelagos, G. J. (1975). The Use of Life Tables in Paleodemography. *American Antiquity*, *40*, 57–70.

Moseley, J. E. (1965). The Paleopathological Riddle of Symmetrical Osteoporosis. *American Journal of Roentgenology*, *95*, 135–142.

Moynihan, D. P., and Glazer, N. (1970). *Beyond the Melting Pot: The Negroes, Puerto Ricans, Jews, Italians and Irish of New York City*. Cambridge: MIT Press.

Mudge, M. K., Wood, V., and Frykman, G. (1984). Rotator Cuff Tears Associated with Os Acromiale. *The Journal of Bone and Joint Surgery*, *66*, 427–429.

Murdock, G. P. (1959). *Africa: Its Peoples and Their Culture History*. New York: McGraw Hill.

Nash, G. B. (1988). *Forging Freedom: The Formation of Philadelphia's Black Community, 1720–1840*. Cambridge: Harvard University Press.

Needles, E. (1849). *Ten Years' Progress: or A Comparison of the State and Condition of the Coloured People in the City and County of Philadelphia from 1837 to 1847*. Philadelphia: Pennsylvania Society for Promoting the Abolition of Slavery. Merrihew and Thompson Printers Manuscript on file, Historical Society of Pennsylvania.

Ortner, D. J. (1976). Microscopic and Molecular Biology of Human Compact Bone: An Anthropological Perspective. *Yearbook of Physical Anthropology, 20*, 35–44.

Ortner, D. J., and Aufderheide, A. C. (1991). *Human Paleopathology: Current Syntheses and Future Options*. Washington, DC: Smithsonian Institution Press.

Ortner, D. J., and Putschar, W.J. (1981). *Identification of Pathological Conditions in Human Skeletal Remains; Smithsonian Contributions to Anthropology Number 28*. Washington, DC: Smithsonian Press.

Otto, J. S. (1975). *Status Differences and the Archaeological Record: A Comparison of Planter, Overseer, and Slave Sites from Cannon's Point Plantation (1794–1861), St. Simon's Island, Georgia*. Ph.D. dissertation, University of Florida, Gainesville.

——— (1982). Race and Class on Antebellum Plantations. In Schuyler (Eds.), *Archeological Perspectives on Ethnicity in America*.

Owsley, D. W (1990) The Skeletal Biology of North American Historical Populations. In Buikstra (Ed.), *A Life in Science: Papers in Honor of J. Lawrence Angel*. Scientific Papers No. 6 Center for American Archeology.

Owsley, D. W., Orser, C. E., Jr., Mann, R. W., Moore-Jansen, P. H., and Montgomery, R. L. (1987). Demography and Pathology of an Urban Slave Population from New Orleans. *American Journal of Physical Anthropology, 74*, 185–197.

Palkovich, A. M. (1987). Endemic Disease Patterns in Paleopathology: Porotic Hyperostosis. *American Journal of Physical Anthropology, 74*, 527–537.

Parrington, M. (1985). Archeological Excavations at the First African Baptist Church Cemetery, Philadelphia, Pennsylvania. Paper presented at the 7th Annual Conference on Historic Preservation, Pennsylvania Historical and Museum Commission, Bethlehem, Pennsylvania.

Parrington, M., and Roberts, D. G. (1984). First African Baptist Church Cemetery. *Archaeology, 37*, 26–32.

——— (1990). Demographic, Cultural, and Bioanthropological Aspects of a Nineteenth Century Free Black Population in Philadelphia, Pennsylvania. In Buikstra (Ed.) *A Life in Science: Papers in Honor of J. Lawrence Angel*. Scientific Papers No.6 Center for American Archeology.

Parrington, M., Roberts, D. G., Pinter, S. A., and Wideman, J. C., (1989). *First African Baptist Church Cemetery: Bioarcheology, Demography, and Acculturation of Early Nineteenth Century Philadelphia Blacks*. 3 vols. Prepared for the Redevelopment Land Authority of the City of Philadelphia. Philadelphia: John Milner Associates, Inc.

Parrington, M., and Wideman, J. (1986). Acculturation in an Urban Setting: The Archaeology of a Black Philadelphia Cemetery. *Expedition, 28*, 55–62.

Paynter, R. (1990). Afro-American in the Massachusetts Historical Landscape. In Gathercole and Lowenthal (Eds.), *The Politics of the Past*. London: Unwin Hyman Ltd.

Pearl, R. (1936). Fertility and Contraception in Urban Whites and Negroes. *Science, 83*, 503–506.

Pennsylvania Society for Promoting the Abolition of Slavery (1838). *The Present State and Conditions of the Free Peoples of Colour of the City of Philadelphia and Adjoining Districts*. Philadelphia: The Society, Merrihew and Gunn Printers. Manuscript on file, Historical Society of Pennsylvania.

———— (1856). *The Present State and Condition of the Free People of Colour of the City of Philadelphia and Adjoining Districts*. Philadelphia: The Society, Merrihew and Gunn Printers. Manuscript on file, Historical Society of Pennsylvania.

Peterson, J. A. (1979). The Impact of Sanitary Reform upon American Urban Planning, 1840–1890. *Journal of Social History, 13*, 83–103.

Phillips, U. B. (1918). *American Negro Slavery: A Survey of the Supply, Employment and Control of Negro Labor as Determined by the Plantation Regime*. New York: Appleton and Company.

Pickering, R. B. (1979). Hunter-Gatherer/Agriculturist Arthritic Patterns: A Preliminary Investigation. *Henry Ford Hospital Medical Journal, 27*, 50–53.

Pitt-Rivers, J. (1967). Race, Color and Class in Central America and the Andes. *Daedalus, 96*, 542–559.

Porter, K. W. (1832). Relations between Negroes and Indians within the Present Limits of the United States. *Journal of Negro History, 17*, 1–81.

Postell, W. D. (1951). *The Health of Slaves on Southern Plantations*. Baton Rouge: Louisiana State University Press.

Price, T. D. (1989). *The Chemistry of Prehistoric Human Bone*. Cambridge: Cambridge University Press.

Price, T. J. (1970). Ethnohistory and Self-Image in Three New World Negro Societies. In Whitten and Szwed (Eds.), *Afro-American Anthropology*.

Project, F. W. (1941). *Slave Narratives: A Folk History of Slavery in the United States*. Washington, DC: Library of Congress.

Raisz, L. G. (1984). Osteoporosis. *Journal of Geriatrics, 21*, 18–26.

Rankin-Hill, L. M. (1990). *Afro-American Biohistory. Methodological and Theoretical Considerations*. Ph.D. dissertation, University of Massachusetts, Amherst.

Rathbun, T. A. (1987). Health and Disease at a South Carolina Plantation: 1840–1870. *American Journal of Physical Anthropology, 74*, 239–253.

Rathbun, T. A. and Scurry, J. D. (1991). Status and Health in Colonial South Carolina: Bellview Plantation 1738–1756. In Powell, et al. (Eds.), *What Mean these Bones*.

Reid, J. D., Lee, E. S., Jedlicka, D., and Shin, Y. (1977). Trends in Black Health. *Phylon, 38*, 105–116.

Reisman, K. (1970). Cultural and Linguistic Ambiguity in a West Indian Village. In Whitten and Szwed (Eds.), *Afro-American Anthropology*.

Roberts, D. F. (1984). Anthropogenetics in a Hybrid Population: The Black Carib Studies. In Crawford and Mielke (Eds.), *Current Developments in Anthropological Genetics*. New York: Plenum Press.

Rose, J. C. (1985). *Gone to a Better Land: A Biohistory of a Rural Black Cemetery in the Post-Reconstruction South*. Fayetteville: University of Arkansas.

Sarnat, B. G., and Schour, I. (1941). Enamel Hypoplasias (chronic enamel aplasia) in Relationship to Systemic Diseases: A Chronologic, Morphologic, and Etiologic Classification. *Journal of the American Dental Association, 28*, 1989–2000.

———— (1942). Enamel Hypoplasias (chronic enamel aplasia) in Relationship to Systemic Diseases: A Chronologic, Morphologic and Etiologic Classification. *Journal of the American Dental Association, 29*, 67–76.

Savitt, T. L. (1978). *Medicine and Slavery: The Diseases and Health Care of Blacks in Antebellum Virginia*. Urbana: University of Illinois Press.

Scharf, T., and Wescott, T. (1884). *History of Philadelphia 1609–1884*. Philadelphia: L.H. Everts and Company.

Schour, I., and Massler, M. (1940). Studies of Tooth Development: The Growth Pattern of Human Teeth. *Journal of the American Dental Association, 27*, 1918–1931.

Schultz, P. D., and McHenry, M. (1975). Age Distribution of Enamel Hypoplasias in Prehistoric California Indians. *Journal of Dental Research, 54*, 913.

Schuyler, R. L. (1982). *Archeological Perspectives on Ethnicity in America*. New York: Baywood Press.

Sciulli, P. W. (1977). A Descriptive and Comparative Study of the Deciduous Dentition of Prehistoric Ohio Valley Amerindians. *American Journal of Physical Anthropology, 47*, 71–80.

Scrimshaw, N. S., Taylor, C. E., and Gordon, J. E. (1968). *Interactions of Nutrition and Infection*. Monograph 57. World Health Organization: Geneva.

Sedlin, E. D., Frost, H. M., and Villanueva, A. R. (1963). Variations in Cross-Section Area of Rib Cortex with Age. *Journal of Gerontology, 18*, 9–13.

Shaw, J. H., and Sweeney, E. A. (1973). Nutrition in Relation to Dental Medicine. In Goodhart and Shils (Eds.), *Modern Nutrition in Health and Disease*. Philadelphia: Lee and Febiger.

Sheridan, R. B. (1975). Mortality and the Medical Treatment of Slaves in the British West Indies. In Engerman and Genovese (Eds.), *Race and Slavery in the Western Hemisphere: Quantitative Studies*.

Shryock, R. (1930). Medical Practice in the Old South. *South Atlantic Quarterly, 29*, 160–163.

Singleton, T. A. (1985). *The Archeology of Slavery and Plantation Life*. Orlando: Academic Press.

Smith, B. G. (1981). The Material Lives of Laboring Philadelphians, 1750 to 1800. *William and Mary Quarterly, 38*, 163–202.

Smith, Edward D. (1988) *Climbing Jacob's Ladder: The Rise of Black Churches in Eastern American Cities 1740–1877*. Washington, DC: Smithsonian Institution Press.

Stack, C. B. (1970). The Kindred of Viola Jackson: Residence and Family Organization of an Urban Black American Family. In Whitten and Szwed (Eds.), *Afro-American Anthropology*.

——— (1974). *All Our Kin: Strategies for Survival in a Black Community*. New York: Harper and Row.

Stampp, K. (1956). *The Peculiar Institution: Slavery in the Antebellum South*. New York: Alfred A. Knopf.

Steckel, R. H. (1973). *Slave Marriage, Fertility, and Society* (Workshop in Economic History No. 7374–4). University of Chicago.

——— (1979). Slave Height Profiles from Coastwise Manifests. *Explorations in Economic History, 46*, 367–370.

——— (1986a). A Dreadful Childhood: The Excess Mortality of American Slaves. *Social Science History, 10*, 427–465.

——— (1986b). Birthweights and Infant Mortality among American Slaves. *Explorations in Economic History, 23*, 173–198.

—— (1986c). A Peculiar Population: the Nutrition, Health and Mortality of American Slaves from Childhood to Maturity. *Journal of Economic History, 46,* 721–741.

Stedman, T. L. (1982). Stedman's Medical Dictionary. 24th ed. Baltimore: Williams and Wilkins.

Steinbock, R. T. (1976). *Paleopathological Diagnosis and Interpretation: Bone Diseases in Ancient Human Populations.* Springfield, IL: Charles C. Thomas.

Stirland, A. (1991). Diagnosis of Occupationally Related Paleopathology: Can it be Done? In Ortner and Aufderheide (Eds.), *Human Paleopathology: Current Syntheses and Future Opinions.*

Stout, S. D. (1978). Histological Structure and Its Preservation in Ancient Bone. *Current Anthropology, 19,* 601–604.

Stout, S. D., and Simmons, D. J. (1979). Histomorphometric Determination of Formation Rates of Archeological Bone. *Calcified Tissue, 21,* 163–169.

Stout, S. D., and Teitlebaum, S. L. (1976). Use of Histology in Ancient Bone Research. *Yearbook of Physical Anthropology, 22,* 228–249.

Stuart-Macadam, P. (1987a). A Radiographic Study of Porotic Hyperostosis. *American Journal of Physical Anthropology, 74,* 511–520.

—— (1987b). Porotic Hyperostosis: New Evidence to Support the Anemia Theory. *American Journal of Physical Anthropology, 74,* 521–526.

Sutch, R. (1976a). The Treatment Received by American Slaves: A Critical Review of the Evidence Presented in Time on the Cross. *Explorations in Economic History, 12,* 386–394.

—— (1976b). The Care and Feeding of Slaves. In David, Gutman, Sutch, and Temin (Eds.), *Reckoning with Slavery: A Critical Study in the Quantitative History of American Negro Slavery.*

Swardstedt, T. (1966). *Odontological Aspects of a Medieval Population in the Provence of Jamtland/Mid-Sweden.* Stockholm: Tinden-Barnaugen.

Swedlund, A. (1990). Infant and Childhood Mortality in the 19th Century United States: A View from Rural Massachusetts. In Swedlund and Armelagos (Eds.), *Disease in Populations in Transition: Anthropological and Epidemiological Perspectives.* South Hadley, MA: Bergin and Garvey.

Swedlund, A., and Armelagos, G. J. (1969). *Demographic Anthropology.* Dubuque, IA: Wm. C. Brown.

Szwed, J. F. (1970). Afro-American Musical Adaptation. In Whitten and Szwed (Eds.), *Afro-American Anthropology.*

Tannenbaum, F. (1946). *Slave and Citizen: The Negro in America.* New York: Knopf Press.

Thomas, R. B., Winterhalder, B., and McRae, S. (1979). An Anthropologic Approach to Human Ecology and Adaptive Dynamics. *Yearbook of Physical Anthropology, 22,* 23–34.

Todd, T. W. (1920). Age Changes in the Pubic Bone, Part I. *American Journal of Physical Anthropology, 3,* 285–344.

—— (1921). Age Changes in the Pubic Bone, Part II-IV. *American Journal of Physical Anthropology, 3,* 285–344.

Torchia, M. M. (1977). Tuberculosis among American Negroes: Medical Research on a Racial Disease, 1830–1950. *Journal of the History of Medicine, 32,* 252–279.

United States of America. (1821). United States Census for 1820. Washington, DC: Gales and Seaton (printers).

——— (1832). 5th Census; or enumeration of the Inhabitants of the United States. 1830, Washington, DC: Duff Green (printers).

——— (1840). 6th Census; or enumeration of the Inhabitants of the United States, as corrected at the Department of State, in 1840. Washington, DC: Blair and Rives (printers).

Valentine, C. (1968). *Culture and Poverty*. Chicago: University of Chicago Press.

Valentine, C., and Valentine, B. L. (1980). Fieldwork in the Ghetto. In Cole (Eds.), *Anthropology for the Eighties*. New York: The Free Press.

Van Gerven, D. P. (1969) *Thickness and Area Measurements as Parameters of Skeletal Involution of the Humerus, Femur, and Tibia*. Unpublished Master's thesis, University of Massachusetts, Amherst.

Van Gerven, D. P., and Armelagos, G. J. (1983). "Farewell to Paleodemography?" Rumors of Its Death Have Been Greatly Exaggerated. *Journal of Human Evolution*, *12*, 353–360.

Van Gerven, D. P., Hummert, J. R., and Burr, D. B. (1985). Cortical Bone Maintenance and Geometry of the Tibia in Prehistoric Children from Nubia's Batn el Hajar. *American Journal of Physical Anthropology*, *66*, 275–280.

Vaughan, J. (1975). *The Physiology of Bone*. Oxford: Clarendon Press.

Vlach, J. M. (1991). *By the Work of Their Hands: Studies in Afro-American Folklife*. Charlottesville: University Press of Virginia.

Walker, J. (1983). *Free Frank: A Black Pioneer on the Antebellum Frontier*. Lexington: University Press of Kentucky.

Walker, P. (1986). Porotic Hyperostosis in a Marine–Dependent California Indian Population. *American Journal of Physical Anthropology*, *69*, 345–354.

Weiss, M. (1973). Demographic Models for Anthropology. *American Antiquity*, *38*, Memoirs No. 27.

Wells, C. (1964). *Bones, Bodies, and Disease*. New York: Praeger Press.

Whitten, N. E. (1970). Personal Networks and Musical Contexts in the Pacific Lowlands of Columbia and Ecuador. In Whitten and Szwed (Eds.), *Afro-American Anthropology*.

Wilkie, J. R. (1976a). The United States Population by Race and Urban–Rural Residence, 1790–1860: Reference Tables. *Demography*, *13*, 139–148.

——— (1976b). Urbanization and De-Urbanization of the Black Population Before the Civil War. *Demography*, *13*, 311–328.

——— (1976c). The Black Urban Population of the Pre-Civil War South. *Phylon*, *37*, 250–262.

Williams, E. (1944). *Capitalism and Slavery*. Chapel Hill: University of North Carolina Press.

———. (1971). The Origins of Slavery. In Frucht (Ed.), *Black Society in the New World*.

Willson, J. (1841). *Sketches of the Higher Classes of Coloured Society in Philadelphia*. Philadelphia: Merrihew and Thompson.

Winch, J. (1988). *Philadelphia Black Elite: Activism, Accommodation, and the Struggle for Autonomy, 1787–1848*. Philadelphia: Temple University Press.

Woodson, C. G. (1968). *The African Background Outlined*. Reprint of the 1936 edition. New York: Negro Universities Press.

Winch, J. (1988). *Philadelphia Black Elite: Activism, Accommodation, and the Struggle for Autonomy, 1787–1848*. Philadelphia: Temple University Press.

Woodson, C. G. (1968). *The African Background Outlined*. Reprint of the 1936 edition. New York: Negro Universities Press.

Yesner, D. R. (1981). Degenerative and Traumatic Pathologies of the Aleut Vertebral Column. *Archives of the California Chiropractic Association, 5*, 45–57.

Zelinsky, W. (1950). The Population Geography of the Free Negro in Ante-Bellum America. *Population Studies, 3*, 386–401.

Zimmerman, M. R. (1980). *Foundations of Medical Anthropology*. Philadelphia: W. B. Saunders Company.

Index

About the Author

LESLEY M. RANKIN-HILL is an Associate Professor of Anthropology at the University of Oklahoma in Norman. Dr. Rankin-Hill received her Ph.D. in Anthropology from the University of Massachusetts at Amherst.

ISBN 0-89789-435-9

9 780897 894357

HARDCOVER BAR CODE